D0540657

MAX CLIFFORD

MAX CLIFFORD

Read All About It

Max Clifford
and Angela Levin

First published in Great Britain in 2005 by
Virgin Books Ltd
Thames Wharf Studios
Rainville Road
London
W6 9HA

Copyright © Max Clifford and Angela Levin 2005

The right of Max Clifford and Angela Levin to be identified as the
Authors of this Work has been asserted by them in accordance
with the Copyright, Designs and Patents Act, 1988.

This book is sold subject to the condition that it shall not,
by way of trade or otherwise, be lent, resold, hired out
or otherwise circulated without the publisher's prior written
consent in any form of binding or cover other than that
in which it is published and without a similar condition
including this condition being imposed on the
subsequent purchaser.

A catalogue record for this book is available
from the British Library.

ISBN 1 85227 237 6 HB
ISBN 0 7535 1100 2 PB

Typeset by TW Typesetting, Plymouth, Devon
Printed and bound in Great Britain by
Mackays of Chatham PLC

DEDICATION

For Liz, Louise, Lily and Frank.
For all the love and laughter.

AUTHORS' NOTE

In some cases names have been changed in the text
to protect the identity of the individual concerned.

CONTENTS

1. PLAYING AWAY

The mobile phone rang loud and clear, echoing across the bougainvillea-filled patio of his Spanish apartment just outside Marbella. Max Clifford climbed out of the swimming pool, wrapped a white towel round his waist and, with his hand still wet, put the phone to his ear. 'Hello,' said the female voice at the other end. 'Is that Max Clifford? My name is Maria and I'm phoning on behalf of a friend who might have a story to sell.'

So started the biggest tabloid exposé for a decade, one that reverberated across the nations and monopolised newspaper and TV headlines for weeks. Its disclosures changed the image of David Beckham, one of the world's most popular footballers and a devoted family man, for good and confirmed that Max Clifford is the image-maker and breaker of the 21st century.

Gossip had been swirling round Fleet Street for some time that England's football captain had been playing around and that his marriage to former Spice Girl Victoria Beckham was in crisis, rumours that were underlined by the fact that she'd stayed pouting at home when the former Manchester United midfielder moved to Spain on joining Real Madrid in the autumn of 2003. Beckham, on the other hand, despite talk that he was homesick, seemed to settle down rather too quickly. Pictures were published of him enjoying the company of a mystery girl, first at Madrid's exclusive restaurant The Thai Garden, then afterwards in the early hours at the Ananda nightclub. Her identity didn't stay a mystery for long. She was 26-year-old Rebecca Loos, employed by Beckham's sports management company SFX to be his personal assistant. Perhaps, it was whispered, she was assisting him rather too personally.

Victoria was certainly not amused, and both Rebecca and the management company were swiftly sacked. Rebecca was shocked and angry at the way she'd been treated, but being a feisty girl, rather than take it lying down, she decided to get advice about what her response should be. She phoned friends in London to ask who they thought she should talk to. The unanimous recommendation was Max Clifford. She rang him in January 2004, calling herself Maria to protect her identity.

Max wasn't fooled for a second. 'Lots of people use a false identity when they first call me,' he says. 'The important thing was whether the rumour about her and Beckham was true. I'd been close to similar Beckham stories over the previous two or three years. One was from a woman in Manchester who claimed she'd had a relationship with him, but couldn't prove it sufficiently to get it published.'

'Maria' told Max she'd heard that one of Beckham's bodyguards wanted to sell his story about life with the biggest name in world football. Did he know anything about it? And did he also perhaps know anything about Beckham's PA who he was supposed to be having an affair with?

'I told "Maria" I'd heard the rumours. She asked me to check whether anything was about to be published in the papers. I said I would.'

Max made a few phone calls then called her back. 'I told her there was a lot of suspicion but no hard evidence at the moment. She then asked what I thought the PA should do. I said that for a certain type of person it could be wonderful, but for others it would be a nightmare. It depended on lots of things, including whether she wanted to continue working as a PA, whether she was resilient enough to cope with criticism from the media and how her loved ones would cope. She said, "thank you" and put the phone down.'

Max calmly went back to continue his swim. 'I am very relaxed about these things and let them take their natural course, partly because there are so many exciting things going on in my life at one time.'

Nothing further happened until March 2004 when Max received another phone call. He was, by chance, again in Spain, but this time sipping an orange juice as he sunned himself by the pool. 'Hello. Is that Max Clifford? My name is Rebecca Loos.'

'Hello,' he replied, instantly recognising the voice. 'Shouldn't I be calling you Maria?'

'I'm sorry,' she said. 'I just couldn't tell you my name before. I'm calling because there are lots of journalists out here asking all sorts of questions about David and myself.'

'I told them I didn't want to talk,' Rebecca later explained. 'I knew not to trust journalists and was unclear how much any of them actually knew or if they were just trying to trick me. I asked Max to represent me.'

'I agreed to,' he says, 'but warned her about the implications of doing such a huge story and how it would change her life. I explained that if she went public she had to accept that all the papers who didn't get the exclusive would attack her and drag up every bad thing they could about her, true or false. But that the money she'd make would provide her with a nice financial nest egg that could buy her a new home.

'I also told her what sort of money she could expect and that, as usual, although my advice had been free until then, I took twenty per cent of any deal I made.'

Max didn't put any pressure on Rebecca to go ahead, but advised her that if she wanted to make a financial killing she needed to make up her mind fast. Rebecca rang her parents, who told her they'd support any decision she made. She also talked it through with some close friends in London. 'I thought about what was the worst thing papers could say about me,' she recalls. 'And I decided it wouldn't be much.' Less than 24 hours later she told Max she wanted to go ahead.

She didn't meet with Max. Nor did he ask her to sign a contract. 'After several conversations with her I felt very comfortable and was happy with that,' he says.

Max then rang Andy Coulson, editor of the British tabloid the *News of the World* and told him Rebecca had agreed to spill the beans and that he could send a journalist to talk to her to evaluate what she had to say before he fixed a price.

Neville Thurlbeck, the paper's chief reporter, went out to meet her. Although Rebecca was street smart, she felt very nervous. Neville told her he wanted to know what sort of man Beckham was in private and, most important of all, what he was like in bed. 'Let's be honest,' he admits. 'I wasn't writing a chapter in the Bible.'

He also asked her to engineer a meeting between herself and Beckham at a hotel, so a *News of the World* photographer could take incriminating photographs, which would make the story more valuable. Rebecca didn't want to. Nor, she insisted, would she go into any sexual detail about their affair. Instead she would talk about their relationship in general terms and say he was a good lover.

The time was ripe to fix the deal. Both Max and Andy Coulson knew the potential of the exclusive and the negotiations didn't take long. 'This was obviously one of the best stories I'd been involved in,' says Coulson. 'Nor did I think twice about the morality of running it. The Beckhams have manipulated the media to promote themselves for years.' Celebrities who use the media are often seen as fair game by the tabloids, and the Beckhams had used the media more than most.

Max finalised the deal over the telephone for £300,000. Neville and photographer Paul Ashton caught the first flight to Madrid, hired an Audi and drove at top speed to Rebecca's parents' £550,000 house in the city where she was waiting for them. Speed was vital. In newspaper terms, she was, at that moment, the hottest media property in the world. Neville needed to reach her, then hide her away to prevent any other journalist from getting a quote or snatching a picture to build up their own story.

He arrived at 4 p.m. and gave her ten minutes to pack. Rebecca neither argued nor made a fuss. Instead she flung some T-shirts, trousers, bikinis and toiletries into a case and grabbed her dog Bu-bu, a one-eyed pug. Then they hit the road. Neville headed south and drove for around 300 miles before stopping at 11 p.m. at a small hotel just north of Fuengirola on the Costa del Sol.

Early next morning they set out again, this time more slowly, keeping off the main roads so Neville could find a place to stay. A villa would be better than a hotel, to avoid her being recognised. But, knowing the press pack would be hot on their heels, he knew it wasn't a good idea to book a villa through a travel agent who might be tempted to sell the details to another paper.

After about an hour's drive they reached the northern outskirts of Marbella. There, down a single-track road, was a large villa with a 'for sale' sign outside. A man, who turned out to be the owner, was in the front garden. Neville asked if he could rent it for two weeks for £3,000 per week. A deal was speedily done and the fugitive group moved in.

To be on the safe side Neville told no one where he was, not the office travel company, his editor, or even Max. The villa had six bedrooms and a pool, but best of all it was surrounded by a high wall so that even if the paparazzi tracked them down, they couldn't snatch any pictures from the road. It was also large enough so that Rebecca wouldn't feel like a caged bird.

Once they'd settled in, the interview started. Rebecca's limited experience of dealing with sports journalists wanting to speak to SFX's clients was barely a match for the polished ways of an award-winning investigative reporter. Although Neville can seem more like a benign Sherlock Holmes than an aggressive tabloid hack, each morning the urbane charmer transmogrified into a master of inquisition. His paper was paying a fortune for the story and it wanted its money's worth.

At the end of each day's session he rang both Andy Coulson and Max to keep them up to speed with how everything was going. Evenings were more relaxed. He and Rebecca chatted, had a meal together, smoked cigars and drank brandy. Some nights Rebecca could barely sleep. 'I felt a mixture of excitement and fear about where my life would go,' she says.

At the end of the first week Neville sent through thousands of words to his office. Andy Coulson guarded his world exclusive carefully. To maximise its impact and outsmart his newspaper rivals, he kept his scoop out of the first editions of 4 April so the other papers wouldn't have time to come out with the same story that day.

Rebecca's alleged affair filled the paper. It was told largely through the voices of Rebecca's 'friends', a common device used to protect the individual actually telling the story. Beckham was described as a 'sensational lover'. He was said to have fed her strawberries and kiwi fruit after a night of passion and to have sent her explicit sexual text messages.

The allegation that Beckham, the idol of millions of football fans – and as many women – had had an affair sent shock waves round the world. Some devoted female fans were as astounded as if they'd read the Pope was secretly married.

Beckham, the golden hero, reacted by quickly putting out a statement that any suggestion of an affair was 'ludicrous' and that he was a happily married man with two wonderful children.

Newspapers and TV channels rushed to jump on the speeding bandwagon. Editors demanded an original angle and reporters were dispatched to get whatever they could from whomever was available. Max's phones rang off the hook and, as he had predicted, a hailstorm of accusations began to rain down on Rebecca's head. These included allegations that she was bisexual, which was true, and had had affairs with a truckload of men, most of whom she'd never met. Max spent hours each day talking to journalists and giving TV and newspaper interviews. It was fantastic publicity for him. 'I get a huge buzz from being in the middle of a great story,' he says.

Although Max had warned Rebecca that her personal life would be put under the microscope, it wasn't how she had seen her story unfolding and she was quite upset. Max, whose handholding skills are as polished as his story-selling ability, understood. Unlike most PRs who do a deal and then move on, he stays closely in touch with his clients after a story breaks.

'It's a big emotional roller coaster for them,' he explains. 'Suddenly from being virtually unknown they become famous, but only famous for a kiss-and-tell. I'm used to how it works, but they are not. I tried to talk Rebecca through it and told her that she must try to stay balanced and rational. I reminded her that the other papers would inevitably buy up anyone who had anything nasty to say about her and that I'd do my best to deny those that were the most over the top.'

There were so many lurid details about her own sex life that, to stay ahead of the pack, the *News of the World* needed to come up with more ground-breaking stuff on Beckham the following week. Rebecca was put under increasing pressure to talk dirty. Nor did they want the story in the voices of her 'friends'. Neville now wanted the specific details of exactly how Beckham had performed as a lover. Rebecca phoned Max again.

'I get impatient when clients become too needy,' he admits. 'They are just involved in the one story, whereas I can have twenty clients wanting me at the same time. But Rebecca was fine overall. I told her to co-operate, but not be dictated to. If she didn't want to say anything, she should stand up for herself and not say it; that she was running them, they were not running her. And if Neville got too bullying she should call me again.

'I also phoned Neville and told him to calm down a bit otherwise she might clear off and he'd lose the rest of the story.'

Although Rebecca's parents kept their own counsel, Rebecca's brother John was upset by the number of journalists camping outside his door wanting a quote about his sister. He rang Max for help. 'I told him that when a journalist tried to press him to say something, he should tell them to speak to me; that if they continued to pester him, he should take their name, and I'd speak to their editor. I explained he didn't have to say anything, that he wasn't on trial or a criminal.' By contrast her parents were fine. They were away when the story broke and once they were back home seemed to enjoy the attention.

The second week in hiding was harder for Rebecca. 'I felt terrified a lot of the time and couldn't sleep,' she says. 'I didn't regret what I'd done, but I had no idea what would happen to me next. It was hard to be locked away without being able to see my friends or family. Luckily I had my pug with me. She is basically my baby and when she is with me I don't feel too bad for long.'

Despite all Neville's precautions, other journalists were hot on their scent. Although no one came too close physically, several managed to get hold of Rebecca's mobile phone number. 'Hi,' said one honeyed male voice. 'Deputy editor of the *News of the World* speaking. Marvellous stuff. Well done. I hope you are being looked after. Now where exactly did you say you were?'

'Good morning,' trilled another. '*News of the World* chief lawyer here, just a few questions . . . And where did you say you were?' Both callers were bogus opportunists and Rebecca, aided by Neville, sent them packing.

Newspapers round the world were now queuing up for follow-up chats with Rebecca and every TV channel was clamouring to get the first exclusive interview. Satellite channel Sky were first.

By chance Sky producer Hazel Stuart had met Rebecca in a bar a few years previously through a mutual friend, Emma Basden, and mentioned the fact at a morning conference when the story broke. 'My bosses nearly bit my hand off in excitement,' she says.

She was told to pull out all the stops to get the first interview. She spoke to Emma and asked her to put a financial offer to Rebecca.

But Max was already in charge and considering various offers from different broadcasters. 'I wanted Rebecca to get the best deal and *Tonight with Trevor MacDonald* on ITV might have been more suitable than Sky,' he says.

As the *News of the World* had Rebecca under contract, Hazel had to deal with both the tabloid and Max to get the interview. 'The difference between them was extraordinary,' she says. 'Max was polite, calm and softly spoken. Whereas everyone I spoke to at the *News of the World* was fraught and uptight.'

The *News of the World* didn't want anyone else to talk to Rebecca until they had extracted every last fact from her, whereas Sky wanted to bring out their interview as soon as they could. For the next ten days Hazel made endless rounds of phone calls to Emma, to Max, and the *News of the World*. 'I held my breath and was so tense my life seemed to come to a complete standstill,' she recalls. 'My bosses at Sky kept asking me if we were going to get it; Emma kept saying she felt sure Rebecca would do it; but Max kept telling me that he was putting Rebecca's interests above anyone else's.

'Each time I spoke to him, which by now was several times a day, he'd say in a totally calm voice, "You haven't got it yet. I'll get back to you." I was like a cat on a hot tin roof. It was awful. But that is how Max does his deals. It is one of his ways of getting the most out of people. You get so frustrated you offer more money just to get the thing sewn up.

'I developed a horrible stitch in my stomach and felt so frustrated that when the second instalment of her story appeared in the *News of the World* on Easter Sunday (11 April), I decided enough was enough. I rang Max and said, "Come on, Max, she's got a bloody good deal. For God's sake . . ." But he's done a million similar stories. He stayed totally professional and utterly calm, which in my agitated state I found quite annoying.'

Max explains: 'I told her I wanted to go with the programme that would get Rebecca the most viewers and asked how many people she thought would watch the interview on Sky. She replied, "About two million". I called Rebecca, and then came back to Hazel. I said she had her deal for £125,000 and gave her Rebecca's mobile number.'

'It was,' says Hazel, 'a massive relief.' The plan was that the Sky team comprising anchor Kay Burley, two cameramen, a sound technician, a director, Hazel and Rebecca's friend Emma, would fly out on Easter Monday, film the interview on Tuesday and broadcast it on Thursday.

They were told to fly to Malaga, but were not told their final destination. All seemed set until Hazel's mobile rang in the departure lounge. There was a problem with the contract over the length of time Rebecca would be tied exclusively to Sky, and her bosses told her the interview might not now go ahead. They flew out anyway hoping for the best.

Neville then took over the cloak-and-dagger operation. He told the Sky team which direction to drive in and approximately how far to go. When they reached the vicinity, he directed them to a point two miles away from the villa, then finally to a particular hotel. By the time they arrived at 3.30 a.m., the problems with the contract had been ironed out.

They collapsed into bed but were up and ready to do the interview at 11.30 that morning. Everyone was delighted with Rebecca's polished on-screen performance. By 4.30 p.m. they were on their way back to London, landing in the early hours of Wednesday morning. After three hours' sleep Hazel began editing the programme. The interview went out at 10 p.m. on 15 April and was seen by just over two million people.

Rebecca, who watched the interview at Max's apartment in Marbella, told the world that Beckham made her feel a 'million dollars'. She also hinted that she knew something about an intimate part of him that could prove her story in court, if it went that far.

After the interview Max arranged for Rebecca to come to London for the second wave of media interest. He likes to give his friends a share in his good fortune when he is working on a good story and on this occasion he picked the television presenter Michael Barrymore's ex-wife Cheryl, whom Max had known since she was fifteen.

Max asked her to hide Rebecca in her central London home and act as her manager for any TV work. Rebecca wanted to become a TV presenter and Cheryl was delighted to help. 'It's not Max's thing to concentrate on one person for weeks on end,' she explained, speaking shortly before her death from cancer in April 2005. 'Whereas I'm good at that. I'm equally good at keeping secrets.

'I hid Rebecca for a total of six weeks. I was a bit taken aback when she first came to stay, because she was the most uninhibited woman I've ever met. She talked freely about intimate sexual things that I'd never talk about, but I got used to it and overall we got on well. She was bright and basically good-hearted.'

Max's role in the story altered again. He was now not only deal-maker but also post-story adviser and gave Rebecca some fatherly counsel about her rampant sexuality. 'I told her she was now under the microscope so anything and everything she did would be blown up out of all proportion, and if she was seen to be a nymphomaniac it would be harder for her to be accepted as a mainstream TV presenter.'

But Max told Rebecca that it was up to her. 'A few weeks later I had journalists from three different papers phoning to say she'd been seen at Stringfellows nightclub with a young lady and that they both went to the toilet together where they were heard to mumble and moan. It was total nonsense. She hadn't been to the toilet with anybody. That sort of thing was happening all the time.' Weeks later Rebecca rang to ask whether he thought she could get away with having a fling with a well-known womaniser. 'I warned her that if it got into the papers she would be torn apart, but that it was again up to her.'

Unlike some of Max's clients who disliked being in the glare of publicity, Rebecca luxuriated in the experience and was determined to milk it for all it was worth. 'Rebecca is a good example of how the attitude of women who kiss and tell today is so different from ten or fifteen years ago,' he says. 'Then most women would have kept their head down and counted their money quietly. Now it's often the complete opposite. They feel absolutely no embarrassment. Perceptions change. Forty years ago you'd feel ashamed if you didn't go to church on a Sunday. But no one would now.

'The only thing that did surprise me was how much blame was heaped on Victoria for not being with David in Spain. I'd anticipated that Rebecca would be the villain of the piece, and poor David the victim, but I thought just for once people might feel sorry for Victoria. But there was more vitriol dumped on her than on Rebecca. So much so you'd have thought that David had nothing to do with it, that he was just an unwilling victim and that Rebecca forced herself on to him and took advantage of him because his wife was neglecting him.

'It was hugely entertaining to read comments in the papers which implied that if you are a man you can do anything sexually with a women and she'd get the blame. It isn't the way I see things.'

Not that Max knows the details of what David and Rebecca were alleged to have got up to. 'I didn't look at the explicit phone texts. Nor did I read a single word in the paper. I'm not in the least interested in reading about other people's sex lives. There are a lot of ironies in my life and that's one of them. I get a lot out of the big stories, but it's the deal I like and then the exposure, not the actual details of the story.'

Vast numbers of people round the world *were* riveted by the detail of the story, though, and Rebecca's disclosures have made her a rich woman.

She earned about £700,000 for talking to the *News of the World*, *NOW* magazine, appearing on TV and through syndication. She's also been given countless media opportunities. These have included presenting programmes, going on *The Farm*, a reality TV show where she masturbated a boar, being given an acting role in the Sky One football soap *Dream Team* and going on *Celebrity Love Island*, another TV reality show where singletons competed for cash, votes and love.

Max, however, only continues to look after his clients if they go along with his advice. Everything went well with Rebecca until the early part of 2005 when she decided she no longer wanted Cheryl as her TV manager. 'I felt this was a mistake as Cheryl had done a very good job for her and was the best chance she had of building a successful career on television. Nor did I think she behaved very well by sending Cheryl a note sacking her shortly before she died, without bothering to speak to her personally. Rebecca and I then parted, but I hope things work out for her. She has a lot of attractive qualities.'

Rebecca has been grateful for Max's help. 'He is so brilliant at what he does, that if anyone has a situation like mine, he is the one person to turn to. But you need to be strong. I have a powerful personality and am very confident, which got me through each day, but not everyone is like that, so it could be very difficult for them.

'He was wonderful at handling the aftermath of the story too. He told me which journalists to speak to and who to avoid. Overall my life is much the same as it was, except I now have new job opportunities, that I wouldn't have wanted to miss out on. But I am equally aware it may not last. If that happens at least I can look back and think I gave everything my best shot.'

Andy Coulson remains delighted with his scoop. 'Max along with our team did a brilliant job on the Beckham story. He is the best PR of his type in the business.'

The story won the *News of the World* 'Scoop of the Year' for 2004 in the Press Awards, the newspaper equivalent of the Oscars. One executive remarked that perhaps the award should have bypassed the newspaper and been given straight to Max.

Ironically, just as it only took one phone call to Max to get the story rolling, it would have taken just one phone call to bury it for good. Max has a unique way of working. He is both poacher and gamekeeper. He knows exactly what's needed to prove a story, and equally what has to be done to stop it. If David Beckham had called him, asked for his protection and become his client, the details about his alleged affair would almost certainly never have come out.

The only way the *News of the World*'s lawyers would have felt confident enough to give the story the go-ahead was through the text messages. So, once the pictures of Rebecca and David at the nightclub appeared in the paper and rumours about the text messages started, Max could have arranged for David to either lose his mobile or lend it to a mate. The friend, who would have been single, would have owned up to having used the phone to send sexy text messages for a laugh. And been paid handsomely to keep his mouth shut.

The call would have made a crucial difference. But David didn't ask Max to help out.

Instead the story started a snowball of indiscretion that gathered so much momentum that it smashed holes not only in the carefully manufactured Beckham brand, but also – though in this case it was SFX and not Rebecca who had been employed by the Beckhams – in confidentiality agreements between celebrities and their staff.

It's a cautionary tale that highlights the fact that whoever has a major story to sell, there is only one person in the UK to go to and that's Max. And if you want to stop one, that's Max too.

2. HARDY ROAD

Curiously there is a strong link between David Beckham and Max's only hero, Johnny Haynes. Both men played midfield and both became England football captain. Johnny, like Beckham, was a high-profile player. He even advertised Brylcreem, the hair gel the image-conscious young man used in the 50s, which by coincidence was also the first product Beckham advertised. Johnny also paved the way for the vast wages available to footballers like Beckham today. In 1960 he became the first player to earn the then mighty sum of £100 per week.

'One of my clearest memories of childhood is going with my dad to watch Johnny play for Fulham, the team my family has been associated with since way back,' Max remembers. 'My great-uncle Fred was secretary of Fulham and Dad, who was quite a good footballer in his time, and one or two of his four brothers used to sell programmes at the grounds so they could watch the games for free.

'Most spectators idolise the guy who scores the goals, but I remember watching Haynes as a young boy and marvelling at his amazing control and creativity and how he always seemed to be at the centre of the game. Although I have followed football all my life, I have never known any one player to have such overall impact in every game. I was too young to understand the psychology of it all at the time, but he epitomised many important qualities. What Johnny was to Fulham I have tried to be in the world of PR. Like him I love to be as close to the centre of everything I'm involved in and to have as much influence and control as possible. I love creating opportunities for other people and defending them against any media attack. Although I later went on to work with many huge stars including The Beatles, Sinatra, and Muhammad Ali, Johnny Haynes still remains the only hero I've ever had.'

Maxwell Frank Clifford was born on Tuesday 6 April 1943 at Kingston Hospital, Surrey, weighing 6lb 4oz. His mother Lillian was 38, his father Frank four years older.

In those days children weren't allowed into hospital wards, so Lillian held up her tiny bundle at the window so that baby Max's 13-year-old sister Eleanor and two brothers Bernard, who was nine and Harold, known as Cliff, seven, could wave at him.

Eleanor, the oldest child and only girl in the family, was absolutely delighted to have a new baby brother. 'His arrival was quite wonderful,' she says. 'We all loved him and gave him lots of attention and, as a result, he was a very good baby. I still think of him as my baby brother. He arrived at a time when the war seemed to be going on for ever and life was hellish. Max's arrival shone a bright light in those dark times.'

Bernard and Cliff both remember the occasion clearly too, but, like many small boys, weren't terribly interested in the new addition to the family. 'The only thing I remember about him as a tiny baby,' says Cliff, 'was that he was a sickly child, covered in veins and went blue a lot of the time. But I soon warmed to him. He was naturally a kind little boy. There was nothing nasty about him.'

Bernard loved Max too. 'From the start there was a strong bond between us and a deep understanding that we would always be there for each other.'

Bernard is convinced Max was conceived with the specific purpose of stopping their mother working. 'Like most women in those days, Mum gave up her job once she got married. But as part of the war effort she was sent to work part time on the production line of Zeals, a factory that made thermometers.

'Dad was furious. He didn't approve of women working. The only way a woman could be excused work was if she was pregnant or had a new baby. So I'm sure they had another child so she could return to being housewife and mother where he felt she belonged. Without the war, Max might never have been born!

'My parents absolutely doted on him from the start, particularly as a few years later both Eleanor and I left school and went on our way. Although Eleanor had been Dad's favourite child, once Max was born Dad really focused on him. It was as if he had a second family.'

Frank Clifford was born in 1900, the third child of a family of ten, eight of whom – four girls and four boys – survived into adulthood. Frank's mother and Max's grandmother, Elizabeth Keatch, was part of a wealthy family of staunch Tories who, in the nineteenth century, owned and ran a large dairy farm in Earlsfield, south London.

They sold some of the land before the Second World War and used the proceeds to build property both on what was left and elsewhere in the locality. Elizabeth was herself one of eight but the only one to marry – to Stephen James Clifford. She was a repressed Victorian lady who played the piano but never showed her grandchildren any affection or even remembered their names. Visiting her was usually quite an ordeal.

'Dad would take us round to see her and it was always very boring,' Max remembers. 'She lived at 10 Pelham Road, Wimbledon, just round the corner from our family home. She had a big house with a nice garden full of apple trees. We children were forbidden to touch the apples, but we always took some if we could.

'Sometimes Grandpa Clifford would sneak us a few windfalls, but if she caught him, she would make us give them back. Otherwise nothing much happened during our visits. She believed that children should be seen and not heard, so we just had to sit on a chair and listen. She never hugged any of us.'

'Grandpa Stephen James Clifford, who came from the West Country, was much kinder. He was the assistant stationmaster at Waterloo station and was genuinely interested in people. Grandma Clifford died in the autumn of 1953, aged 83, and Grandpa Clifford the following January.

'About the only thing Dad had in common with his mother was a love of music and playing the piano. He was so keen that his parents bought him an organ to play at home. When he was fourteen – in 1914 – he volunteered to fight in the First World War. He served as a marksman in the infantry and became a sniper. He was in Cologne on Armistice Day, played the organ in Cologne Cathedral and desperately wanted to become a concert pianist when he left the army.

'In 1923 he was invited to join the Savoy Orpheans, a dance band who played at the Savoy Hotel, but he turned the opportunity down because he wanted a solo career. He became very frustrated when it didn't happen. He was at that time a typical 1920s man-about-town who loved parties.

'Politically his views put him at odds with his family. They were active Conservatives on various councils, but he came back from the war hating aristocratic Field Marshal Sir Douglas Haig, later Earl Haig, who was called the 'Butcher of the Somme' after British forces suffered massive losses in 1917.

'The horrors Dad saw turned him into an ardent socialist. He loathed the fact that ordinary people had been sent to the front while the aristocracy in the army stayed back and remained safe. It coloured his view of the upper classes all his life. Dad always voted Labour except when his older brother Philip stood unsuccessfully as a Tory candidate for Wimbledon Council.

'When Dad realised he wasn't going to make it as a concert pianist he took a job lighting the streetlights, then became an electrician, working for the Wimbledon Electric Light Company. He earned a decent living, but was poor all his life because he was a compulsive gambler. He mainly bet on horses and the football pools. The family suffered more before I was born as there were three dependent children, and sometimes my brothers and sister were virtually destitute and starving.

'Dad had also upset his family when he married my mother Lillian in 1928. She was a maid and they felt she was beneath him. Mum was born in 1905, thirteen years after her parents married; she had a younger sister Eleanor. Her parents also adopted two boys who she thought of as her brothers.

'Her background was very religious. Her mother Annie was a major in the Salvation Army. Her father, Charles Boffee, owned a couple of grocery shops, but gave them up to work full time for the Salvation Army. They married in Bermondsey in 1892 and first lived in Kingston Road, Wimbledon before moving close by to 41 Hardy Road; a house owned by the Salvation Army.

'My family moved into the house next-door-but-one to them five years before I was born. My mother's parents worked in the East End, which was a rough and deprived area.

'My grandfather was a gentle giant, about six feet tall, and a devout Christian. Salvation Army officers wouldn't consider going into a pub at that time. It was much too sinful, so he used to stand outside waiting for people to come out, then try to preach to them and sell them *Warcry*, the Salvation Army newspaper. The drunken louts used to goad him and wind him up and there were lots of fights.

'I can get angry very quickly, but my grandfather was completely opposed to violence of any sort and would just stand there and refuse to retaliate however hard he was hit, or however many times he was knocked down.

'He became ill in his late forties and was taken into Brookwood lunatic asylum in Woking, Surrey. His illness was shrouded in mystery. My grandmother used to say he had a creeping paralysis but my mother said his illness was due to all the blows he took on the head. In those days mental illness wasn't talked about, so no one really knew. He died in hospital in 1916 and my grandmother received the news of his death in a curt printed letter with his personal details added in ink. It informed her that if she didn't collect his body immediately he would be put in a lunatic pauper's grave. He was fifty-three and my mother was a little girl of ten when he died.

'I was three when grandma Boffee died aged eighty in the summer of 1946. Apparently seventy members of the Salvation Army stood outside her house playing music very loudly for her as she passed away. They hoped that even though she was deaf, she'd be able to hear them. I'm sorry I didn't really know her because, by all accounts, she was a wonderful person.

'When her husband was taken ill, and there was no money coming into the home, Annie Boffee took in laundry and looked after other people's babies, often given to her through the Salvation Army.

'One of the babies was John Ricard. His mother never came back for him so, as poor as Grandma was, she brought him up as one of the family until he was eighteen. He then went into the navy, but apparently deserted quite soon afterwards. She tried to find out what happened to him but never could and was terribly upset that he never got in touch.

'She adopted another boy called Norman, who she was very proud of. He joined the RAF, became a wing commander, got a DFC with Bar and led the raid on Munich in the Second World War.

'My brothers loved my grandma very much and not just because she always bought them comics like the *Beano* and *Dandy*. Living so close meant they popped round a lot to see her. As she was deaf, instead of knocking, they would put a hand through the letter box and pull on a black leather shoelace to open the door.

'Her brother Richard Pink, who we called Uncle Dick, also lived with her. He'd been blown up and gassed during the First World War and was rather slow, poor man. When Grandma died he stayed on in the house but took all his meals with us. He didn't have any teeth so Mum used to cut up bread and put it in hot milk for him with lots of sugar. He made terrible slurping noises as he ate, so we boys used to wait until just before he started to eat and then make terrible slurping noises too.

'Dad was five feet nine inches tall, thin, handsome and quite vain. I am supposed to look rather like him. Mum, on the other hand, was five-foot-two and weighed about sixteen stone. She had red hair, a big bust, liked loose floral dresses and was wonderful to cuddle. Perhaps that's why I've always loved a good cuddle myself. Mum was the first of three very important women in my life.

'Mum and her sister were put in service at the age of thirteen, because Grandma was struggling to feed them. They worked for various families who lived in large houses in Morden, Surrey. Dad was 28 and Mum 24 when they married at Trinity Road church in south Wimbledon on 17 April 1928.

'They first lived in a couple of rooms in Latimer Road, Wimbledon. My sister Eleanor was born in 1930 and Bernard, who we called Bunny because his ears stuck out, four years later in 1934. Cliff was born two years after that in 1936. He was given the name of Harold, but hated it so much that he told us he wanted to be called Cliff.

'In 1938 the five of them moved round the corner to 37 Hardy Road. The house, which then cost eleven old shillings (55p) a week to rent was in a row of terraced properties. They were built of brick at the turn of the twentieth century. They had rounded brick arches over the doors and tiny front gardens. There was an alleyway at the end of every ten houses where the dustmen used to collect the rubbish. They are now described as artisan cottages and fetch over £300,000, but in those days they were very modest properties. At one point Dad was offered the chance to buy it for £300, but unfortunately he wasn't interested.

'They were originally built without a damp course and water ran down the inside walls, so it always felt very dank. There was no bathroom or inside toilet. The toilet was a horrible smelly place and always freezing, so none of us stayed in there long. Our toilet paper was squares of newspaper Mum cut up and hung on a butcher's hook. Dad used to buy the *Daily* and *Sunday Express* because he loved the cartoonist Giles, and he'd give them to Mum when he'd finished reading them.

'We had a front room with a settee, two chairs and an upright piano, which we children weren't allowed to go into except at Christmas. It was saved for when the vicar or the doctor came round. There was a passage that led to a ten-foot by ten-foot middle room which had a coal fire, the only proper fire in the house, and where we all lived most of the time. In the room were some upright wooden chairs with rush seats plus a couple of easy chairs.

'There was also an inlaid oval wooden table with flaps. The top came off and during the war my parents would prop it up against the windows so that when a bomb blew out the windows, which apparently happened quite a few times, the shattered glass didn't scatter too far. We didn't have a shelter and when there were air raids, Grandma Boffee would come round and tell my brothers and sister stories to keep them calm.

'The kitchen or scullery was at the end of the passage. It had a wood-burning boiler in the corner where Mum did the family washing every Monday. This was replaced in the 50s by a gas boiler, and an Ascot water heater was also installed over the kitchen sink. When it was freezing Mum would also light the gas oven and keep the door open.

'Upstairs there were three small bedrooms. Mum and Dad originally slept in the front room, which was the largest. When I was a baby I slept in a cot alongside them. My sister had a tiny box room and my brothers slept head to toe in the back bedroom, which was little more than eight foot by seven foot. Mum used to foster children given to her by the Salvation Army. Some of them stayed during the day, others were with us for years at a time and somehow squashed in with my brothers.

'There were sometimes so many children coming and going you didn't always remember who was who. Mum loved kids and it was also a way of earning a little extra money. Once I became a toddler, I slept with my brothers in the larger front bedroom and Mum and Dad moved into what had been my brothers' bedroom at the back.

'None of the bedrooms had any heating and in winter there would be ice not only on the inside of the windows but also down the walls. We didn't have pyjamas, but used to sleep in whatever we had on. I'm sure that's why I don't feel the cold now.

'Mum made sure all of us were clean. We used to brush our teeth in the kitchen sink and have a wash down in the middle room in front of the open fire. There was a zinc bath that balanced on the garden fence, but it was only brought into the kitchen once in a blue moon. It was a real performance filling it up with water from the boiler and, like most boys, I was never interested in using it.

'If we were made to have a bath we'd usually go round the corner to the public baths in Latimer Road, which is now the Wimbledon Leisure Centre. They were closed on Sunday and there was always a queue on Saturday, so it was best to go during the week. It cost about three old pennies for a towel and soap and we'd go into a small numbered cubicle that contained nothing but a bath.

'The water controls were outside in the corridor. We used to shout "more hot water for number nine", and whoever was patrolling the corridor outside would turn on the tap. You could only have one lot of hot water. If you asked again you'd be told your time was up. I remember looking down into the cellar through the windows when I arrived at the two men whose job it was to keep the boilers stocked and thinking that was one job I didn't want to do.

'We had electric lights at home, which were fitted on the walls alongside our gaslights, but no power at all, so we didn't have an electric fire or fridge, although Mum later got a gas fridge. Instead we had a larder under the stairs and Mum would put milk and anything else that was likely to go off outside on a cold windowsill. The gas meter was in the larder too and took old shillings. When we ran out of money Grandma Boffee would come round and feed the meter for us.

'There was a wonderful sense of community in our road and nearly everyone left their doors open so neighbours could pop in and out. Nothing was ever stolen, but of course there wasn't anything to steal.

'Mum always kept the house spotless and did the cleaning wearing a floral wrap-around pinafore. The only thing of value we had was the piano in the front room. As soon as the family moved to Hardy Road Dad went to the piano shop Barnes & Co in Tooting, south London, and bought himself an upright iron-framed piano.

'It was quite selfish of him because there was often not enough money left at the end of the week for food, but it was his priority. Dad was quiet and just got on with his own thing. He was also stubborn and single-minded. I'm the same, but hopefully not as selfish.

'When I was older I loved listening to him play and music remains one of my passions. We didn't have a radio until after the war. If any of us wanted to listen to something, we went to Grandma Boffee. We became the proud possessors of her radio when she died.

'Mum had a lot to put up with from my father, but I never heard her complain. She thought the world of him and even though his constant gambling caused her considerable hardship, she was always in awe of him and grateful that he had married her. She did, though, get very upset when he got into debt. She often had to pawn her wedding ring or a pair of shoes to pay the bills. Occasionally she'd have to pawn our sheets and we'd sleep directly on the mattress.

'Being so much older than me, my brothers and sister had the worst of it. Life could be very tough for them. In the 30s workers used to get paid cash at the end of the week. Dad earned about three pounds and ten shillings (£3.50). He would often collect his money, then go straight to a local club called Messengers that had a café on the ground floor and billiard and card tables upstairs and blow the lot in the afternoon. Mum used to try to stop him by sending Eleanor to persuade him to give her a few shillings before he started gambling so she would be able to feed us.

'Dad had a soft spot for Eleanor, probably because she was the only girl, and if anyone could get money out of him, she could. But the timing was crucial and sometimes she arrived too late, or he was in a mood to refuse. Dad didn't mean to be unkind, he was just unworldly. He'd never had to worry about money before he married Mum and he found it hard when he became responsible for looking after a family.

'When Mum didn't have enough money to buy food she'd send Bernard and Cliff to the local bakers late in the afternoon with a ha'penny that she'd managed to save. They'd ask for some stale bread. Sometimes the baker would take pity on them and hand some over for nothing.

'Mum knew that hungry children couldn't sleep so she would try to make as much as possible out of very little by pouring hot water on the bread and adding some pepper to give it some taste. My brothers and sister would eat it before they went to bed so they could sleep with full stomachs.

'When Dad was gambling heavily that was the only meal they had all day. Bernard doesn't remember having breakfast until he was eleven and in those days there wasn't school lunch. But when Eleanor managed to get some money from Dad, Mum would make stews with everything in them and bread pudding for afters. They might even have bread and jam for tea. There was also always a pot of tea on the go, which is possibly why I drink so much of it today.

'During the war Mum made cakes with our egg rations. Cliff would never eat them but it was years before he confessed why. He claims Dad used to cut his toenails in the kitchen every Sunday and a few hours later he'd sometimes spot bits of toenail surfacing in Mum's cakes.

'Luckily good old Grandma Boffee used to help us out when times were bad. Norman used to send her food parcels from wherever he was with the RAF and she always passed them on to us. Mum and Norman were always close and she never referred to him as anything other than her brother.

'Round the time the Second World War started Dad took an additional job working in the evenings as a dresser at Wimbledon Theatre. He loved the theatre, ballet and opera and much enjoyed being with artists. Unfortunately he spent all that money at the bookmakers too. He was 39 when the war began, so too old to be in the forces, but he served as a local defence volunteer in the Home Guard and was also seconded to work as an electrician at the American Forces' aerodrome in Buckinghamshire.

'The pay was good, but it meant he was away for periods of time. During the war my brothers and sister were evacuated from London twice, but luckily I was too small to be sent anywhere alone and went instead with Mum to St Neots, near Huntingdonshire, where Dad was working.

'Although I love my brothers and sister we've never been that close – partly because of the age gap. Nor was I as close to Dad as I was to Mum. I always felt he was a nice person, but like most men at the time he didn't get very involved with us children. But as I grew older I do remember listening to his political views, and his experiences in the First World War. Basically if you were rich you voted Conservative and if you were poor you voted Labour. I wasn't at all interested in politics then. I just wanted to play sport, and particularly football, but Bernard was actively involved and later became a local Labour councillor in the London borough of Merton, then mayor and alderman.

'My interest in the Labour party developed differently – more the PR side of politics than active participation. Some people have said I was significantly responsible for the downfall of the Tory government in 1997 because of my involvement in the stories that led to it being tagged the party of sleaze, and that the party has still not recovered.

'One of my earliest memories is sitting under the oval table in our middle room listening to the radio. I'd get a cushion, crawl underneath, pull the flap down and pretend it was a little house. There I'd listen to programmes like *Variety Bandbox*, the *Goon Show*, *In Town Tonight* and *Dick Barton Special Agent*. Hiding under the table also meant I could stay up late, because Mum often forgot I was there.

'Being the youngest of four meant I was competitive from a very early age and always had the impetus to do well, but only in the things that interested me, like football. I'd play in the street or at the recreation centre down the road. I've been passionate about sport since childhood and good at it too. It's one of the things that has given me confidence. I've played cricket, water polo, boxed and run, but football has always been my favourite sport and at school I was always in the first teams.

'Sport is about ability, talent and strength, but psychology also comes into it. I noticed from an early age that although there were several players who were more talented than me, they often had the wrong temperament.

'As a young boy I often played with a local lad who was a brilliant winger, but if someone kicked him he'd quit the game. Whereas when I got injured, I'd get up and carry on running. I never wanted the opposing side to see that I was injured or in pain. Pride and a will to win are two characteristics that were always with me on the football pitch and have stayed with me throughout my life.'

Max's attitude on the pitch was deadly earnest. His long-time friend Mac McCormick, who played in the same football team, clearly remembers their schoolboy matches: 'Max would get so angry if one of us missed a pass or goal, that he could become quite sinister and some players were scared of him. I'd often try to calm him down and remind him it was just a game. He wouldn't listen at the time, but once the game was over, he'd quickly recover his good humour.'

Max has always had lots of energy and found sport both physically and mentally stimulating and a good way of getting rid of tension. 'I need to take exercise regularly,' he says. 'I don't play football any more. Instead I play a lot of tennis, but I'm not a good sport and have always been a terrible loser. I can get really angry.

'I also swim. I have a fifty-foot swimming pool at home where I swim about twenty lengths a day, including front crawl and butterfly. I also swim in the pool at my apartment in Marbella. Working out makes me feel sharp, sparkling and alive. I miss the adrenalin and feel stale without it.

'By the time I came along, the family finances had improved a bit. Once my brothers were seven they had started doing milk, paper and bakers' rounds and gave the money to Mum. The introduction of rationing helped, too, as Dad couldn't gamble our rations away and we would always have food. Also the school clinic gave out orange juice and cod-liver oil to pupils.

'Mum used to buy some of our clothes at the local Co-op store and if she didn't have enough money to buy what she needed outright, she could pay smaller amounts weekly until her debt was paid. Being the youngest most of my clothes were hand-me-downs. I didn't mind, nearly everyone who lived around us was poor too. And I didn't realise until I was much older that our parlous financial state was largely due to Dad's gambling.

'Every Sunday we had to go to Sunday school. We'd all been christened in the Church of England, but the Sunday school was Methodist. I never really entered the spirit of it, but I used to love Sunday afternoons when we went out as a family to Bushey Park or Epsom Downs.

'In the summer we'd go to Hampton Court, which I enjoyed too. They used to have classical concerts in the music rooms and open the windows so you could hear them for free in the grounds. Dad loved them, but my brothers and I were more interested in rolling down the grass slopes. Holidays consisted, if we were lucky, of a day trip to Hastings or Brighton.

'Although parents smacked their children in those days, and Mum had given Bernard a few beatings when he was young, I was never hit. If I'd done something naughty, Mum would sometimes chase me with a rolling pin or the copper stick she used to pull out the washing from the boiler, but as she was a big lady, I was always too quick for her. I used to run up the stairs, jump on the shed roof and then down to the alleyway and disappear. When I got back she'd be laughing.

'My parents were quite strict with my brothers, but by the time I came along, they'd mellowed. It was just as well. As a small child I hated being told what to do, what to eat or when to go to bed. Even today if someone tells me something, you can be almost sure I'll do the opposite. From a very young age I felt I was best at controlling my own destiny. It's one reason I have to be self-employed.

'I always knew my brothers and sister loved me, but being so much older they also thought I was a pain. When I was six, Eleanor was already nineteen and when she brought a boyfriend home I would run into the room stark naked, fart and then run out again. She would understandably go mad.

'To get her own back, she developed a habit of pinching my bottom. I used to undress in the middle room where the coal fire was, but by the age of ten I became so self-conscious about my bottom, that when Bernard – then twenty – brought his girlfriend Iris home, who later became his wife, I'd undress, then stand in the nude in the corner to hide my bottom. I wasn't at all worried about exposing myself in front. Apparently Iris felt extremely embarrassed.

'Cliff, as the one nearest in age to me, was often given the task of looking after me. From when I was five he'd have to take me swimming. There were two pools round the corner from us. Cliff and I would go to the cheaper one which had a painted concrete floor and cost one penny as compared to the more expensive pool that cost two pennies and had floor tiles and cubicles. He hated going with me because, as he was just entering his teens, he wanted to talk to girls without his small brother hovering close by. Also, although I later became a very strong swimmer, at that age I stood around shivering because I didn't want to go into the water.

'My first school was Pelham Primary School. Then at eight I started at All Saints Junior School, a dark and gloomy place where my brothers and sister had been. I've always been very physical and got into a fight on my first day when I saw one of the older boys picking on an obviously weaker lad. Even though I was a new boy I went up to the older boy and told him to leave the small boy alone. Not surprisingly he ignored me. So I hit him.

'He turned out to be the headmaster's son, but the head couldn't say too much to me, because he knew his son was in the wrong. I told Bernard about it when I got home and he told me to be careful of the boy as he would be looking out for me, but it was fine. Then as now I've always hated bullies and was often involved in skirmishes and fighting other people's battles. If any of my mates were picked on by another boy, especially those who were small, I'd pick on that boy.

'From the time I was little Mum told me stories about how good the Salvation Army were at helping people. Both she and Dad brought us children up to be fair and help people who had less than you, rather than look down or take advantage of them. It's something I've always tried to do, although not many people know that side of me.

'From a very young age I would help old ladies cross the road or carry their shopping. My school friends wouldn't notice them or run off, but it was instinctive to me. In fact I have always helped people and supported the underdog, both financially and in practical ways.

'Sport was my way of showing off and helped make me a lot of friends. I was very sociable, but not particularly well behaved, partly because I've always enjoyed playing practical jokes on people. I remember a lad in my class had a speech impediment and I used to flick something at his ear, which made him yell out. But by the time the teacher turned round I'd be head down doing my work and because he had difficulty in talking, it was hard for him to explain what had happened. So he was often sent out of the class for something I'd done. I should have felt sorry for him and don't now remember why at the time I thought it was incredibly funny.

'I always disliked sitting down for ages learning things. Some of the pupils in my class were very slow and would take what seemed for ever to understand what the teacher was saying. Whereas I picked it up in five minutes and once I got the gist of it, I got bored very quickly. I've never been academic but I'm quick thinking and adjust to and manipulate situations very easily. I also have a very low boredom threshold, which is why I'm so lucky in my work; I have so many things going on at the same time.

'As a child I was always finding ways of entertaining myself and got up to all sorts of trouble. I would see opportunities for mischief that others wouldn't. It's an ability that has served me well throughout my working life. I got away with it most of the time too, and barely got detention or told to write lines.

'When I was nine, my mother was summoned to school by the head. He produced an exam paper where I'd written my name on the top and then covered the rest of the page with drawings of footballs and goal posts. She told Dad, but neither of them told me off. There was never any pressure or indeed much interest in me being academic and they weren't at all upset when I failed my eleven-plus – which meant missing out on going to grammar school – and went instead to Pelham Secondary Modern School. They were more interested in me earning money. My sister was the only academic one in the family.

'When she was fifteen she won a scholarship to Wimbledon Commercial School, where she became head girl. She soon got a job as PA to the Vice President at Morgan Guarantee Trust Bank, a very up-market bank, and she was very well paid.

'She used to give a lot of her salary to Mum so our fortunes and the food we ate improved considerably. She later went into the colonial service, became a PA to various High Commissioners and eventually emigrated to South Africa, where at 38 she married an accountant with his own business and had two children. Although we are friendly, I've hardly seen her in the last forty years, but I'm very pleased that she's done well for herself.

'One of the things I've always loved is shopping for food. I've done the supermarket shopping all my adult life and even as a boy I was happy to help Mum with that chore. I remember going into the local butchers one day when I was nine and him reaching under the counter to get something he wrapped up in brown paper and gave to me saying, "Here, son. Take this home and it will see you through the week."

'I was thrilled because there was still rationing at the time. I ran all the way home and proudly gave it to Mum. She opened the parcel and found a sheep's eye. Hence the joke that it would "see" us through the week. I felt so disappointed but Mum thought it was hilarious.

'All in all I had a wonderful upbringing. I adored my mother and know she doted on me. She had a great sense of humour, a love of the ridiculous and took most things with a pinch of salt, all characteristics I have inherited. She also had a real temper. I do too. I'm a bit better now I'm older, but that red mist still descends from time to time.'

3. LUST AND LOVE

Max's position as youngest in the family suited him well. When he was small he had all the advantages of being part of a large family and was doted on by his older siblings. Then as he grew older he had all the benefits of being like an only child and enjoying the full focus of his parents' attention.

'Our parents spoiled him,' remembers Bernard. 'They gave him everything they couldn't afford to give us. When he needed a new leather football, football boots or kit he always had them, whereas they had so little money when Cliff and I were small, that we didn't even have a football.

'Mum also washed all the kit for Max's entire team and encouraged him to bring friends home and made them cakes and tea. She never did that with us, because in those early days we didn't have enough food to share.'

'Max even had different food from us,' adds Cliff. 'Once Eleanor was helping to support the family financially we used to have food like kippers or roe, but Mum often bought a steak for Max instead. We never resented it. I'm not sure why.'

By the time Max was a teenager, his sister and brothers had virtually left home.

Bernard left school at fourteen, worked for Bradbury, Wilkinson, the now defunct banknote printing business in Surrey, and became an active member of the print union Natsopa. He did his national service and married Iris soon after he returned to London. They had three children.

Cliff left school at fifteen to work at Elys, a department store in Wimbledon. Following his National Service, he trained to lay floors and worked as a freelance flooring subcontractor for various companies including Elys. His first wife Pam died of cancer in 1968, leaving him with two small sons. He married again and had another son by his second wife Jane.

Max's attitude to life as a teenager was very much as it is today. 'I thought life was a race and I had to cram in as much as possible, do everything in top gear as fast as I could and have a great time,' he says.

'When I was fifteen I discovered water polo, which was a terrific sport for me as it combined swimming with a ball sport and the referee is virtually irrelevant. He can only see about twenty-five per cent of what is going on, so you can mete out your own justice and particularly make up your own rules, which is something I've done many times in my adult life.

'I also took up boxing at Earlsfield Boxing Club. It was an outlet for my aggressive side, but I didn't do it for long, as I much preferred football and swimming. In amongst all the sport, though, I started a skiffle group with four friends. I played the guitar, but I was hopeless.

'I crammed a lot into my school lunch break too, and would do things like rush to the swimming baths to take life-saving classes.

'I even managed to lose my virginity during my lunch break. I was fifteen. She was called Christine, was sixteen and had glasses, big boobs, lovely skin, brunette hair and dark sparkling eyes. She also had a bit of experience, so from my point of view she was a mature woman.

'I'd gone round to my friend Chris's house, which was about a hundred yards from the school. She was there too and it all happened very naturally. We were in the sitting room and she told me to lie down on the floor. She got undressed and I followed, taking my clothes off as quickly as I could.

'She then sat astride me and it was wonderful watching her lovely boobs bounce up and down in my face. The whole thing lasted all of ten seconds and wasn't in the least romantic. But I really enjoyed it and wanted to do it again. I learned quickly and it was much better and lasted longer the second time. That time I was on top. It suited me – being on top is the position in life where I always want to be.

'Over the next few weeks I got into the swing of it. Christine and I didn't have a relationship. I didn't fall for her and we didn't talk much. It was more a case of grabbing every opportunity. Sex became another sport for me. I enjoyed it like I enjoyed football and swimming. I spent a lot of time with her at Chris's house that summer. His parents always seemed to be away, so it became a den of iniquity with lots of teenagers experimenting and finding out about sex.

'At the end of the summer it stopped as naturally as it began. Since then I've nearly always gone for brunettes with big boobs, bright sparkling eyes, who could make me laugh. I found that well-rounded boobs often meant a well-rounded personality, whereas skinny girls tended to be a bit uptight. I love women's bodies and the fact that every one is so different and I have always wanted to please them sexually. Knowing a woman is enjoying herself enhances my own enjoyment and I have taken a personal pride in giving women pleasure.

'As a young man I never thought of myself as either Jack the Lad or Casanova and never rushed around like a headless chicken looking to get laid. Luckily girls seemed to be attracted to me, but I was never the ideal partner. I was too greedy to be faithful. I didn't even feel guilty about it, but I did want my girlfriend to be happy when I was with her.'

Unlike many teenagers whose early sexual exploits are little more than tentative fumbles, Max seems to have hit the ground running. From the start he was unshockable, confident and amoral. Any kind of sexual behaviour was fine by him, as long as no one was forced into doing something they didn't want to do. Sex was a jolly romp and as natural as breathing.

He's also always preferred the company of women to men. 'Although I love sport, I've never been macho and don't like to go to pubs with men,' he says. 'I prefer to be with women, not only because sex has played an important part in my life and I've never been sexually attracted to men, but also because I'd rather talk to someone I felt attracted to.

'Throughout my life women have always talked to me about their problems and I've never found it difficult to keep their secrets. It's been essential in my work. But I don't pour my heart out to anyone. I've always seen it as a matter of pride to rely on myself.

'I've also always loved dancing and as a teenager I was very keen on the twist. Most lads of my age were too shy to ask a girl to dance and instead would hang around the bar, but I couldn't see the point of leaning on the bar when I could be out on the dance floor bopping away and enjoying myself. I used to love the slow dances too because it was a good excuse to get very close. I also preferred to wait for a woman to give me signals that she was interested in me before I'd approach her. I'm proud and I didn't want to waste my time.

'Not long after Christine and I stopped seeing each other, I started going out with a girl called Valerie Harding who I met at Wimbledon Palais. The Palais was then the centre of everything, but has long since been demolished. We were the same age and went out together for a year. She was lovely, but much too nice for me and it came to an end when she realised I wasn't being faithful. I felt rotten about how I had treated her, but there was so much going on that nothing was going to break my young heart for long.

'I was sexually adventurous from an early age and if I wanted to do something specific like having sex with a girl when her parents were in the next room, I'd keep on trying until I found someone who wanted to do it too. Almost anything went, including having two girls at a time, having sex with girlfriends' mothers and watching others have sex. It all seemed very natural to me. When I look back now at the risks I took, I realise I could have had all kinds of sexually transmitted diseases but luckily I never have.'

Although Max had innumerable girlfriends, he also yearned for stability. The little boy who made his first 'home' under the dining table at six has, as a grown man, always needed a traditional base where he could be quiet, live simply and recharge his batteries. The more energy he puts out into the world and the busier he gets, the more essential this has become.

And although he's always made friends easily, he never identifies with any one group of people. Contrary to his reputation for endless socialising, deep inside he's a loner who needs a lot of private space. He was only nineteen when he met Liz Porter and quickly knew that she was the girl who could give him the stability he needed.

'We met at Wimbledon Park, a little social club by the side of Wimbledon Park Station, in 1962,' he recalls. 'It was quite near where we both lived and I often used to go there on a Friday night with my friend Stanley Fry who'd been a winger in my football team.

'His mum, who had a florist shop in Wimbledon, bought him a small Renault. In those days it was almost unheard of for someone of nineteen to have their own car and that particular evening he drove me to the club.

'As usual I got straight on to the floor and started dancing very energetically. It wasn't long before I noticed a young girl dancing nearby with her friend and taking the mickey out of my dancing. I thought "that's cheeky" but I also admired her spirit. I liked her round, open face and big smile too, so I asked her to dance.

'She told me her name was Liz and that she was eighteen. Stan started dancing with her friend Sheila who he fancied. At the end of the dance we asked them rather nonchalantly if they would like a lift somewhere. They were so astonished that they'd met a couple of lads with a car that they accepted immediately. Liz later used to tease me that really she'd fancied Stan because of the car, and only put up with me.

'We started going out as a foursome. Stan and Sheila didn't stay together long, but Liz and I got on very well from the start and I quickly fell in love with her. She'd left school, was working as a secretary for London County Council and was a very natural person with a lovely giggle. She told me she had been born in Glasgow but had come to England when she was three. Her father Richie worked in a factory. He was also a good golfer and a quietly spoken man until he had a bit to drink, and then he loved to sing.

'Her mother Jeanette, who everyone called Etta, was a housewife. She was quiet too, but had a lovely nature and I enjoyed making her laugh. Liz also had a younger sister Christine.

'Liz was different from my other girlfriends. She instinctively knew how to cope with me. She lived on a council estate in Putney and I remember one early date when we were on the 93 bus going to a dance club in Putney, I started bragging about a flat I pretended to own in the exclusive Cheyne Walk, Chelsea.

'I did it to impress her, but she just looked at me full in the face and said, "If you have a flat in Cheyne Walk, why are we on a bus?" I loved the fact that she was not taken in by me at all. Our relationship always felt so natural.

'Liz and I also used to whiz about on a second-hand 190cc motorbike I bought, which I rode as fast as I could. I didn't wear a crash helmet, took terrible risks and came off several times, but I never hurt myself. Looking back I realise I was very lucky not to have killed her.

'When we first started going out I was still seeing one or two other girls, but those relationships petered out and luckily she didn't insist on being a virgin until her wedding day. Liz was the second of the three most important women in my life, and we married on 3 June 1967, when I was 24. We had 35 happy years together before she tragically died of cancer in April 2003.

'She was the love of my life, my wife and the mother of my only child Louise and, although I did occasionally play away, I would never have left her. Nor did I stop loving her.'

Max, who lived at home until he got married, was welcomed by Liz's parents as a future son-in-law. His mother was, however, a little tricky about Liz.

'Mum thought the world of her three sons and never believed any girl was good enough for any of us,' he explains. 'She was always difficult with Bernard and Cliff's girlfriends and later wives, but by the time Liz came along, she'd mellowed a bit and was just about OK.'

Although many grooms feel very nervous about their big day, Max was his laid-back self, packing in as much as he could in the hours before the ceremony and cutting his timing down to the wire. 'I was a little late arriving at the church because I'd gone swimming that morning and only made it just before Liz arrived,' he remembers. 'Everyone was anxious about where I was, but I knew I'd be OK.

'The ceremony took place at St Barnabas' church, in Southfields, south London. Cliff was best man and Liz's bridesmaids were her sister Christine and two of her friends. I wasn't at all nervous. It all seemed so right.

'Liz, who was 22, and very slim, wore a simple, long white dress with a veil. She looked lovely. The ceremony started solemnly, but then everyone started giggling because one of the local loonies came into the church and pretended to make a phone call against the wall, and chatted away in a very loud voice.

'Luckily it didn't spoil things. The reception with dancing followed at the local community hall of the Argyle council estate in Putney where Liz and her parents lived. The only sad thing was that Cliff's wife Pam had just been diagnosed with cancer and was going into hospital the next day for a major operation. Tragically she died almost a year to the day afterwards.

'The whisky flowed freely at the reception so my father-in-law Richie was happy. I didn't touch any but put the leftover bottles in the back of my car, a green Vauxhall, when we left. We spent our first night at our own home, a two-bedroom brand-new maisonette in Florence Avenue, Morden, Surrey that I bought for £4,750. We'd just got into bed when the phone rang. It was Richie asking for his whisky back. I told him I'd leave it outside the front door and he came round later to pick it up.

'Richie always used to sing the song "I Left My Heart in San Francisco", which everyone associated with Tony Bennett. I did some PR for the singer in the late 60s and so when he appeared at the Lakeside Country Club in Camberley, Surrey, I took my parents-in-law and Liz to hear him.

'Tony was such an easy-going man that I mentioned to him that my father-in-law was a huge fan and I'd like to bring him backstage afterwards to the artists' lounge. He was happy for me to do that. After the show he came straight up to Richie, put his arm round him and said how good it was to meet him. Richie was a very shy man and so flabbergasted that he didn't know what to say. He stuttered a bit and then blurted out, "I've been to San Francisco, you know."

'For years afterwards he used to laugh at himself and say, "What on earth made me say that? At the time I was so taken aback I couldn't think of what to say."

'Liz and I didn't have much money and largely furnished our home with things we borrowed, including a set of dining chairs with wooden arms. The first time I sat on one I went right the way through it. Liz and I roared with laughter. Laughter was always the key to our marriage. We both had very similar senses of humour. But whether she was laughing with me or at me I was never quite sure. Probably a bit of both.

'A day or two later we left for our honeymoon – a few days in Bournemouth on the south coast where Liz had an aunt. We stayed in a boarding house and spent our time walking along the beach hand in hand and swimming in the sea.

'One of the things I loved about Liz was that she was very down to earth. She said what she thought and felt, regardless of my views. She wasn't interested in hearing about my work. Nor was she ever star-struck. I didn't mind. I spent so much time with artificial people in unnatural environments that I found it therapeutic to come home to someone as natural and unaffected as Liz. I liked knowing she married me when I had very little and didn't love me because I was successful.

'It also meant I could relax and totally cut off when I was with her. I rarely asked her advice about work either. In fact if she told me not to get involved with something or that I had too much on my plate, it would almost without exception make me do whatever it was. It's part of the cantankerous side of me.

'Liz was a very loyal person, but also very private and self-contained. She used to get terribly embarrassed by me, but luckily she also found me very funny. She never shouted at me, but she had a temper and if I knew something made her cross I used to enjoy deliberately teasing her, which would inevitably make her even angrier.

'She enjoyed the fact that I earned well as she loved nice clothes, luxury holidays and going out to eat, but she didn't like people recognising me and coming up to say hello when we were having dinner in a restaurant. She also resented people constantly phoning me for help and guidance. She'd say, "Why can't they sort out their own problems and leave you alone?"

'Unlike my mother, Liz wasn't the sort of woman who would tell you she loved you, but I know she did. She never actually told Louise, who was born in June 1971, that she loved her either, but she was devoted to her. Liz gave up working as a secretary once we had Louise. I was pleased. I preferred to be the provider and for Liz to be like my mum; run the home, cook and look after our child. I wasn't a chauvinist, though, and before Louise came along I used to help out with the domestic chores. I went to the launderette, did the food shopping and made tea without any problems.

'A few months after the birth we moved to a typical three-bedroom suburban semi in Park Way, Raynes Park, which I bought for £11,500. Liz chose the décor, which was fine because she had the time and our tastes were similar. She never got pregnant again. I would have liked to have had a son and it would have been nice for Louise to have had a brother or sister, but we never saw a gynaecologist to investigate the problem, or even talked about it. I don't think that Liz was that maternal. If she had have been I'm sure we would have been more actively concerned. Perhaps she was on the pill without telling me. I didn't mind. I was happy enough with one child, and once Louise was diagnosed with juvenile rheumatoid arthritis we were so busy running backwards and forwards to hospitals over so many years that in some ways just having one child was better.'

4. WORK, PLAY AND ROCK 'N' ROLL

The only subjects Max enjoyed at school were sport and English. He didn't take O levels and left at fifteen with no qualifications or plans. It didn't worry him at all. 'I've never set out to do anything,' he says.

'Things have just come to me and I've had the luck to be in the right place at the right time.' He was, however, both ambitious and driven. He had an iron will to win and an innate ability to recognise a lucky break and grasp it with both hands. He would also work hard at anything that interested him.

'I've always been better in practice than in theory and very good at seeing opportunities,' he says. 'If there are twenty people round a table, ten won't recognise an opportunity when it's right under their nose; five can't make a decision, four keep changing their mind, but I've always been decisive and seized the moment. It's something that has helped make me successful and brought me a lot of money.'

His first job was following in his brother Cliff's footsteps to train as a salesman at Elys. He was manifestly and deliberately unsuited to the task.

'It was unbelievably dull and full of snooty old ladies from up the hill in Wimbledon Village who wanted me to bow and scrape to them, which I couldn't do. I've never been that kind of person.'

Bernard remembers: 'It was Dad's idea Max should work at Elys, but he was plainly not interested in the job. He began to play all sorts of pranks like putting chewing gum on shop assistants' or customers' chairs. He also smeared carpet glue on to the manager's chair and watched with a straight face when he stood up and ripped the seat of his trousers.

'The final straw occurred after only a few months when Max was working in the carpet and lino department. A customer who was active in the local women's guild asked him to show her something for her back passage. Max pointed to some candles in the hardware department. She was not amused and immediately reported him to the store manager.

'When Max told Mum he'd been sacked she phoned me to say I had to do something. I was father of a local Natsopa clerical chapel, part of the print union at the time and spoke to the branch chairman, who was also father of the chapel at IPC, to ask if he knew of any vacancies. He told me there was a job going as editorial assistant on the *Eagle* comic. Max went for an interview and was offered the job for the annual salary of £761/15. The editor took a shine to him and gradually began to let him write one or two small pieces.

'After two years they had to move offices and Max took voluntary redundancy. He got about £1,200, which was about eighteen months' money and used some of it to buy his first home with Liz.

'He had by then joined the National Union of Journalists and they helped him find a job as a trainee reporter for the South London Press, first on the *Wimbledon Borough News* and then on the *Merton and Morden News*, which turned out to be his early training for his knowledge of the press and how it works today.'

'I felt extremely lucky,' Max says. 'I had no qualifications so I started by making the tea and went on from there. Maggie Britain, the chief reporter, was very patient and taught me a lot. I eventually wrote about anything and everything that was going on in the local community from police calls, to the local magistrate court, sport and entertainment.

'Sometimes, once I'd written my story, she'd ask me to take out one hundred words or so without losing any meaning. It was good training, educational and something I found very easy. Maggie was great and we had a very warm and friendly relationship and she seemed very happy with my various creative endeavours, enthusiasm and energy.

'I was instinctively good with words and took to it like a duck to water. By the end of six months I think I was doing a reasonable job.'

In the early 60s Max seized the first of many opportunities that proved to be vital stepping stones on his career path. He began writing a record column for the paper. 'Unlike nowadays that sort of column barely existed,' he recalls, 'but I suggested we start one on the paper because record companies used to send free records to us and I wanted to encourage them.'

One advantage of Max's job was that he got to know the local characters. One of these was Richard Freshwater, the publican of the Crown in Morden. Richard liked seeing his picture in the local paper and Max often wrote about the charity functions he put on in the pub. Some of these took place in a large room at the top of the pub that Max noticed was otherwise left empty.

Here, he realised, was another opportunity ripe for the picking.

'I came up with the idea of putting on a regular disco up there. I felt sure it would work and spoke to Richard, who said I could have the room for nothing. I played records that had been sent to me by record companies, so the music cost me nothing too, and borrowed a turntable from the local record shop.

I asked Mum to run the cloakroom. It was havoc because her way of looking after the coats was to put them anywhere. But Liz agreed to go on the door and, being Scottish, she was very good at looking after money. I charged a nominal entrance fee because almost everything I made was profit. The first evening was so successful that it became a regular Friday night event for about two hundred people. It was helped by me promoting the event in the paper. Sometimes I'd write that a popular pop star would be coming. It was totally untrue, but I kept the room so dark you wouldn't have known who was standing next to you.'

The amount he made tripled his wages and is an early example not only of Max's inventiveness but also his ability to put his ideas into practice. He also regularly booked a different local room for a 'social event' for his football club where he showed blue movies. He branded them as coming from 'Max Clifford's Climax Productions', but they were in fact films that had been confiscated by the police, but given to Max by a policeman friend.

'I got the films and the room for nothing. About one hundred men would come along each time so I made quite a bit of money. Compared to today's standard the films, which were in black-and-white, were very tame. Nevertheless on the rare occasions the landlord popped in, the film would quickly be turned off and all these middle-aged men would start talking about various football fixtures.'

Max's record column also brought him into contact with record companies, which led to his next – and one of his most significant – career moves. Syd Gillingham, then chief press officer for EMI, regularly sent Max records to review, and when in 1962 he needed someone to help out in his office, he contacted Max to see if he was interested.

'I remember Max coming to see me,' Syd says. 'There was something very impressive about him and I sensed he could easily do the job. He was obviously both street-wise and down to earth. I persuaded him to join me by telling him how fascinating the job was.'

Max had never heard of a press officer – 'not many people had in the early 60s' – but relying on his instinct, something he's continued to do professionally and personally throughout his life, decided to give it a go. 'I liked Syd and accepted his offer. It's amazing how opportunities have come to me.'

It proved to be a good decision. There were four others in the department, but only nineteen-year-old Max had journalistic experience. His job was to get publicity for new artists when their record came out. He had to write their potted biography, and from that try to pick out a news story to sell. He would then send both to London and provincial papers, and hope something was published.

Syd left his staff to get on with their job with minimum interference, which was just as well. 'I've always had the sort of nature that I can only work under someone else if they let me totally do my own thing,' Max admits. 'It was a wonderful adventure, I had such a good time and I got results, so he was delighted.'

What Max learned at EMI formed the basis of his future career. This was not merely the nuts and bolts of how to be a press officer, but the more relevant experience of watching how stars behave. He learned how to cope with them and deal with their ego, mishaps and self-obsession. He also absorbed how those who came into contact with the stars conducted themselves.

It was a fast-track lesson in human nature and helped consolidate his attitude to the rich and famous. He decided from the start that he would deal with it by continuing to behave as he had done at Elys and not kowtow to anyone.

He remembers his PR beginnings very clearly. 'The first task I was given when I joined EMI in October 1962 was to promote a new group whose first single was about to come out. They weren't expected to amount to much, and I remember one of the directors saying to me, "Don't waste much time on that lot, son. They haven't got a chance." The single in question was called "Love Me Do" by a then unknown group called The Beatles. Obviously you don't get any luckier than that.'

To the surprise of some EMI executives, 'Love Me Do' reached number four in the charts. A few months later their next single, 'Please, Please Me,' reached number two, and, a couple of months after that, their third single, 'From Me To You', became their first number one hit. A phenomenon had been born.

'My part in their success story was nonexistent,' Max admits. 'But their part in mine was huge. They became famous so quickly that almost from the start journalists wanted to talk to them and in those very early days they all had to come through me at the EMI Press Office.

'The record business is now a huge, sophisticated, savage industry, but in the early 60s it was much softer. There weren't that many journalists covering music, so if you knew a dozen national journalists plus a dozen in the provinces reasonably well, you had everywhere pretty well covered.

'Because the Beatles were a red-hot client, journalists instantly became my best mates and would chase me to find out about albums or what was going on in the studios. I could always think up a line for them even in those early days. It wasn't anything to do with foresight, good planning or creative ability on my part. It all came instinctively and within a year I had built up tremendous contacts worldwide. It was a fantastically lucky break.

'I didn't get particularly close to the Beatles because after about six months they got their own people to handle their publicity, but of the four I liked John Lennon best. He was their driving force and really impressed me. I enjoyed his sense of humour and his anti-Establishment attitude, which was similar to my own. Ringo Starr was a bit of a clown. He liked to muck about and play the buffoon. George Harrison was likeable, quiet and shy, but I personally found Paul McCartney too wishy-washy and self-obsessed for me and I didn't have much to do with him.

'But I loved their music. The melodies were wonderful and I thought they would go far, but I didn't anticipate them conquering the world as quickly as they did. It was amazing how John and Paul came out with one world hit after another of such original music. It is virtually without parallel.

'EMI threw a reception party for them a year after they had signed up with them, and I watched several executives go up to John, congratulate him and say they always thought the group would do well.

'John was shrewd and knew that there hadn't been much excitement at EMI about them at the beginning, so he looked whoever it was straight in the eye and said, "You must think I'm stupid. I can't believe what I'm hearing. You thought we were crap. Why can't you be honest?" George, who was standing close by, winked at me, but didn't say anything. One director started stuttering, "Oh, no, no ..." But John interrupted and said, "Bollocks. I can't be bothered talking to you."

'As soon as the Beatles were successful, all these people who had previously been uninterested in them, suddenly tried to be their best friend. They wanted to invite them to dinner and show them off to everyone they knew. John saw through it all, which I really admired. It was an early eye-opener for me too and I've learned from it. I've never sucked up to anyone and have always hated hypocrites and sycophants. It's a lesson that meant I was pleased to expose various members of the Tory party who were preaching family values in public, but getting up to all sorts of mischief behind the scenes.'

When Max joined EMI it was the centre of the record industry universe. Cliff Richard, Russ Conway, Ronnie Hilton and Adam Faith were amongst the British artists contracted to them. They also distributed the Capitol Label that had legendary American artists like Frank Sinatra, Nat King Cole, Nelson Riddle and Judy Garland.

Max tried to avoid working with Cliff Richard. 'I always found him too precious, like a big girl's blouse. I worked more closely with

Adam Faith because we both had the same attitude to what we did, which was that it was better than working for a living.'

Max also met Cheryl St Clair at EMI. She later married Michael Barrymore, but was then a fifteen-year-old pop singer who'd been given the name Alice Wonder. Max was delegated to be her PR man. 'He promoted my record "Once More With Feeling",' she remembered, talking shortly before she died. 'I was very young and although he was still only nineteen himself, he was very protective of me.

'When I went on TV to promote my single, he'd make sure I was at the studio on time, properly looked after, and he always introduced me to the producer. He was handsome, confident, good at his job, attentive, ambitious and never missed a trick. Not very different to how he is today. We liked each other from the start but there was never anything romantic between us. Our relationship was purely professional. Little did I know that later when my once so-happy marriage to Michael fell apart as a result of his drug-taking and his declaration that he was gay, Max would save my life.'

Max quickly realised he had fallen on his feet; he loved his job and was good at it too.

'I was at EMI at a very exciting time when it seemed that everything we touched turned to gold. We handled the UK launch for many Motown black artists including the Jackson Five where Michael Jackson began, Stevie Wonder, the Four Tops, Diana Ross, the Temptations, and Marvin Gaye. Soon after the Beatles, Billy J Kramer came along and had a number one hit with a song written for him by Paul and John called "Do You Want To Know A Secret". Then there were the Seekers, who in February 1965 had their first number one hit "I'll Never Find Another You".'

At this point Max was still doing straightforward, traditional PR work, 'I really enjoyed helping to make it happen for those and other artists. It was like playing midfield in football, only this time I was orchestrating things for singers to score hits. I don't say they wouldn't have been successful without me, just that I helped them make it bigger quicker.'

Syd was delighted with his young member of staff. 'We got on well together. I liked his tongue-in-cheek attitude and that he found the job fun. We existed in a world of egos but from the start nothing seemed to faze him. Not even big stars. He made friends with some of the artists and was always very good at sizing someone up quickly; as he has done throughout his career.

'He also built up quite a collection of records. We had to in a way because we needed to listen to everything we put out.'

Max took full advantage of this useful perk. 'The bloke who lived underneath Liz and me in Morden used to cut hair for the Irish Guards at Chelsea Barracks. I offered him some of my albums at half the retail price and he flogged them to the guards. It helped boost my wages considerably.'

The records also made ideal raffle prizes when he put on fundraising discos for his local amateur football team. He even managed to persuade 60s stars like singing twins Paul and Barry Ryan to perform live. The money raised was ploughed back into the team and covered all their expenses.

Another of Max's tasks was to meet Capitol Records' American stars at Heathrow, and when necessary escort them to a press interview at the airport and then on to their hotel in London. It could be a difficult assignment. When jazz singer Ella Fitzgerald came over in the mid-60s, she was thoroughly searched by customs looking for drugs. By the time she was let through she was absolutely furious and Max had a tough job calming her down.

He also helped organise press receptions in the basement of EMI's central London offices in Manchester Square. Syd remembers: 'Some stars like Nat King Cole were easy to deal with, but others, like Judy Garland, were a terrible pain. I remember fetching her from the Savoy Hotel and on the way reminding her about the hordes of press and BBC disc jockeys who would be waiting for her. Her reply was, "Tell them to fuck off." I'd never heard a woman use the f-word before and I was very shocked.

'I asked Max to circulate and keep everyone happy until I persuaded her to make an appearance. He was brilliant at chatting to journalists. He could always think on his feet so when she finally agreed to meet everyone, he'd done such a good job there was no ill feeling against her.'

Max himself was unimpressed with Judy Garland. 'The few times I saw her she was always drunk and, like so many stars, seemed emotionally unstable.'

Situations like these taught Max a lot. 'I noticed how so many of the stars were unhappy and insecure. They would often throw tantrums, start crying and create all sorts of dramas. So although there were some wonderful highs being in their company, I was never in awe of them.'

In fact it was quite the opposite. As young as Max was, he developed a paternalistic streak, and from these early days took it upon himself to look after his clients – at least those he liked – and when necessary help get them out of trouble. In later years, as he became more established, his protection extended to keeping potentially damaging stories about stars out of the papers. He now earns most of his money from preventing stories appearing rather than selling them.

He also learned to back his own judgment. 'It was instinctive to me. I've always thought I know better than anyone else, and the way stars behaved confirmed in my mind that I should never be guided by anyone.'

Max was by now experiencing a lifestyle that was very different to the one he grew up with. 'One minute I was going around on a scooter and the next sitting in the back of a limousine taking someone famous to an appointment. I started staying in smart hotels and eating in the best restaurants.'

Many young lads from his modest background might have felt self-conscious and inhibited but Max's innate confidence saw him through. 'My self-esteem was never dented. A lot of the rock stars were talented but didn't have a clue about how to present themselves. Many of them were also out of their brains on drugs and sometimes when we were in a smart restaurant they'd even eat with their hands. Compared to that I was very sophisticated and never needed to worry about which knife and fork to use.

'Because they were stars anything they did was OK. I remember on one occasion one pop star ordered caviar with HP sauce and you don't get more ridiculous than that.'

Going abroad for the first time on business for EMI was exciting for such a young man. 'It was in February 1964 and I accompanied the Beatles to the United States. It was their first visit and they were performing in Washington, New York and Miami. As we were touching down at New York's John F Kennedy airport we saw hundreds of kids waiting below. George Harrison turned to me and said, "Look at all those people down there. There must be someone famous flying in."

'It turned out, of course, that they were all screaming for them. I felt incredibly lucky to be there and see the Beatles adventure evolve.'

One of the many highlights of Max's time at EMI, and an early example of his flair for publicity, took place in the late 60s when he put on a concert at the Royal Albert Hall made up entirely of buskers. 'I got the idea because Don Partridge, who was then known as king of the buskers, had a hit with a song called "Rosie". He was a one-man band and played an acoustic guitar whilst simultaneously playing a drum on his back using beaters attached to his elbows.

'I did publicity for him, we became friendly and I thought it would be an original thing to do. Don, who lived rough and had a great personality, helped me. Between us we gathered a whole range of street singers. There were so many characters involved including the Earl of Mustard who used to wear a top hat, tap dance and jump over imaginary obstacles. The concert wasn't part of my work at EMI. I did it as a freelance, but everyone in the office who heard about it told me it wouldn't work. It made me more determined to succeed.

'I decided not to advertise it, but, because it was so unusual, I persuaded several journalists to write about it in the national papers. It got great coverage and was a complete sell-out. On the day itself all went well until about an hour before the show when one of the female buskers Meg Aitken, who had cerebral palsy, came rushing to find me because four of the other buskers were fighting each other backstage.

'It was quite a punch-up, but luckily I was strong enough to force them apart. Apparently a couple of them wanted to busk the queue of ticket-holders waiting outside, while the other two insisted they couldn't because they were the very people who had paid to see them. I managed to calm everyone down and convince them that on this occasion it wasn't a good idea to busk. It was a great night. I made about fifty quid, but that wasn't the point. I was young, and it was a challenge to sell out a concert at the Albert Hall when everyone said I couldn't.'

It was always unlikely that Max would stay too long as a small cog in a large business wheel, and when in 1968 Syd left to work as a PR with Chris Hutchins and asked Max to join him he quickly agreed.

'I hadn't thought about leaving EMI but I decided it was potentially a good move. Among the artists we continued to represent were Don Partridge, Paul and Barry Ryan, Joe Cocker, who had a number one UK hit in 1968 with his version of the

Beatles' "A Little Help From My Friends", Tom Jones, Engelbert Humperdinck and the Bee Gees.'

Paul and Barry Ryan had by this time introduced Max to their stepfather, impresario Harold Davidson, who looked after a clutch of Hollywood stars including Frank Sinatra and Judy Garland. Davidson liked Max's style and began to ask him to keep an eye on his celebrity clients when they came to town, which was a huge vote of confidence for such a young man.

As well as looking after stars, the agency also handled the PR for the Batley Variety Club in Leeds, Yorkshire. The club covered a wide catchment area and was extremely successful in the 60s. Great names including Shirley Bassey, Gracie Fields and Louis Armstrong would come to perform for a week at a time.

It was never rowdy. The audiences traditionally didn't drink too much, preferring instead to tuck into chicken or scampi and chips. Sadly it closed in the early 80s as it could no longer afford the stars. Shirley Bassey, for example, asked for a fourteen-piece orchestra to back her, which made it difficult to make money.

Back in the late 60s the acts changed on a Sunday evening and Max and Syd would usually go up on Sunday afternoon to make sure all was well with the next star. Max, however, had firm boundaries as to how far he would go to make any star happy. When he liked him or her, nothing was too much trouble. If he didn't, he'd barely have anything to do with them. It was the same tough, resolute, uncompromising side to his nature that scared some of his team-mates on the football field and can still make some friends and clients wary. On the surface they don't seem ideal characteristics for a PR but, as time has proved, they helped distinguish Max from the many sycophants in the trade.

He did, for example, take an instant dislike to the flamboyant, kitsch pianist Liberace, who played at Batley in the late 60s. 'He was a homosexual, and fawned over his fans, but was horrible to the people who worked for and around him,' he says. 'I found him utterly repulsive and when he instructed me, rather than asked me, to get him something to drink, I told him to get it himself. He was furious and marched straight up to Syd to demand he sack me. Syd told him he would, but merely told me to keep out of his way, which I did.'

Nor did Max like the American singer Solomon King, who died in January 2005. 'He came from Kentucky and had a powerful operatic voice and an ego as large as Mount Everest. He had one big hit, "She Wears My Ring", and we in the press office had to get journalists to talk to him. It was difficult because he was such a prat.

'We used to take the journalists to a pub next to the office where there was a jukebox and at some point during the conversation Solomon would get up to go to the toilet and on the way press the number for his song on the jukebox. He'd then saunter back with an expression of mock surprise on his face that his song was playing, then sing along with himself in front of everyone. I'd cringe with embarrassment and want the floor to open up.'

Max also had a hot-tempered confrontation with Bob Dylan when he was handling the PR for the Isle of Wight Festival in 1969. 'It was the British version of Woodstock, a massive open-air event with over 150,000 people attending,' he remembers. 'It lasted for three days and lots of big names performed, including Dylan.

'Although he wrote some good songs, particularly "Mr Tambourine Man", I couldn't bear the nasal way he sang. As soon as I met him I could tell he was a legend in his own mind and saw himself as a prophet as well as a poet.

'I also thought he was pretentious. There'd been an agreement that he would do a certain number of interviews at the festival and when I began filling him in on the journalists he was going to see, he suddenly said he didn't have the time or the inclination to see anyone. I was furious, but managed not to lose my temper. A short while later he asked me to arrange some transport for him. I told him to sort himself out and that he could walk as far as I was concerned. I was annoyed because he hadn't been professional. Dylan and people like him, who only want PRs who will suck up to them, are better off choosing someone other than me. I'm not interested.'

This take it or leave it attitude could have sounded the death knell for many budding PRs, but in practice it hasn't hindered Max's rise to the top of his profession.

His close proximity to pop and jazz stars also brought him to the borders of the seedy world of drugs. Max has never been remotely tempted to try any soft or hard drug. 'I've never wanted to be out of control, and I can't see any sense in taking drugs if, like me, you are keen on sport. Nor, for the same reasons, do I drink or smoke.

'Unlike a lot of rock stars I've never needed drugs to feel confident or creative. Some pop stars I've worked with tried to make the excuse that it made them more creative, but I disagree. For example, I thought the Beatles wrote great songs before they were on drugs. There's always been a lot of drink and drugs in the world of jazz, and rock and roll became an extension of that culture.

'What did surprise me was seeing how some managers and record company executives encouraged drug-taking by giving their artists all sorts of substances as a way of controlling them. I often saw it happen, including at Batley. As a result some major stars at times didn't know where or who they were and would rely on their manager for everything, which was presumably just what the manager wanted.

'In the late 60s drug-taking was the norm, rather than the exception. All too often it became part of a rock star's image, but I hated seeing anyone destroy himself through drugs and could rarely keep my views to myself.

'Ray Charles, who performed at Batley several times, was into all kinds of substances. People could be unkind to him too over his blindness. I remember one occasion when someone with a perverted sense of humour put his chair back to front on the stage so that when he came out to perform he sat with his back to the audience. Fortunately it didn't take him long to sense what had happened and turn it round. I thought it was a rather nasty trick.

'Joe Cocker was another one heavily into drink and drugs. I often told him he didn't need to get high to perform well but it was a waste of time. It was very sad to see someone who was basically a kind sweet person almost kill himself through drugs. He must have the constitution of an ox to come through that time alive.

'I had a similar conversation with Marvin Gaye, who was a wonderful singer and a great-looking guy, but became addicted to cocaine. I kept saying I couldn't understand why he was taking all that stuff when he had such a great talent and could get all the women in the world. All he'd reply was, "It's just a different thing, Max." He became so addicted, it destroyed his career and his two marriages. It was such a waste. Eric Clapton was yet another heavy user of drugs, but I didn't get close to him.'

The gulf that he saw between the needy, drug-driven private face of a star and their slick but contrived public image had a profound effect on Max. He decided that, for him, being a PR involved more than just getting them publicity. As young as he was he wanted to protect them. 'Excesses were part of a rock star's image, so it didn't matter what appeared in the media about them. What was important was helping them stay alive.

'I couldn't be with them all the time, particularly when they were touring, but I tried to get the right people around them, especially if I felt they were in danger of overdosing. For example, I'd employ a new road manager or PA who would try to look after them and keep them away from the wrong influences.'

Max, the mischievous child and promiscuous teenager, was developing his unique moral code. One that, at this stage, perhaps even his Salvation Army grandparents would have approved of.

He was now ready for the next big step in his life. After a year working with Chris Hutchins, Syd told Max he was going to call it a day. Max, who neither liked nor admired Chris, decided to quit too. Nor did he want to be employed by anyone again. It was time to branch out on his own.

5. MY WAY WITH SINATRA

M ax was 27 when he took his first giant leap to professional freedom. He rented a small room on the top floor of 5 Shaftesbury Avenue in central London, part of a suite used by Joe Cocker's manager Nigel Thomas. He called his company Max Clifford Associates. 'I didn't pay rent. I got the room as part of a package deal for doing public relations for Cocker and some of the other rock bands Nigel managed.'

Max's approach to running his own business was individual, idiosyncratic and, for a young man with no capital and a wife to support, rather defiant. His aims were clear and simple. 'I wanted to be successful, do things on my own terms and enjoy life. I didn't want vast numbers of people working for me, or high overheads. I assumed that if I got results, everything else would fall into place.'

Several of his former clients, including Paul and Barry Ryan, Don Partridge and Marvin Gaye, wanted Max to carry on looking after them. Harold Davidson also wanted him to continue looking after Sinatra. It was an enormous compliment to someone from his modest background, and proof that not only could he be relied on to be efficient, trustworthy and discreet, but that in spite of (or perhaps because of) his determination not to be sycophantic, global stars felt comfortable with him.

'My association with Sinatra lasted until his death,' Max reveals. 'But I didn't often contact him directly. Harold Davidson would phone to tell me when he was coming to London, usually once or twice a year, and ask me to keep an eye out for him. Sometimes I was paid a monthly retainer. On other occasions I'd be given an all-expenses-paid luxury holiday in one of the best hotels in the world with a chauffeur-driven car and meals in top restaurants.

'Sinatra was a great artist and singer and a legend in his own lifetime. He had amazing charisma, something I've only seen with other megastars like Marlon Brando, Jack Nicholson and Muhammad Ali. But I didn't warm to him. Although he'd sometimes do nice things, he could be extremely cruel. He had close connections with the Mafia, was surrounded by henchmen and obviously enjoyed people being frightened of him. But I was neither scared or in awe of him and he was always fine with me.'

One of Max's more tricky jobs occurred in the mid-60s. 'Sinatra was fifty and had just married twenty-one-year-old Mia Farrow. They were coming to London and Paul and Barry's mother Marion Ryan, who was a pop singer in the 50s and was married to Harold Davidson, bought a beautiful apartment for them on a short lease in Grosvenor Square. Paul and Barry stayed in it the week before Sinatra and Mia arrived. One night they were feeling very hungry, looked into the freezer and found it was full of Häagen-Dazs coffee ice cream.

'They immediately got stuck in and over a day or so ate the lot. Marion came round just before Sinatra arrived to check that everything was OK and had a complete fit when she saw what they'd done. Apparently that ice cream was all Mia wanted to eat at the time and, as it wasn't yet sold in London, Sinatra had hired a private plane to fly some over. Marion immediately phoned me to say they were in real trouble and that Sinatra would go absolutely mad when he found out it had all been eaten.

'I tried desperately to buy some more, and rang every shop I could think of, but I couldn't. Instead I suggested we tell Sinatra that someone had mistakenly unplugged the freezer, that it had totally defrosted and we had to throw out all the ice cream. Luckily he believed us and was all right about it.

'My best and most memorable recollection of him was the gala concert he gave at London's Festival Hall in 1971, a year after I set up on my own and the same year Sinatra announced one of many retirements. It was a star-studded black-tie occasion. Sinatra was introduced by Grace Kelly, his co-star in the film *High Society*. Bob Hope, Prince Rainier, Nelson Riddle and Princess Margaret were also amongst the host of celebrities present.

'I had a great seat near the front behind Paul and Barry. Paul was with a girlfriend and Barry was with Princess Mariam, the daughter of the Sultan of Johore, then one of the world's richest men, who he married in June 1976. Sinatra sang lots of his old favourites including "I've Got You Under My Skin" and "Strangers In The Night" and then about halfway through the show announced, "Ladies and gentlemen. I'm now going to sing a new song, by a wonderful British songwriter, Paul Ryan. It's called 'I Will Drink The Wine' and I'm about to record it."

'Paul had decided to quit performing to write songs, and was desperate for a big name to sing one of his compositions. He'd sent a few songs, including "I Will Drink The Wine", to Sinatra about a month before the concert. Sinatra would probably never have known about them, except that unbeknown to Paul, Harold mentioned the songs to him. He then looked through them and picked out that particular melody.

'When he finished singing, he pointed to Paul and asked him to stand up and take a bow. A spotlight followed Sinatra's hand and settled on Paul, who was so taken aback he stayed rooted to his chair. I leaned forward, gave him a push and shouted in his ear, "Get up, get up." He did and the entire audience applauded him. It was an amazing and unforgettable moment and very generous of Sinatra. There he was, the biggest star in the world, thanking Paul, a young songwriter. It was an example of Sinatra's generous side and showed how kind he could be when he wanted to.'

Max was one of the select few to be invited to the intimate post-concert party. Most people would just focus on how lucky they were but, when Max is involved in a big occasion or story, he inevitably works out how he can also get other clients, or someone who had fallen on hard times, involved too. It's the sort of multi-thinking that has enabled him to promote several clients in one go and give a treat to those he cares about.

So, despite being young and unknown, he had the chutzpah to take along an uninvited guest to Sinatra's dinner just because he knew she would be thrilled to be there.

'Through a friend I heard about an elderly recently widowed lady who was having a very bad time. Apparently Sinatra was her all-time hero and she'd tried but failed to get a ticket for his concert. So I invited her along to the dinner party that was taking place in his Grosvenor Square apartment. We arrived before him and were having a drink when the doors opened and in he walked.

'She didn't have a clue he was coming and her face was a picture when she saw him. He was in a good mood that night and when she was introduced to him, he shook her hand warmly and chatted to her. We then all sat down to dinner and afterwards Oscar Peterson played the piano and Sinatra and Tony Bennett sang together. I was delighted I'd managed to get her just feet away from her idol and she could listen to him at a private concert. She couldn't believe what was happening and has never forgotten it. I've done that sort of thing throughout my career.'

But not even the overpowering presence of Frank Sinatra could inhibit Max from getting up to mischief.

'One night I booked a private room for dinner for Sinatra and some friends at Annabel's, a London nightclub. If you were organising food for Sinatra you had to make sure what he liked was available. He ate simply: steak, potatoes and pasta and lots of Jack Daniel's. The other guests included Paul and Barry and actor Roger Moore, who was a huge Sinatra fan. My role was to keep an eye on everything but for fun I also brought along a young, very busty eighteen-year-old model.

'She'd obviously not heard of Sinatra because at first she didn't seem too happy to be there. But after a while she was clearly affected by Sinatra's charismatic presence. She got up, moved to where he was sitting, tickled his chin and said, "You're cute, big boy." The whole table went silent. Sinatra's mood could instantly turn nasty, particularly if he was approached the wrong way, and when he lost his temper things could get quite hairy. Instead he burst out laughing, chatted to the girl and the evening progressed very well after that.'

Perhaps Sinatra secretly liked Max's cheek. In the mid-70s he invited Max to one of his lavish parties at his home in Palm Springs. 'Although he could be quite insular, if he got to like you he relaxed and was a fantastic host,' Max recalls. Harold and Marion had by then moved to Los Angeles and Paul, Barry and I flew over to stay with them for a few days before going to the party. Sinatra's mansion was vast and the grounds were so enormous there was even a small train to take you round. He had two large swimming pools, one built to get the morning sun and the other the afternoon sun. Barry, Paul and I had been invited to stay overnight and we were put up in one of the many luxurious guest suites built round the pools.

'Sinatra was by then with Barbara, his last wife. She was older, more mature and self-possessed than his former wives and she'd previously been married to Zeppo, one of the Marx Brothers, and was therefore used to dealing with celebrities.

'She seemed to accept Sinatra for who he was, handled him well and didn't try to change him. Although most big stars are only capable of being in love with themselves, he was obviously fond of her too. Amongst the other guests at the party were Sammy Davis Jr and Liza Minelli, plus lots of extremely well-dressed and polished older men with attractive, much younger women on their arms. There was an enormous buffet, lots of champagne and, of course, Jack Daniel's.

'Sinatra and I chatted a bit during the evening. When he was in good form he loved telling stories and was genuinely funny, though towards the end of his life he became less chatty and more guarded and didn't seem to trust anyone. That particular night he asked me a lot about the English music scene and the Beatles and Rolling Stones. I also told him about Matt Monro, who I'd met when I worked at EMI. Monro was a modest man, who had been a bus driver and was described as a British Sinatra. I told him he specialised in singing just like he did. He roared with laughter and said he'd better watch out. Years later he used to describe Monro as his favourite English singer.

'The Beatles fascinated everyone at the party and later that evening a much older man sat next to me and asked me about them. I told him a few things and at one point he said, "They don't sound much to me." I said he was wrong and that they were very talented and had taken the UK by storm. We chatted for quite a while and later, when we'd gone our separate ways, another guest came up to me and said, "You seem to get on well with that man."

"Yes."

"It's interesting that Sam took quite a shine to you."

"Is his name Sam?"

"Don't tell me you don't know?"

"No."

"He's Sam Giancana."

'I was taken aback. Giancana was a Chicago mob leader and one of the Mafia's most ruthless men. He'd brought about scores of deaths, shared a mistress called Judith Campbell with President Kennedy and was later murdered at his home in Illinois.

'It then clicked that most of the exceptionally well-dressed males at the party belonged to the Mafia. It was fascinating to see how terribly charming and impeccably behaved they were on the surface, but you knew that if you upset them you'd end up buried in the desert. I was pleased my conversation with Giancana had gone well!'

Ironically it wasn't Max's conversation with Giancana, but his relationship with Sinatra that sparked the first of the many threatening phone calls he's received during his working career. 'It was the mid-70s when someone phoned my receptionist and said, "Tell him not to get mixed up with people like Sinatra otherwise he won't stay around." She told me about the call, and I said it was obviously a game and someone was winding her up. But I took it seriously and thought about telling the police. In the end I decided against it on this one. Nor would I let it inhibit me from doing what I wanted to do. As it happened he didn't call again.'

Marlon Brando was another occasional client Max looked after when he came to London. As with Sinatra, he rarely dealt with him directly, but was told by his lawyers or a member of his staff when to expect him. His role again was to keep an eye on him. 'Brando was a pushy, difficult, temperamental and demanding man,' he recalls. 'I coped by letting him be. I didn't try to make him content or get close to him. I just did my job. At the time he was still physically very attractive, but also very greedy. He liked lots of small dark girls, particularly Polynesian, Thai and Hawaiian, either together or one after the other.

'My most memorable evening with him happened in the 80s. I knew how much he liked to both eat and cook, so I arranged for him to come along to my friendly local Chinese restaurant Mann's in Raynes Park, which at the time had a particularly good Chinese chef. Brando arrived and went straight into the kitchen and spent the whole evening cooking.

'The chef didn't speak a word of English so I popped back every so often to check Brando was OK. It was extraordinary to see this large man who was such a huge star talking in such an animated way to a tiny unknown chef. They spoke different languages to each other so obviously didn't understand a word each of them was saying, but cooking together seemed to transcend that and they were obviously both enjoying themselves. The highlight of the evening was when Brando came out of the kitchen carrying an enormous lobster he'd prepared. The mouths of the other customers who hadn't known he was there dropped open in astonishment.

'He had a great time, but what struck me most about him was that he seemed to despise the very thing that he was at the centre of – fame. He enjoyed the trappings, wealth, power and success with women, but he obviously hated show business itself and the sycophants drawn to it. There was a sadness about him that I felt no amount of success could rid him of. It was as if he was chasing something that didn't exist. I've seen it in lots of other big stars too. They seek fame as a means to an end, but when they have it, it doesn't seem to give them the satisfaction, peace of mind or contentment they were seeking.'

Megastars usually want to keep their name out of the paper as far as their private lives are concerned and Max soon proved his worth by both protecting them from the prying eyes of the press and keeping their intimate secrets safe. Most people find keeping secrets a huge burden and sooner or later off-load what they know on to someone else, with the almost inevitable consequence that the secret slips out.

But for Max it became the rock on which his reputation has been built. 'I pride myself on being an ace secret-keeper, especially when it comes to stars. It's not difficult. In fact I enjoy it and it's had huge rewards. It helped, too, that Liz was never remotely interested in celebrity gossip, so I didn't feel under pressure to tell her anything.

'Over the years I've had thousands of secrets. People find me easy to tell things to because I'm not judgmental. Protecting my clients and anticipating what they might get up to has always been an important and substantial part of my work and covered not only sexual misbehaviour, but any sort of wildness that could rebound on their careers.'

It's put Max into a unique position; selling salacious stories to the newspaper with one hand and protecting his clients from journalists' and friends' prying eyes with the other, while making money from both. 'I've done extremely well financially, but if I'd wanted to blackmail people I could have been a multimillionaire years ago, or dead' he says.

He was meanwhile building up a portfolio of different clients. These included several wannabe stars who, unlike the established version, craved the oxygen of publicity. Even in those early days Max could produce the goods from the most unlikely of sources.

One mediocre rock band became Max's clients for a short while soon after he set up on his own. They were at the other end of the celebrity spectrum from Sinatra and Brando; just one of a glut of rock bands in the late 60s and early 70s who earned a lot of money quickly from one record, spent it just as fast, often on buying drugs, and disappeared without trace.

This particular group wanted some publicity before embarking on a European tour. The national newspapers weren't very responsive as there was nothing particularly original about them, but Max, who doesn't do defeat, had a brainwave.

He knew his seventeen-year-old secretary Shirley Porter came from Stratford in east London. Her local paper, the *Stratford Express*, had a masthead that looked very similar to that of the national *Daily Express*. Max contacted the paper with a made-up story about the band's connection to the area. The paper was delighted to send a reporter to interview them. Max didn't tell the band specifically that he could only get a local journalist along, leaving them to make their own assumptions. Nor did he tell the journalist that the band had never been to the east London suburb, but had instead visited Stratford-on-Avon in Warwick-shire.

The result was that when the reporter asked them all sorts of questions about their time in Stratford, the members of the group assumed she meant the beautiful town of Shakespeare's birth and responded positively. The reporter was thrilled, although perhaps also a little perplexed by their unbridled enthusiasm for the area. The result was a long, glowing article about them, which became the perfect cutting to encourage more press coverage in Europe.

'No one abroad would query exactly what "Express" newspaper it was,' Max remembers. 'As a result they got much more press attention than anyone had anticipated.'

A popular but pointless fad among rock bands at the time was trashing hotel rooms. Max, combining the qualities of a close friend and the best kind of boarding school housemaster, tried to keep his clients' bad behaviour out of the papers. 'I used to check their rooms before they left and make sure the hotel was paid for any damage that had been caused so the management wouldn't complain to the press.

'I'd also go through their luggage and often remove towels, bathrobes, radios or whatever else they'd taken from their suites. Whenever I caught one of them, I'd say, "You've got enough money to buy the hotel and a hundred bathrobes, why do you need to pinch one?" The individual would usually just mumble a reply. Most of them came from working-class homes and were so insecure they'd pinch anything they thought was free. It taught me that it was important, and made life so much easier, to have as much control over a situation as possible.

'By this time I'd also had a lot of experience of the type of musician who goes to extremes; the I-can-resist-anything-but-temptation kind of person. Sometimes a rock singer would set himself the target of having sex with six different girls in one week then, if he achieved it, set another target of doing the same with ten girls the next. As there were always lots of girls hanging round concert halls and TV studios it was all too easy. It was an obsession rather than something they wanted to do and reminded me of little kids in a sweet shop when the owner says, "help yourself" and even if they don't like one particular type of sweet, they'd try it because it was on offer.

'When I had to look after someone like that I'd keep my eyes open to make sure there weren't any journalists around to witness what was going on. It was easier in the 60s and 70s. There was nothing like the press hunger for scandal and the obsession for celebrities of the last fifteen or so years.'

After a couple of years Max decided he didn't see his future doing PR for spaced-out rock bands and wanted to move on. His decision coincided with the deterioration of his relationship with Nigel Thomas. It had never been particularly good and was soon to end in a dramatic fashion.

'I was out at lunch one day when Shirley called the restaurant to speak to me. She sounded very distraught and was obviously in tears. Although Nigel had a secretary of his own, and my operation was independent from his, he'd asked Shirley to type some letters for him. When she said she didn't have time, because she was busy working for me, he turned thoroughly nasty and decided to use his master key to lock her in our office. She was desperate. I rushed back, unlocked our door and after I'd calmed her down, marched straight into Nigel's suite. Despite the fact that he was in a meeting, I punched him so hard he almost flew across the room. I couldn't stand that type of bullying, and Shirley and I moved out that same day.'

The following morning Max and Shirley visited several estate agents and within a few days moved into the third-floor offices at 109 New Bond Street, above a hairdresser. There was no lift and the stairs were steep and narrow, but the location was perfect. The office itself consisted of two rooms, a kitchen and reception area. It looked a bit grubby so Shirley and a friend painted the walls yellow and Max bought a couple of second-hand desks.

Max, who had been so used to seeing his mother count the pennies, continued to watch his overheads carefully. Even though he was paying a peppercorn rent, he decided to keep his costs right down by letting off one of his rooms. There were several willing takers, including Barry Ryan who used it for a short while to do some writing, Max's friend Alan Fields, a celebrity manager, and Greg, a tailor from Trinidad, who did alterations for some of the top Bond Street designers and answered Max's phone when he wasn't around.

It was about this time that Max invented a character that has been invaluable to him for over thirty years and became an original but effective way of extracting information and testing a person's loyalty.

As his anonymity still needs to be preserved we shall call him John Brown. Max explains: 'He is a man who works behind the scenes in his chosen profession. He contacts ambitious women who have been in touch with me and, after carefully establishing a rapport, says he doesn't really like me, that he would love to know what I'm up to and effectively asks them to spy on me and the people I represent.

'None of the women have realised it's me on the other end of the phone pretending to be this character. Over the years some of them have immediately aligned themselves with John Brown against me and promised to keep him posted about my movements. Other times they've told him in no uncertain terms to get lost and shown me touching loyalty.' John Brown has helped Max, in the deceitful world of show business, to weed out the genuine from the untrustworthy.

'Sometimes I've been even more mischievous and, using John Brown's voice, I've phoned a woman who has shown a romantic interest in me, and said that the way to make me jealous was to have sex with one of my friends. I've then told the friend and left it up to the two of them to take advantage of it or not. Certain friends have enjoyed themselves a lot.

'Some of the things the women have said about me have been eye-openers and it's always been a quick and easy way to find out where I stand with them. Occasionally, a short while before the phone call, the woman in question has looked me in the eyes and told me I'm wonderful. Then shortly afterwards she's told John Brown that I'm arrogant and she wouldn't fancy me if I was the last person on earth. It's the funniest thing in the world to do, but you need a broad back and not take yourself too seriously to carry it off. It's certainly helped keep me humble!'

There is one woman, however, who is not a show-business star, client or friend, whose approval Max has always sought.

6. LOUISE

'Louise has always been the be-all and end-all of everything for Max,' says Bernard. 'She also became Liz's life's work.' As the third most important woman in Max's life, he's always had an incredibly powerful bond with his only child Louise.

Louise came into her parents' lives at 3 p.m. on 1 June 1971 at Atkinson Morley's Hospital in Wimbledon. She weighed a healthy 7lb 10oz and seemed in fine shape physically. Max was at the birth and, like many first-time fathers, was overwhelmed by the experience.

'I cried when I first saw her because I thought she was the most perfect baby,' he recalls. 'She grew into a beautiful little girl with an open smiley face and an adventurous spirit. As a toddler she loved to run, swim and jump. She doted on me too, like lots of little girls do on their dad.'

'Dad and I have always been very close,' Louise agrees. 'He's always had a way of putting his arms round me and making me feel everything is OK.

'I was like Dad when I was little as I was always up to mischief. When I was three a neighbour found me very early one morning marching up and down the local common in my nightie and wellies, dragging our dog Brandy behind me. I'd managed to pull him through one of the sitting-room windows at the back of the house, while my parents were still asleep.'

Her earliest memory of her father is of him teaching her to swim when she was three. 'I was fearless in water and became a good little swimmer very quickly, and was as fast as Dad at breaststroke by the time I was five. I remember going to Brighton with my mother and her parents when I was four, stripping off and rushing into the water to swim without a second's thought and before they had time to stop me. They were panic-stricken, but I was fine.' Sadly these physical adventures were soon to be a thing of the past.

When Louise was three Max's father Frank died. He'd been a heavy smoker and passed away in September 1974 after suffering a leg thrombosis. Max immediately took his mother under his wing. He'd always been the closest to her of all the children and saw her most weekends.

He'd collect her almost every Sunday from Hardy Road and drive her to his home in Raynes Park for lunch and tea. 'Sunday was always family day,' Louise remembers. 'I would wait at the window for Grandma to arrive and then at about 2 p.m. we'd have roast beef, pork or lamb for lunch. I'd also go with Dad to visit her most Saturdays; he always took her food parcels. She was called Lillian and when we arrived we'd sing "Lily The Pink" through her letterbox so she'd know we were there. She was a traditional Grandma, big and fat, and she would always save me Penguin biscuits with the red wrappers.

'Although she was always lovely to me, she had a sharp tongue and could be quite difficult, especially to her sons' wives. Mum used to tell me about the power struggles between the two of them, but the only disagreement I saw was over Brandy. After lunch Grandma would put one of our dinner plates on the carpet so Brandy could polish off our leftovers. But Mum was so house-proud she wanted everything to be scraped into his bowl. Grandma always refused and Mum had to accept it.'

Max also regularly gave his mother money and took her out to buy clothes. Cliff remembers: 'He liked taking her to Elys where he'd buy her a new dress, coat or anything she wanted. She accepted very reluctantly. If, for example, a dress cost twenty pounds in the shop, she'd tell Max she could have bought three from the local market for the same price. He kept trying to improve her living conditions too. The house in Hardy Road was very damp and he tried to persuade her to let him install central heating but she refused, telling him she preferred her paraffin oil stove. She died three years after our dad in 1977. I think she wanted to go. She didn't like living without him.'

Her will specified that Max was to have a pair of elephant-skin boots that Eleanor had had made for their father. 'I couldn't initially understand it,' says Max, 'but when I took them I found she'd stuffed bundles of the pound notes I'd given her into them. I suppose it was her way of giving me the money back.

'I thought the world of my mother, still really miss her and often talk to her in my head.'

At five Louise had become a lively bundle of fun, and a real tomboy who preferred building camps to playing with dolls. Neither of her parents suspected that within a year her health would rapidly deteriorate and her condition would from then on challenge and change their lives for good.

She was just six when Liz and Max noticed that her knee and finger had become badly swollen.

'Liz took her to our local GP, who initially thought she'd knocked herself,' Max remembers. 'When the swellings didn't go down he arranged for her to be seen by a specialist at the local children's hospital in Carshalton, Surrey. There we were told she showed signs of juvenile rheumatoid arthritis.' Louise was then referred to St Helier's Hospital in south London where the diagnosis was confirmed. An appointment was then made for her with Dr Barbara Ansell, a leading specialist in the field who was working at Northwick Park Hospital in Harrow, Middlesex.

'We were concerned, but not too worried at that stage because we'd never heard of the condition,' Max adds. 'Dr Ansell confirmed the diagnosis, but no one ever sat down and talked through with us exactly what it meant and what might happen. Nor were we offered any kind of counselling or training. We had to find out everything about it for ourselves as we went along.'

Juvenile rheumatoid arthritis is a chronic autoimmune disorder. The body attacks some of its own cells and tissues, which results in inflammation that causes pain, stiffness and swelling that can eventually destroy the joints. Other major organs can also be affected. Each child can have different symptoms and require different treatments. Powerful medication is often prescribed to reduce the inflammation and pain. This in turn can cause side effects that include bleeding in the stomach and upper intestine. The symptoms can come and go; one child might have one or two flare-ups and never suffer again, while others like Louise have symptoms that rarely go away.

'As the years went by her arthritis became more active and damaging,' Max adds. 'It was a nightmare for all three of us.'

Louise remembers first being in pain when she was six and a pupil at Hatfield Primary, her local state school. 'The church club I was going to in the school holidays took us all on a four-mile hike round Richmond Park. Towards the end I just couldn't walk any more. My big toe had gone rigid, my ankles hurt and the vicar ended up having to carry me.'

She then began having physiotherapy as an outpatient at St Helier's, the local hospital, but found the sessions very painful. 'They tried to force my joints to do exercises they didn't want to do, so it hurt a lot.'

It was agonising for Max to watch Louise in so much pain. 'It's hard for anyone who hasn't experienced it, to imagine what a parent goes through when you have to sit with the daughter you idolise while a physiotherapist pushes and pulls at her fingers and she screams in agony. I wanted to wrench the therapist's head off, but of course she was only trying her best to stop Louise's hands seizing up.'

Louise's condition continued to deteriorate, so she was admitted to the Canadian Red Cross Memorial Hospital in Taplow for intensive physiotherapy. The hospital closed shortly afterwards, but at the time Ward 2, the children's ward, contained about thirty beds. It was a scary, dilapidated, unwelcoming place for a six-year-old and Louise didn't want to stay.

'I was in pain and very tearful,' she remembers. 'Eventually I asked a nurse to phone my dad. I begged and pleaded with him to let me come home. I was crying so much I could hardly catch my breath. Dad tried to tell me I had to stay in hospital for a little while to help me get better, but I carried on crying and begging. In the end he said, "Louise, I'm going to have to put the phone down now."'

'He told me later that he was in a complete state because I was so upset, but that he felt he had to be cruel to be kind. On that occasion I stayed in hospital for three months and although I was inconsolable at first, within a few weeks I made friends with other children on the ward and felt more comfortable. Also after a few weeks I was also allowed home at weekends, while Dad stayed with me most Mondays and Wednesdays, which helped.'

Once out of hospital, Louise went back to school, but it was the start of a fifteen-year continuous cycle of pain, drugs, hospitalisation, operations and physiotherapy. During her childhood Louise had to undergo twelve major operations. Both her hips and knees were replaced to try to counteract the damage caused by her arthritis and she had several tissue-release operations to ease her twisted limbs.

She's also had a rib removed, a rod put down her spine and, in 2003, a kidney transplant. 'Louise's health became the centrepiece of our lives,' Max says. 'Liz and I were forever backwards and forwards to hospital and we suffered so much emotional pain seeing our beautiful little girl in anguish. Some marriages break up under that sort of strain, but Liz and I stayed positive and wrapped ourselves around our only child.'

Liz's mother Etta was also a strong support. 'She and Grandpa lived in Wimbledon, which was only fifteen minutes' drive away, and she came round a lot to see me,' remembers Louise. 'She was funny, gentle and good company. After her husband died when I was eleven she came every Sunday and we'd do crosswords together after lunch. I thought of her as one of my closest friends. She visited me regularly in hospital too, particularly when Mum felt under pressure, but I know seeing me in pain upset her a lot.'

'Etta was a laugh and so good to Louise,' agrees Max. 'She'd always baby-sit if we needed her and she and Louise became very close. Sadly in the early 90s she was diagnosed with cancer. It seemed to be under control but when she went on a pensioners' trip to Brighton in 1996 she contracted food poisoning and never got over it. She went into Roehampton Hospital and died eight weeks later.'

Louise became a regular in-patient at Wrexham Park Hospital which, following the closure of the Canadian Red Cross Hospital, opened a new rheumatology unit that became a centre for the country. Max spent a great deal of time with her, and experienced the state of the health service at first hand. It strengthened both his commitment to the NHS and his dislike of the Conservative Party, which was then in power. 'I saw how the Tories were ruining hospitals, closing wards and cutting down on nurses,' he says.

'The doctors were patently exhausted from their ever-increasing workloads and management obviously didn't understand the practicalities of what they were trying to do. One result was that patients were left increasingly on their own and I saw for myself the pain and indignity they suffered from the decline in the services provided.

'I used to wander round the hospital and find cups of tea left by old ladies' beds that had gone cold because no one was available to help them drink them. Whilst I'm not praising what the Labour Party has done since it came to office in 1997, they did inherit something in terminal decline, which is inevitably difficult to turn round.

'Watching Louise suffer so much for so long also helped clarify my priorities. As I worked for myself I made sure I was at the hospital with her whenever I needed to be. It also made me determined to increase my involvement with charities.'

In practical terms it meant that his life now followed two very different tracks. One was maintaining his successful and expanding business. The other was coping with the huge and unceasing demands of a disabled child. Both required enormous efforts on his part, but he remained resolutely positive and didn't complain about the extra demands or constant worry. His daughter always came first. No business commitment, no deal, no demands from a star, no social event ever took precedence when her health was poor.

Louise, who in many ways is a chip off her father's block, also kept up a positive attitude to life. As a result she's coped with her disabilities with extraordinary courage. 'I felt lucky that I had parents who cared about me so much, and dedicated themselves to me,' she says. 'Dad was the demonstrative one. He continually told me how much he loved me and the two of us became a very tight unit.

'He was always full of surprises too, and would make me laugh. I remember him coming to see me in hospital on one occasion with a huge bin liner. "I've a few cards for you," he joked. He then pulled out a gigantic polar bear from the bag that he'd just bought from Hamleys. He'd also bring in lots of people to see me, including tennis champion Pat Cash and Tom Watt, who was then Lofty in *EastEnders*.

'Mum was the practical one and would bring me nice things to eat in hospital. She also paid great attention to detail. When I had a doctor's appointment she'd make sure I wore matching knickers and vest and pretty socks. It made me feel safe, loved and well looked after. Emotionally she was very reticent though: I knew she loved me but she never actually said so. She was very self-contained, happy with her lot, and at times a little selfish. She also had a wry sense of humour, could read Dad like a book, and knew how to handle him. When necessary she would give him a look to keep him under control. When she said "no", she meant "no". He respected that and they both accepted each other's independence.'

Louise was regularly in and out of hospital after her diagnosis but, despite the doctors' efforts, little could be done to halt the relentless and cruel pace of the rheumatoid arthritis. By the time she was twelve she was in a wheelchair, where she was virtually confined throughout her teenage years.

She had her first operation for soft-tissue release a year later. This involved cutting tendons and sinews on her legs that had become hardened and shortened from the arthritis. After the operation Louise was immediately put in traction. She had to lie flat for two weeks and was in constant pain. Three other similar operations followed in quick succession.

She also had two operations to break a bone in her knee so it could be straightened. 'It was a cruel time because I was aware of how different I was from other teenagers,' she remembers. 'Between the ages of thirteen and seventeen, I also had to inject myself with steroids three times a week, to counteract the effects of the arthritis. They made my face puffy so I also felt very self-conscious.

'I lost several girlfriends during those years because they were going to parties and discos with boys, which I couldn't do. Hardly any of them came to visit me, partly because the hospital was thirty miles away from home. It meant that at a time when most children start to become independent of their parents, I had to rely even more heavily on mine. Dad was particularly brilliant when I was a teenager and organised lots of dinner parties in restaurants for me.

'Fortunately I love being with him and never tire of his company. I've always felt blessed to have a father who has such a big personality and warmth. I'm not surprised that people gravitate to him when he is in a room. He has real presence. In retrospect he's probably unwittingly held me back a bit because he's always such good fun that I preferred to spend a Saturday night with him than anyone my own age.

'It was hard for my parents to cope with the stress of my constant operations. I know that Mum used to find them particularly distressing and would worry so much about me she couldn't face coming to the hospital just before or immediately after an operation. I understood and luckily Dad was always there.'

'I made sure I was the last person Louise saw before she went under the anaesthetic and the first she saw when she came round,' he says. 'I always went down to the theatre with her and when she was injected with the anaesthetic, I'd hug her and wish her sweet dreams. The hours she was under the knife were always terrible for me, however many times I went through them. I couldn't help thinking what might go wrong. I was OK once the nurses brought her back to the recovery unit, and I could hug her again.

'Fortunately as I do so much of my business by phone, I could carry on working in hospital waiting rooms or corridors. I regularly stayed overnight in the hospital too, especially for the first few days after an operation. Sometimes I'd just lie on the floor by her bed and snatch short spells of sleep as and when I could.'

Life for Louise out of hospital was also very difficult. For years she had to be on traction at night to try to keep her hips straight, and help her stand. Max took total responsibility for this complicated procedure that involved bandaging her legs tightly then threading straps that hung by the side of each of her legs through loops at the end of her bed that were connected to weights.

It effectively immobilised her and when she needed to go to the toilet, which happened at least twice a night, she had to call out for help. 'Mum used to sleep very soundly and not hear me, but Dad, even though he is naturally a very heavy sleeper, would instantly be alert.

'He'd get up, unwind the bandages and disconnect me from the straps, help me walk to the toilet, then connect me up again. Just disconnecting me took about five minutes each time, the whole procedure more like ten. I suppose it was a bit selfish of Mum to carry on sleeping when Dad had to go to work the following day, but that is how it was and I never once heard him complain.'

Max's chronic lack of sleep combined with the continual demands of his business could well have taken a toll on his health, and during the late 80s he began to have 'funny turns'. 'I'd be talking to someone and suddenly I'd see a sort of aura around them,' he remembers. 'At the same time I'd also start licking my lips and making sucking noises. I wasn't aware of it, but after several people told me what was happening, I went to see a doctor.

'He initially said it could be a middle-ear infection, but after a while it became obvious that it wasn't. Over the subsequent eighteen months my turns became more frequent and increased from once a month to about twice a week. I kept making appointments with various doctors. One even thought I might have a brain tumour, but that was ruled out after a brain scan. I also tried all sorts of alternative medicine including acupuncture, but nothing seemed to work.

'It came to a head in 1992. We were living in Raynes Park at the time and I regularly used to take several neighbours' children swimming on a Saturday morning at a pool in New Malden, Surrey. That particular Saturday was no exception. I drove everyone there in my Jag along the A3 travelling at speeds of up to 70mph. We then went into a greasy-spoon café for an early lunch. I started looking through the menu and the next thing I knew I was in the back of an ambulance. I'd had a full-blown epileptic fit. It must have been horrible for everyone with me, but I knew nothing about it.

'It was so lucky it didn't happen when I was driving as I could have killed all the kids. I recovered reasonably quickly, and refused to go to hospital. Instead I went home and had a good sleep. I then made an appointment with a Harley Street specialist. He said he thought I'd been having the symptoms of epilepsy for as far back as two years. It was extraordinary that none of the other doctors had recognised what turned out to be fairly classic symptoms.

'Tests eventually traced the source of the attacks to scarred brain tissue between my right ear and the top of my head. There were a few possible causes: a blow to my head while I was boxing or playing water polo, or a car accident I'd previously had when someone went into the back of my car. Although I wasn't badly hurt I did smash my head against the windscreen.

'Alternatively they could have been brought on by stress and exhaustion. I was working long hours running my business and I was then up several times during the night taking care of Louise.

'No one knew for sure. The specialist told me not to drive for eighteen months, or to do any intense exercise, such as playing squash, and gave me some Tegretol tablets. Tegretol is an anti-convulsant drug that has long been used in the control of epilepsy and doesn't make you drowsy. I took the pills and listened to him about driving, but within days I was back playing squash and swimming.

'I had about five more fits over the following months. One was in a car taking me to Central Television's Birmingham studios where I was due to appear in a programme with my client Antonia de Sancha, who it is alleged had been the former Tory cabinet minister David Mellor's lover. The press reported that I'd had a stroke.

'The remainder of the fits were at home, which was horrendous for Liz. I never remembered any of them, but apparently I was like a wounded animal, making horrible noises, foaming at the mouth and flaying my arms. Fortunately Liz learned how to deal with my fits, laying me on my side and putting something in my mouth to stop me choking and biting my tongue. Afterwards I'd sleep for hours and feel a bit dozy the following day.

'I didn't get scared, although when I was on a railway platform, I'd often think, if I have a fit I could fall under a train, but it didn't stop me travelling.

'I stopped the pills after a year. I'm lucky in that I've been fine ever since and I don't give it a second thought now.

'Once I started having the fits, though, I became aware of the terrible stigma attached to epilepsy, and how so few people would admit to having the problem. So I volunteered to talk about it for the National Association of Epilepsy. I told whoever would listen that I was no more peculiar after the fits than I had been before, that epilepsy hadn't stopped me having a busy and successful business, and that other sufferers should continue to do whatever they wanted to. I said that if people didn't want to know me because I'd had a few fits, it spoke volumes about them rather than me and that I had no time for that sort of ignorance.

'As a result I had loads of letters from other sufferers and know I gave a lot of comfort to many people. I refused to be downcast by what had happened and made sure something good came out of it; I turned a negative into a positive. Being positive is fundamental to me and extends to everything I do. I instinctively try to find a solution to whatever problem I come up against. I believe that if I can't do one thing, I must be able to do another and go on searching until I find it.'

As well as trying to instil this feeling of positivity into Louise, he also encouraged her to stand up for herself.

'Dad empowered me whenever he could,' she says. 'It was particularly important when I was a vulnerable teenager. For example, when I was booked in to have my first hip replacement operation at Wrexham Park Hospital when I was six weeks away from being sixteen, the doctor gave the operation consent form to Dad to sign.

'He immediately handed it to me saying, "You're the one having the operation. You read it." The doctor made a fuss, said I was a minor and that the form was for Dad, but he felt equally strongly that I should be in control of what was happening to me and said he would only sign it if I gave him the OK.

'I liked how he treated me and that he always questioned authority. It helped me feel stronger. He also kept me fully informed about my drugs. When I was given diazepam at fifteen to help stop spasms in my muscles and hips, the doctors didn't bother to tell me that it was also an antidepressant. But Dad did, saying they would help cheer me up. In fact I wasn't depressed at the time, but I was homesick.'

Max always wanted the best for Louise, which sometimes led to confrontations with the medical profession. 'I had my moments, particularly when there were problems with any of the operations,' he admits. 'I remember one incident which occurred during the time I was suffering from epilepsy and couldn't drive.

'My friend Mac McCormick offered to drive me to Wrexham Park Hospital. We set off in good time but there was so much traffic on the M25 that day that it was touch and go whether we'd make it before her operation and I became increasingly agitated. When it got to 8.30 a.m. and we still had some way to go and the operation was due to start at 9 a.m., I insisted Mac drove down the hard shoulder of the motorway, telling him that if we got into any trouble with the police, I'd take full responsibility.

'By the time we arrived with just minutes to spare, I was as tense and nervous as hell. I ran through the hospital to Louise's bed. She'd had her pre-med and was about to be taken to the operating theatre, when a nurse arrived to say the operation had been cancelled. We weren't given any explanation so I went off in search of someone in authority who could tell me what the problem was.

'I eventually found the hospital administrator in his office and barged in. Someone there looked me up and down and then asked, "Who are you?" I was so angry by this time that a red mist descended and my anger overwhelmed me. "I'll tell you who I am,"

I snapped. "My name is Max Clifford and my daughter was due to have a hip replacement this morning and there has been a cockup somewhere along the line. No one has bothered to give either of us an explanation and I want to know exactly what has happened. If you don't find out I'll ensure you will be the most famous hospital in the country for the wrong reasons."

'I got my explanation. Someone in the hospital had ordered the wrong size hip and we would now have to wait a few days to get the right one delivered.

'My rage was so terrible because Louise was defenceless and I wanted to protect her. I've battled for lots of other people over the years too, particularly if I see bullying. It's an instinct.

'When I lived in Raynes Park I used to jog round a forty-minute circuit on the common every Sunday where there was a football pitch. One morning I saw a load of six-year-olds playing football. As I ran I heard one man on the line shout, "Get stuck in. Kick him. Kick him." I recognised him from my old school so I stopped and told him he should be ashamed of himself telling a little kid to kick his opponent and that he was the biggest coward on the pitch when we'd played football at school.

'There was also nearly a nasty confrontation on Robert Kilroy-Silk's BBC morning talk show in January 1997. It was a programme about freedom of the press and I was going to be in the hot seat on stage above the audience.

'I was given the impression there were going to be about half the audience supporting my view and half against, but looking at everyone there I realised Kilroy's people must have phoned almost every Tory they knew to speak against me and that I had walked into a lion's den.

'Particularly because placed right opposite me in the centre of the audience was Roger Gale, then chairman of the Tory backbench media committee, who always makes me cringe. Just a few minutes before the programme went on air I could see him silently mouthing something at me across the studio floor. I jumped up, stormed towards him and said, "Why don't you repeat what you said openly to my face?"

'Kilroy and my friend Derek Hatton, the former deputy leader of Liverpool Council, rushed over and began pulling me away from him. As they did so, one of them brushed against Annabel Heseltine, a journalist and daughter of Tory cabinet minister Michael Heseltine. The first editions of the next day's papers said I had hit her. As it happens I didn't even brush against the woman, something that was later borne out by the video.

'I also lost my temper in 2004 on a shopping trip to Sainsbury's. As Louise was with me, I had a disabled badge in my car and parked perfectly legitimately in a disabled bay in the supermarket car park. I got out first and was on my way round to the passenger seat to help Louise out of the car when I heard this bloke shout, "You don't look like some 'effing cripple to me."

'I spun round and said, "What did you say?" He ignored me and walked off, so I chased after him and grabbed him. I was so angry he could call someone who was disabled an "'effing cripple" I said, "Repeat what you just said if you dare." By this time the security people had run over to us and begun pulling us apart. He then ran off. I know it was wrong of me to do something like that, but people like him make my blood boil.'

With Louise, however, Max's patience is boundless. He also has enormous admiration for her courage.

'She's never said, "Why me? What have I done to deserve it?" It's easy for me to be positive because I've been very successful, but for someone to go through all that pain and so many operations and still remain upbeat is a huge achievement. I am immensely proud of her as a person as well as a daughter. Her quiet dignity is extraordinary too.

'Sometimes, when she was in hospital, she would be bandaged like a little Michelin Man, with tubes everywhere and on traction to keep her legs straight, but rather than think about herself, she'd ask me to feed or cuddle someone else on the ward, who she knew needed cheering up as their parents couldn't be with them that day. Seeing your child put her own suffering aside for someone else puts the rest of your life into a proper perspective.'

There were, however, occasions when Louise did feel low. 'I hated my secondary school, Ricards Lodge High School, a comprehensive in Wimbledon,' she admits. 'I felt so different from the other pupils, partly because I was in a wheelchair and partly because I was dropped off and collected in Dad's Jaguar. Some of the pupils, especially those who came from troubled backgrounds, obviously didn't like the fact that I came from a comfortably off home.

'They would deliberately be unkind to me and call me a cripple. It made me hate my useless legs. The teachers weren't particularly supportive either. They didn't help me to catch up on the schoolwork I missed when I was in hospital, or even aid me physically to get round the school. Instead they made me feel I was an inconvenience.'

Max and Liz hadn't considered sending Louise to a private school. 'I'd always believed that if someone was bright enough, they'd do well anywhere,' Max insists, 'something I'd based on the fact that I'd only had a basic education myself and been successful. Also, Louise was away from school so much with her health problems, that Liz and I were less interested in her academic progress than keeping her well and happy. Her education came way down our list of priorities. I felt she'd catch up as and when she was able to. She's done brilliantly, so it's all worked out for the best.'

Louise had a particularly difficult year when she was fifteen. 'My hips were giving me terrible pain and I hated having to rely on my wheelchair. It was the year I had four operations; two soft-tissue removals and two hip replacements. I became so run-down in hospital that I caught an infection and spent weeks in isolation. All in all I was in hospital for eight months.'

Like father like daughter, she did, however, manage to find something positive amid the gloom. 'After the hip replacements it was so important to move me carefully and not shake either of the joints that it took four people to put me on a bedpan. Dad was often one of them. As a result I lost all self-consciousness about my body. I am not coy or awkward about anything, in fact I believe that my body is a testament to medical science!'

Her life cheered up the following year when she reached sixteen and became eligible for a small disability grant. She loved having money of her own. She also began boarding at Lord Mayor Treloar College in Alton, Hampshire, for people with physical disabilities. For the first time in her life she began to have a social life independent of her parents and with people of her own age.

'I made lots of friends, which was good for me especially as I'd been institutionalised for the previous eight months. The college didn't push me academically and neither did my parents, but I wanted to push myself. I did GCSE in English and maths as well as various courses in business studies.'

She left at eighteen but shortly afterwards needed yet more surgery. 'Mum noticed that my shoulder blade was coming out of its socket and I was beginning to develop a hump. We went to see a specialist who said I had scoliosis and that my spine had a 64 per cent curvature.

'It wasn't connected to the arthritis, but meant I needed a major operation to straighten it, which would have to be done in two parts. The first part consisted of removing a rib, putting a metal rod down my spine and then inserting pins through the rod to keep it and therefore my back straight. The second, to be scheduled ten days later, would involve a bone graft to fuse the rod and the pins.'

'It was,' says Max, 'the only time I saw Liz break down. She sobbed her heart out outside the hospital during the first operation. Louise had been through so much that it seemed too cruel, frightening, horrible and unfair that she had to have this problem too. I felt terrible for Louise but I tried to keep her and Liz upbeat and cheerful.'

Max was, as usual, with Louise as she went into the operating theatre and waiting when she came round. It was a very difficult time for her and Max spent many nights by her side.

'The first operation was awful,' Louise remembers. 'I reacted badly to the anaesthetic and was terribly sick for ten days. It meant the second operation had to be postponed and took place three weeks later instead of ten days. I also had one knee replaced at the same time and was in hospital for six weeks in all. When I went home I had to wear a brace like a thick corset that encased me from my hips to above my chest for six months.'

The operations meant that she no longer needed to rely entirely on her wheelchair, although she still used it for longer distances.

As Louise slowly recovered, she wondered what to do with her life now she was nineteen, but didn't take long to decide. She went to Merton College and took and passed six GCSEs in a year. 'Mum and Dad didn't push me, but I pushed myself. I felt so encouraged by my results that I decided to take A levels in sociology, English and media studies.

'I did the course in a year, but the first time I tried to sit the exams, I had to give up. My shoulders were so painful, that however hard I struggled, I couldn't write the essays. Dad then bought me a computer with a dictation package and the night before my second attempt at my sociology exam, I spoke all the technical names into the machine, so that it would recognise them easily the following day. Two exam invigilators sat in the room and I passed with two A grades and one B.'

Max was again in awe of his indomitable, hard-working daughter. 'She was so brave and determined and insisted on going to night school even on cold winter's evenings, somehow managing to get herself round the old building on an electric scooter, despite the fact that it didn't have a lift. Liz and I were immensely proud of her because she'd had such a huge battle just to stand, let alone anything else.

'Hearing she had passed all three subjects was absolutely bloody wonderful; like getting presents on Christmas Day.'

'Dad was tickled pink,' Louise remembers. 'I think he told virtually every journalist and editor he knew about my results and I had so many bouquets of flowers. Then for ages afterwards he'd introduce me to people saying, "This is my daughter, Louise, who has A, A, B, for her A levels." '

Louise's grades were good enough to get her into Bournemouth University to do a communications degree. Max again marvelled at her self-discipline. 'She used to put hours and hours of work in. I've never struggled to do things that don't come easily to me. Even if I'd had the academic potential, I didn't have the discipline or dedication to study, but Louise was terrific.'

Being at university was the first time that Louise had lived away from home in a normal environment. Although she had a carer to help her cope with day-to-day routine like getting dressed, she enjoyed her independence. Home, however, was still where her heart was and she regularly returned to be with her parents.

'Dad had bought me a Ford Escort to learn to drive in when I was seventeen and then a Clio while I was at university, so I could be mobile. He's brought me up to be as independent as possible and also encouraged me to have a good time. He used to get me tickets for all sorts of pop concerts and I remember seeing Whitney Houston and Janet Jackson among others. They were good fun, but Mum used to worry in case I was trampled on in the crush.

'I never had to be back by a certain time. Dad felt it was more important for me to enjoy myself. He never even complained when I came home at 4 a.m. and he had to get out of bed to carry me upstairs to my bedroom.'

One of Max's proudest moments was when Louise received her degree. 'I remember the occasion clearly,' he says. 'The ceremony began at 11 a.m. on 11 November and every parent who attended was naturally full of pride. But seeing my Louise not only collect her degree but also manage to walk across the stage after she'd been in a wheelchair for so many years, added a huge extra dimension to the day.

'I cried with joy and almost burst with pride. She'd had to fight so hard, but that day I felt not only had she won a huge battle, but that she'd done so with such style and without any bitterness.'

One reason Max coped so well with Louise's ongoing condition was because he found a surprising and liberating way of managing the continual strain.

7. SEX PARTIES AND THE SECRETS OF THE STARS

At home Max was the rock Louise and Liz relied on as he tried to keep them both strong and positive. But his own anxieties remained bottled up inside him. He became an expert at juggling the demands of his work with those of his chronically sick daughter. He leaned on no one, but escaped from his worries through his work, playing sport and organising sex-based parties.

Max's parties were legendary in the 70s and early 80s, but only amongst the trusted few. He describes them as 'good, honest filth', but they helped him professionally too. 'The parties were quite small and developed a reputation for being discreet. Stars and producers mixed with ordinary people,' he explains. 'No one kissed and told and nothing was leaked to the press.

'Sometimes various film and TV agents would ask me to look after megastars, so that if they wanted to misbehave, which most of them did, they could do so in safety.'

Max had been to similar parties in the mid-60s at the Berkshire home of Diana Dors, the blonde-bombshell actress and 50s pin-up.

Diana was then living with Troy Dante, a singer, in a huge house with tennis court and pool in Sunningdale. 'Although she was a lot older than me, we got on very well and had the same sense of humour,' he says. 'She briefly took a shine to me, but blondes have never been my type.'

Troy remembers the parties well. 'They were mainly for an older crowd, who liked to swap partners and drink heavily. There was also a lot of drug-taking, which Max hated. But Diana's games were fun. One was called "Hot Seat" where a guest had to sit on a chair and be asked lots of sexually based questions.

'If he or she gave an answer the other guests disagreed with, or could prove to be untrue, they'd have to do a forfeit, which usually involved taking their clothes off, which in those times was quite risqué.'

Max's own parties began spontaneously in the early 70s, soon after he'd set up on his own. He and a group of pals used to meet for dinner on a Friday evening in a local restaurant near his home in Raynes Park. One night one of the group invited everyone back to his house and the nature of the gathering changed from then on. 'After that there always seemed to be plenty of offers of premises,' he says. 'The venues varied from a small flat to a mansion with a pool, when we'd all go nude swimming.

'The parties initially took place about once a month, then weekly. I became the ringmaster, a role I like to have in many aspects of my life, and particularly when I'm in the middle of big stories. The parties became my circus and various people performed in different ways.

'I didn't allow drugs to be taken or anyone underage to come. Otherwise it was all very relaxed, spontaneous and easy-going. After all, sex is a natural part of life. I never had any problem finding people to invite. Men were always available and my phone would start ringing on Monday morning with girls asking if there was going to be a party that Friday and if so, could they come.

'Often they were both beautiful and randy and, because some of the male guests were TV and film producers, they saw the parties as a way of getting an Equity card. In those days the actors' union was a closed shop and getting a card was like finding gold dust. Fortunately I knew one or two agents who would issue false contracts in return for sexual favours.'

Max didn't have a conscience about the double life he was leading. 'I didn't tell Liz about the parties because she had absolutely nothing to worry about. They didn't change what I felt about her and I'm sure she never found out. It meant I could enjoy the parties and then go home and enjoy being domestic. I've always been able to separate the various parts of my life and give each my full attention.

'The parties stopped years ago but I loved them at the time. It was like watching sport and most people came along for the fun of it, knowing that no one would find out what they were up to. Interestingly enough, once they relaxed, the women were usually more active than the men.

'Bisexuality wasn't as fashionable then as it is today, but many women learned to enjoy it at these parties. When I knew a girl was curious about a bisexual experience, I'd invite her along and make sure another woman who was experienced at seducing women came too. Then I'd put them together.

'A classic example was a young woman Wendy, who was a regular guest for about two years. She was in her mid-twenties, rather upper crust, married and a teacher at a top private school. She told her husband she'd joined an amateur dramatic group that rehearsed every Friday night, and she'd strip off soon after she arrived and thoroughly enjoy herself.

'Sometimes I'd invite a mate along as a special treat. One was a plumber, but I pretended to the girls at the party that he was a film producer. I made sure he had a wonderful time with a couple of them who thought they might get a part in his next film. The girls did OK out of it too, as I had already persuaded a real producer to give them a small role.'

After a year or so the parties mainly took place in a maisonette in Colliers Wood, Surrey, the home of Max's friend Mac McCormick. 'Mac worked nights in the print industry so his maisonette was free until the morning,' Max explains. 'I used to organise lots of games. Sometimes the guests got so excited I felt I'd taken them all to a toyshop where they could play with every toy, as long as they didn't do any damage.

'One game involved getting a beautiful girl to kiss a male guest and rub her boobs against his chest, but he wasn't allowed to have an erection. If he did, he had to do a forfeit – something like putting his Y-fronts on top of a lamppost. Most of the games ended with a forfeit. I remember one night in November when I told a stand-up comedian, a huge UK star, that his forfeit was to go outside and jump up and down fifteen times stark naked. To my great amusement he agreed, even though it was 3 a.m. and freezing cold.

'An elderly couple lived in the flat below and I often wondered if one of them got up in the night to go to the toilet, looked through the window and woke the other to say, "You just wouldn't believe who I saw outside."

'As well as the parties I gave alibis to the various stars I was looking after who might need them. I'd often suggest they tell their husband, wife, boy or girlfriend that they were with me, as I knew I could instantly make up something believable to get them off the hook. It worked equally well when I was away with a star at a film festival. I'd always claim he or she was doing an interview whatever time of the day or night it was, even if they were misbehaving with someone in the next room.'

Max's inventiveness was as versatile as it was prolific.

'A major singing star who was having a passionate affair with his wife's best friend was desperate that neither she nor the press found out about it. He asked me to help and I created a scenario where I convinced the wife that I was the one having a relationship with the woman rather than the star. It meant that when I accompanied the star on a tour, his mistress Fran could come too, ostensibly to keep me company.

The star and I had adjoining suites and if Fran answered the phone when his wife called, I'd speak to her afterwards and talk about Fran in loving terms. The result was that the star had a relationship with Fran for three years without being found out. Of course, if he had been caught I'd have had to sort out the mess, but anticipating problems usually stops them occurring. I was also well rewarded financially.'

Just occasionally things didn't work out entirely as he'd planned. One top international celebrity came over to give a concert in London in the early 70s. He took a suite at a five-star hotel and told Max he wanted a bit of fun that night. Barry Ryan, who was with Max, suggested they asked a couple of girls they knew who lived in Shepherd's Market just off Piccadilly, which was then a notorious haunt for up-market call girls, to come along.

'The girls were dancers and did a naughty double act,' Barry remembers. 'They agreed to come to the hotel. We knocked on the star's room and he opened it himself. One of the girls looked at him, screamed and fainted on the floor. She couldn't believe who she'd seen.

'Soon afterwards one of the hotel staff came rushing along the corridor to find out what was going on. It was totally against hotel rules to bring in those sort of girls, so we quickly picked her up off the floor then bundled them both out of the hotel as fast as we could, before the star got into trouble.'

Max built up a host of contacts during his party period, which he's been able to call on ever since, particularly when protecting global stars. 'Protection comes in lots of different shapes and forms,' he explains. 'Sometimes it's protection from the individual himself, or from the media or sometimes from those out to destroy or damage them. The key to protection is anticipation. If a man wants a variety of women I make sure that both the madam supplying the girls, and the girls themselves, are trustworthy and that he doesn't go anywhere with them where he can be spotted. I've built up good relationships with several madams who run escort and dating agencies and they've always been happy to help me protect stars from being exposed in the press. They are often the first people to hear rumours about them and mark my card.'

This aspect of Max's life hasn't dented his moral conscience.

'Although what I've done is certainly immoral, sexual procuring has never bothered me as long as the people involved have been old enough to know what they're doing. I take protecting my clients very seriously. To do it properly I have to know the star well, including their weaknesses and tastes, which can take a long time, as they don't trust people.'

'Over the years I've represented stars who have enjoyed almost every kind of sexual permutation including mother-and-daughter situations. Others have been secretly gay, but don't want to come out, so I've sometimes arranged so-called girlfriends for them and even made up heterosexual kiss-and-tells for the tabloids to write about.

'I have told whoever is going to be interviewed to think of her last sexual experience and talk about that. I've then rehearsed it with her and added a bit from my own past experience. It's something that has become more necessary over the last fifteen years, as the public have become increasingly prurient about people's sex lives – a situation I accept is partly due to me.

'Many of the things my well-known clients have got up to have also been hysterically funny. One powerful businessman liked to be naked apart from an apron and be smacked by a woman while he was dusting. A powerful politician used to get turned on by being wrapped in black plastic and locked in a cupboard. One day the madam in whose house he was staying forgot about him and went out. When she came back three hours later he was sweating profusely and had almost suffocated to death. To add insult to injury, I think he had to pay her for the extra time he was there too!

'There was one terrible occasion when three men were watching a couple have sex through a peephole in a small cupboard. When it was all over two of them noticed that the third voyeur had stopped breathing. He'd had a fatal heart attack, possibly as a result of all the excitement. Luckily there was no investigation.

'There was also an extremely wealthy Tory MP who liked to walk round Piccadilly at night in stockings, suspenders and a bra, which he covered with trousers and a coat. He used to be accompanied by a girl supplied by a madam I knew, to keep an eye on him and make sure he wasn't discovered.

'My experience has convinced me that even though England has the most intrusive and savage media in the world, the rich and famous can still have an exotic private life, if they employ someone to take care of it. But I admit it's becoming increasingly difficult to organise.

'It's an adventure I seem to have tapped into without even asking, and in one way it's like being involved in an ever-changing game of chess. Many stars like risk, especially when it involves sex. The excitement and element of self-destruction that comes from not knowing the consequences of a particular action turns them on. When there's no risk, they're not interested, so my job has been to minimise the risk often without them realising what I'm doing, so they can still enjoy themselves.

'For example, when a big American star, who likes to have sex in unusual places, or in unusual ways, comes over to the UK, I ensure what he wants to do happens in a safe environment. I supply a driver who will take him somewhere safe where the girls will, without the star knowing, have been checked out for their discretion in advance.

'If, for example, Hugh Grant had been my client in all probability he'd never have got into trouble with Divine Brown, the prostitute he picked up in Los Angeles in 1995. He was caught with her in his white BMW and charged with lewd behaviour in public. But I would have found someone who could have taken care of all his fantasies so that what he thought was happening spontaneously, would in fact have been stage-managed. Plus any car he'd been in would have had blacked-out windows.

'The problem is,' Max acknowledges, 'that the rich and famous know I am good at protecting them, and want to push boundaries even further and take more risks.'

One of the easiest and most obvious ways of keeping stories out of the papers is, Max has found, to make sure the papers don't get hold of the story in the first place. One potentially career-ruining story that never reached the papers involved an aspiring, young, good-looking male actor whose first major role in a film turned him into an overnight sensation. But within weeks his past threatened to come back to haunt him.

'Two young men came to see me wanting to sell their story. They had a gay porn video the young star had made when he was a teenager and showed him having sex with other young boys. I talked to them for a while to find out what sort of money they were looking for. When they left I contacted the star's lawyer, who understandably was desperate to stop the story coming out and asked me to help protect his client.

'I negotiated with the young men to buy the master video and only copy for a sum around £100,000, which was much more than they would have got from any newspaper deal. It was cheap at the price too, as it would have destroyed the star's career. The lawyer paid me a fortune for sorting it out, but it was worth it, as the star's past mistakes will now remain secret. The star himself is now an international success and worth millions.

'There have been all sorts of other sexually incriminating videos that I've taken out of circulation, including one of a powerful American politician having sex with a woman. I later found out she had also had a sexual relationship with his wife.

'Another story I kept out of the papers involved a married English woman who for six years had a relationship with a very famous married American. An American lawyer who was a friend of a friend contacted me saying she'd been led to believe that the woman might want to sell her story, because although she was happy to be his mistress she was furious there was now another woman in the man's life.

'By chance I'd met the English woman, an attractive, tall, busty blonde. I called her, told her I knew what was going on and that I didn't think it was a good idea to sell her story. And that if it was simply a question of money, I could get her more by stopping the story coming out. I knew that her own husband had some business connections with the man in question and said I didn't think either he or her family would want to be put under the spotlight. She listened and so far nothing has appeared. Persuasion can be a very powerful tool in this situation.

'Over the years I've protected huge stars, tycoons, millionaires, multimillionaires and billionaires. For example, one married multi-millionaire American middle-aged businessman came to see me to ask for help in ending his twenty-year relationship with his mistress. She was now fifty rather than thirty and he didn't fancy her any more. The difficulty was that he was known as a very respectable Catholic, and was wisely worried about what she might do when he told her it was over. He'd heard her mention my name in conversation and assumed, probably rightly, that if he broke up with her and she decided to sell her story, she'd come to me.

'I agreed to help and charged him around £20,000 a month. By chance she did come to see me shortly afterwards and it was obvious that she had seen better days. I felt very sorry for her because he had led her on and said that he would eventually leave his wife but I advised her not to sell her story. Although the businessman was financially very successful, he wasn't a well-known figure and she was unlikely to get more than £25,000 from a paper. She was very upset, but I tried to comfort her by saying I'd do my best to help her. There was no conflict of interests. I was confident I could satisfy them both.

'From the multimillionaire's point of view, any publicity about his affair would do him untold damage. His wife may well have left him, which could have meant a twenty-million-pound divorce settlement for starters. There would also have been a lot of heartache. I explained to him that he had to make it worth his mistress's while not to say anything and provide some financial security for her. He then offered her about £50,000. I thought it was a ridiculously low amount bearing in mind how much he was worth.

'Over the next few months I negotiated a deal where he gave her a million pounds plus an annual income of £50,000 for the next twenty years. It was enough for his ex-lover to get a beautiful flat and have something to show for the relationship. Meanwhile his reputation and marriage remained intact. I didn't get a cut of the amount I negotiated, but he was so pleased that, as well as my monthly fee, he gave me a generous bonus.

'I've done many similar deals over the last twenty years and now have a standard three-page contract, which I draw up between the two parties involved. The mistress has to sign, amongst other things, that she guarantees her former lover total anonymity, and that she will deny any relationship took place between them and will never help anyone write a story about it. This particular mistress signed that should the story ever come out in any shape or form she would agree to forfeit a sum around £500,000 plus the annual income.

'I don't say the agreements are watertight or that they would stand up in a court of law, but I doubt that it would ever come to that because it just wouldn't be worth the person's while. The key thing is to come up with something that both sides feel happy about.'

Sorting out tricky, failing or complex relationships has become yet another lucrative string to Max's ever-expanding bow. However bizarre or perverse the problem, Max can come up with an equally outlandish or original solution.

'One major American film star came to me for help,' he remembers. 'He had problems performing with his female partner. So instead he paid someone to do it for him and got his satisfaction from watching them. His arrangement had worked well for several years, but the guy in question suddenly demanded a lot more money and threatened that unless the star paid up, he'd go to the papers with his story.

'I worked out a plan based on the fact that the guy, Jo, thought he was very macho and a good lover. I also knew that he liked champagne. I got him invited to a party, made sure champagne was served, and that his glass was constantly topped up. I also hired a very attractive young lady and a young gay guy for the evening. The young lady was very affectionate towards him and at one point in the evening, by which time he was very drunk, he took her to bed. At a given signal, she slipped out of the bed and the gay guy slipped in.

'He was then filmed for two or three minutes in a compromising position with this young man. It all went so smoothly and happened so fast that Jo, who wasn't remotely gay but was completely out of his head, didn't realise what was going on.

'A few days later I got in touch with Jo and asked him to come and see me. I told him that I'd heard rumours that he wanted to sell his story and advised him it wasn't a good idea because it was bound to come out that he was bisexual. He said he didn't know what I was talking about. I then showed him the film and told him there were two or three witnesses. He didn't know what to say.

'I then added for good measure that the boy was only just seventeen and everyone would be disgusted by his behaviour. The conversation got a bit blue but he left and nothing has ever come out in the papers about his relationship with the star's partner. He did, though, stop having sex with her, so I got someone else in instead, and the star was happy.'

Even newspaper editors have turned to Max when they have problems with women.

'One editor in particular came to me after he'd had a night of passion with two young ladies while he was abroad and they'd threatened to expose him. I stopped the story coming out by arranging a deal between them whereby the editor gave each of them a five-figure sum, which he managed to put through the books for a fictitious story. He also got them tickets for a whole range of parties and premieres. In return they kept quiet about what happened.'

Nor is it just men who ask Max to protect their sexual secrets. Over the last ten years an increasing number of women have sought his professional help.

'Several American lawyers, who work for major American female actresses, singers or TV personalities, have asked me to keep an eye out for them when they are in the UK and let them know if anyone they've been involved with comes to me to try to sell their story. It used to be just women who would kiss and tell, but now, with the knowledge of the sums of money that are out there, and the increase in powerful and famous women, there are plenty of guys looking for an opportunity to sell their story.

'Women have also become a lot more sexually adventurous over the last few years – some not just with another partner but with a woman or a much younger man. There are lots of successful rich women in their forties who are bored and feel physically unfulfilled. They were often hot and horny in their twenties, which suited their young husbands or partners very well, but over the years the man's passion has diminished while theirs has not. I believe they find having sex is the best of all therapies, so instead of going to the gym or talking to a counsellor they want a young man who will make them feel good inside and out, make their skin glow and their eyes shine.

'The guys involved know they are on to a bloody good thing and have a great time doing what comes naturally. And if they ever come to me to sell their story, I buy them off and keep it out of the papers.'

Either with money or by negotiation or both, it's always easier to prevent a paper getting hold of a story, than stopping it once they have, particularly as newspapers now crave scandalous stories about celebrities of any sort. When Max has a hard time keeping the story out of the papers, he makes sure the celebrity knows about it. 'I tell whoever it is that they've been very lucky to have got away with it this time. I explain I've managed to get them off the hook because there hasn't been enough to substantiate it, and they've been given the benefit of the doubt. But if they do it again and the papers are offered a similar scenario they will very likely run with it. I also remind them how frightened they've been waiting to hear if the story has been killed.

'I've discovered over the years that for a star, the most important thing in the world is to preserve his or her fame. It's at the very core of their existence and nothing remotely comes close to it. So the best way of containing them is to convince them that what he or she has done could destroy their fame. It's a case of not only stopping their story coming out but also trying to make sure they change their behaviour, which most of the time they do.'

In return for his help, every celebrity on Max's books, from the best behaved to the most difficult, will at some time be asked to help him out. But not for his own ends.

8. CHARITY BEGAN AT HOME

M ax has always been a man of contrasts and contradictions and, at the same time as he was masterminding sexual extravaganzas, he was also becoming increasingly involved in various charities.

His charitable work began in the late 60s when he was working in the press office at EMI. People would make contact to ask if their seriously sick child could meet one or other of the company's recording stars. 'In the early days the requests often came through a charity called Dreams Come True that provided treats for terminally ill children,' he says. 'They mainly wanted to meet pop stars and I was very happy and keen to help.

'Many of the children were being treated for leukaemia at the Royal Marsden Children's Clinic in Sutton, Surrey, which is how my subsequent long relationship with the hospital began. At the time I would put in a request for the child to come to a recording or TV studio. Sometimes I'd get a reply from the studio that said, "Hopefully in a couple of months." It was hopeless as the child was unlikely to live that long.

So without asking anyone I'd usually just take the child into a studio and tell him or her to sit quietly at the back and watch.

Sometimes the star didn't know he or she was there until afterwards, when I'd quickly introduce them and have a photograph taken of the two of them together.

Alternatively I'd smuggle a child into my office and when the star arrived to do a press interview I'd ask him to spare a couple of minutes to say hello, and be photographed. Most stars were more than happy to be involved – it didn't take long and the child was always thrilled. Major celebrities like Dustin Hoffman, John Lennon, George Harrison, Paul Newman and Adam Faith have all been photographed with these very sick kids. I wasn't supposed to do that sort of thing and was still quite junior, but I've always broken the rules. I knew from early on that it was best to take control and do something without waiting forever to get permission. It's been much easier to arrange treats for seriously ill children as I've got older and become well known.'

Max has supported the Royal Marsden Hospital for decades. Professor Ray Powles, the consultant who carried out the first bone-marrow transplant on a child, and has recently retired as head of haemato-oncology at the Royal Marsden, got to know him well.

'I've been particularly impressed by the low-profile way Max has donated money to the hospital,' he says. 'All too often people say, "Here is fifty pounds, now where is the plaque?" But not Max. For years various cheques would come to the hospital from newspapers or television channels without any explanatory note.

'It took a while before we discovered that they were fees due to Max for brokering stories or TV appearances, but which he'd asked to be sent directly to the hospital. I believe he's given at least £100,000 to the hospital. He's also spent a lot of his time visiting patients and on several occasions each year brought different stars to see the sick children.'

These visitors have included Muhammad Ali, Marlon Brando and Frank Sinatra. 'Brando mumbled to the children, while Sinatra was wonderful and sang "My Way" to a group of sick ladies,' Max remembers. One of his regular visits takes place just before Christmas and for the last three years he has brought the boyband Westlife along to sing to the children.

Max inevitably likes to make his own arrangements, and his dislike of being told what to do in any sphere of his life has sometimes led to difficulties with the hospital management. 'In the early days I didn't warm to the official side of the Marsden,' he admits. 'There were some pompous officials on the board – I like to think they were probably Tories – and they don't like me being involved. But then it's not the officials I'm out to help.'

Professor Powles, who now runs Parkside cancer clinic and serves on several government think-tanks for the National Health Service, sees Max's problem from a different perspective. 'Bureaucracy is anathema to Max, mainly because he wants to get things done fast. But there are inevitable barriers in his way like clearing visits with a committee and sorting out patient confidentiality, which fortunately or unfortunately Max has trouble accepting.'

Max was also involved in saving the South Kensington branch of the Marsden in the early 80s when there was speculation that the then Conservative government would either close or resite it.

'I did everything I could to get positive spin on stories about the Marsden in the press and on TV,' he says. 'I also tried to get Sean Connery on board, because he was thought to be having treatment for throat cancer at the time, but he declined. I pulled favours, spoke to editors and did my best to make sure they were sympathetic.

'I tried to persuade them to give the story a high profile in their papers and point out that there were more advantages in keeping the hospital going than closing it. And of course I didn't charge the Marsden a penny for my work.'

It wasn't the first time, nor would it be the last, that Max tried to influence what newspaper editors put in their paper, but this was one of his most worthy causes. 'Max and a bunch of others brought a lot of influence to delay the hospital's closure,' remembers Professor Powles. 'As a result the Marsden survived long enough for the government mood about how the health service was to be structured to change. It helped enormously that there was big media coverage about the hospital's possible closure. I believe Max influenced what was written, because he understands what the hospital stands for and supports our global fight to try to beat cancer.'

'It's deeply ironic,' adds Max, 'that having put so much time and effort into the hospital, Liz spent the last days of her life in the Marsden.'

He rigorously rejects the notion that his charitable work could be in penance for the more carnal side of his life. 'I don't see them as contradictory aspects of my character. I am very instinctive, get an awful lot out of life and like to think I've put a lot back. I like the balance in my life. I can expose the people who deserve to be exposed and protect and help those who are most in need. The older I get the more I am able to maintain both.

'Even the naughty side of me has given a lot of pleasure to a lot of people. Although I can be a so-and-so and take the mickey out of people, I've always had a compassionate side, a powerful social conscience, and find helping others hugely rewarding.'

Although Max was encouraged to be charitable at his mother's knee, Professor Powles thinks he became a philanthropist largely as a result of Louise's chronic illness. 'It's put a purpose into his life and made him want to do what he can for those in need,' he says. 'I know him well and see him as a man of total integrity.

'We are not talking about a goody-goody here, but someone with extraordinary insight who I admire enormously. I don't think he does so much for charities to compensate for whatever else he is doing. It is part of the package of the man.'

In 1996 Max became involved with Barry and Carmen Daniels, whose son Rhys and daughter Charley were suffering from the cruel and terminal Batten's disease – an inherited disorder of the nervous system that eventually causes blindness, dementia and loss of motor skills. Sufferers rarely live beyond their teens.

Little Rhys captured the heart of the nation when at three he underwent various bone-marrow transplants that sadly didn't save his life. The media was keen on the story and the family had no idea how to cope with the throng of journalists hanging round their home, the constant phone calls plus caring for two demanding and very sick children.

'Everyone wanted to talk to us but we felt stressed as virtually all our time was taken up with the children,' remembers Barry. 'Our friend, actor Ian McShane, said there was one person who could and would want to take care of us and that was Max. We rang him and he willingly gave us free advice and took all the strain away. He told us to be level-headed and work with as many people in the media as we could. He later also helped us set up our charity The Rhys Daniels Trust that now provides homes for families with very sick children so they can stay close to them when they are in hospital.

'He's spoken at many of our events and has been involved in putting together an annual fundraising golf tournament in Spain, which is sponsored by Majestic, a local property development company that is on his books. He's also arranged for several celebrities including Brian McFadden, Bobby Davro, Jeremy Beadle, Simon Cowell and Des O'Connor to come to our fundraising events. In December 2003 Max became one of our vice-patrons along with actress Pauline Quirke.' Max and Pauline also raised £32,000 for the charity in the celebrity version of *Who Wants To Be A Millionaire* in December 2004. When it came to deciding whether or not to go for the £32,000 question and possibly lose £15,000, Max said that if he did lose he would give the charity the £16,000 from his own money. He's been the only celebrity to make such a gesture.

Max likes nothing better than getting one of his clients to help another, especially when a charity can benefit. His own generosity is often spontaneous too. At one charity auction he paid £50,000 for a Chelsea football shirt, then donated it to another charity for them to auction again.

Since 2003 Max has been involved with Chase, a voluntary organisation that provides a wide range of services for terminally ill children and in 2005 agreed to be a patron. Chase is also behind Christopher's, a children's hospice in Ardington, near Guildford in Surrey. Max has so far donated over £250,000 of his own money to the hospice, which has gone towards a new conservatory and a therapy room.

'I often visit Christopher's and after Kerry Katona won *I'm A Celebrity Get Me Out Of Here* in 2004, she and her then husband Brian McFadden came along. They were both brilliant with the children.'

Bridget Turner, director of care at Christopher's, can't speak highly enough of Max. 'What Max has done has made a huge difference to us,' she enthuses. 'It's not just the money but because he's taken time to understand how we work and talk to our families.'

Once again, Max doesn't publicise what he does or how much he gives and, just like the Marsden, cheques go directly to the hospice from his TV appearances. 'I've often rung him to ask if a particular sum of money has come from him,' she adds. 'He absolutely doesn't want any fanfare or public accolade. I've never once seen him doing the "I-am-a-big-celebrity number". He prefers to chat quietly to a worried parent over a cup of tea.

'He has even come to my own rescue. In June 2004 we had to cope with the deaths of five children one after the other at the hospice, and all the staff were very badly affected. I was telling Max how down we all were, when before I knew it he had given me six hundred pounds and told me to take all forty of my staff out to dinner to thank them for doing a terrific job. I now think of him as my fairy godfather.'

Max is also involved with the Bubble Foundation, a charity that raises funds for babies born without an immune system who cannot survive without a bone-marrow transplant. The specialised unit, one of only two in the country, is based in Newcastle upon Tyne. It also helps children suffering from leukaemia and severe forms of arthritis.

He heard about the foundation from agony aunt Denise Robertson. 'I rang Max because I needed some publicity in the press for the work of the unit and asked him how to go about it. He immediately said he would do it for me and didn't charge a penny.'

He also helps Phoenix Survivors, a web-based support group set up by and for the victims of child sexual abuse. He gives advice on dealing with the media and helps those who have been abused but who want to talk to find a newspaper outlet.

Apart from the charities he supports, Max also likes giving money to individuals. 'I love to see the pleasure on their faces,' he says. 'Sometimes I can be a soft touch, but I wouldn't want people to know that.' There are literally hundreds of examples of his generosity. If he is in a restaurant and sees an elderly couple having a meal, he often arranges to pay for it, just to see their faces when they ask for the bill and discover it's already been settled.

He's taken an impoverished local single mother and her child to a toyshop just before Christmas and told them to pick whatever they wanted. In addition he sent her a cheque for £1,000 inside his Christmas card. Max is particularly generous at Christmas time; each year he asks friends if they know anyone who is having a really bad time and then just sends them a cheque, even when he doesn't know them.

He's paid for first-class flights from the USA for the parents of a very sick baby, when the child unexpectedly took a turn for the worse and they needed to get back to see him. He paid for a stretch limousine to take a terminally ill boy to spend the day on the set of *EastEnders*; the child died the following day. He bought a football shirt signed by Michael Owen and David Beckham to give to another child with not long to live.

Max also bought a deluxe wheelchair costing £18,000 for a seriously ill nine-year-old boy called Joseph and his parents a suitably sized van so they could take him out in his wheelchair with his siblings.

'I like to go to bed at night, close my eyes and see the little fellow whizzing around in his wheelchair, knowing he wouldn't have been able to leave his home without it,' he says. 'I also find it hugely satisfying when the parents of a child with a crippling illness who are really up against it come and shake my hand and say how much they appreciate what I have given them. I like the feeling of being able to do something to help a child, a family and the hospice.

'It is, of course, often emotionally very draining. When I first visited terminally ill children many years ago I was so moved I sometimes had to sit in my car for ages to compose myself before being able to drive off. But the older I get the more I think this work is what I am meant to do.

'In 1998 I became a governor of Rydens School, my local comprehensive where my nephews went. The headmaster David Hebden called me when he heard I'd moved into the area. I went down and chatted to him and I liked his enthusiasm. I told him I didn't have time to come to the governors' meetings, but that I'd help out when I could with publicity, planning of events, fundraising and public image.

'I've got all sorts of people down for prize days, including Piers Morgan and Simon Cowell, and I sometimes talk at an education conference. Each year I also take about twenty sixteen- and seventeen-year-olds and a few teachers to an Oxford or Cambridge debate that I'm taking part in. I hire and pay for a coach. I show them round the universities and then we go to one of the debates.

'On one occasion I finished up with a split eye. I'd just got back on the coach after the debate when I noticed a gang of local louts swaggering up to some of the kids. They started picking on them, pushing them around and swearing. I got off to find out what was going on and one of the yobs walked up to me and hit me in the face. My instinctive reaction was to punch him straight back, but luckily I managed to control myself. The other kids were quite shocked. I think some of the yobs must have been as well because they quickly disappeared. A picture of me with an enormous black eye subsequently appeared in a couple of papers, which didn't do me any harm.'

Often the individuals Max helps are those he knows. One of his female staff, Lucy Murphy, recalls, 'I started getting blackouts for a while, and after one particular collapse I was found to have an irregular heartbeat. There was a twelve-week wait to see a cardiologist, which Max said wasn't good enough. Instead he packed me off to see the best cardiologist in the country and within four weeks I was operated on. He paid for everything and I was unbelievably grateful as there was an eighteen-month waiting list for the operation on the NHS.'

Marjorie Cunningham, a former neighbour now in her eighties, also tells of his generosity. 'I've known Max for over thirty years,' she says. 'We've always been close and since my husband Jim died in 1990, he's visited me regularly every week. I'm very disabled and I can't get out of the house unless I'm in a wheelchair, so for the last few years Max has done all my shopping. Before he arrives he goes to Waitrose or Sainsbury's and brings me some ready-to-cook meals and lots of treats. When he arrives he unpacks the shopping for me, makes me a cup of tea and we have a natter.

'He's also my salvation. At the beginning of 2005 my doctors told me I had to go into a nursing home. I got terribly upset because I want to stay in my own house. When I told Max he said I could stay put and that he would pay for a full-time carer for me, which he now does. I know it costs him three thousand pounds a month.

'I don't know anything about him being a celebrity PR person. My son Greg, who doesn't live close, tells me he leads a very glitzy life, but there is nothing glamorous about visiting me, I can tell you. To me he's just Max my former neighbour and very dear friend.'

Greg, a social worker, is equally extremely grateful. 'I know the image of Max is that he is making a mint out of scandal and mischief, but no one could be more kind or generous to my mother. However busy he is, he always comes and the continuity of their relationship has been vital to my mother's wellbeing.'

On occasion Max's visits to Marjorie have sent editors into a spin. Phil Hall, a former *News of the World* editor, remembers: 'In the past I've had a big story from Max on the go and been under huge pressure, but if I've needed to get hold of him on a Wednesday morning, which is usually his time with Marjorie, she took priority and his mobile could be off.

'When in desperation I've rung Marjorie to ask to speak to him she'd often say, "I'm sorry, he can't talk now, he's making my drink." I'd reply, "But it's really urgent." She'd then say, "Hold on," and I'd hear her call, "Yes please, Max, just hot milk and water as usual." I felt like tearing my hair out.'

While this is not Max trying to be awkward, there are countless occasions when Phil and many others have never known whether or not they are the butt of Max's mischievous sense of humour.

9. FREDDIE STARR AND THE LEGEND OF THE HAMSTER

$\mathbf{M}$ax has an insatiable appetite for practical jokes and his friends, clients, family and business colleagues have all been his victims. Some pranks could have come from a *Just William!* story rewritten by television comic Dom Joly. Max thinks them up in the blink of an eye and, if he is spinning the yarn on the telephone, often uses a range of voices.

It's mostly just devilment, but sometimes he uses them to deflate someone he dislikes, and occasionally they can be hurtful.

In the early 80s he was asked to handle the PR for a three-day summer county show near Aylesbury in Buckinghamshire that included a gala concert with Suzy Quatro, Jerry Lee Lewis and Boy George. Max was employed to deal with the national press while an elderly, rather prim woman, Mary, was handling the local press.

Before the festival opened Mary sat in the doorway of a marquee earnestly discussing the flower-arrangement and home-made jam competitions with a couple of other ladies. Then the phone at the side of the tent rang. Max picked it up. The line went dead but Max was feeling mischievous and began to have a conversation with an imaginary journalist.

He said loud enough for Mary to hear, 'That is absolutely disgusting. She is a respectable married woman and if you repeat that in the paper I will get the lawyers on to you.' He paused, then shouted, 'She did what! Believe me, I know the lady and she wouldn't do such a thing and in any case she'd have to be a gymnast.'

He paused again. 'Look, she doesn't wear anything like that. She's a respectable woman who has been publicising county shows since 1948 and I am warning you again if you print any of those allegations, you will be sued.'

He carried on for about fifteen minutes, and then put the phone down. Mary rather anxiously asked Max who had called. He told her a reporter had phoned accusing her of wild sexual antics with the organiser of the festival, a respectable married businessman. He then reassured her, saying he'd convinced him not to print the story. 'Don't worry,' he said. 'Although many journalists today are nasty, cynical people I've sorted it out for you.' Throughout the show she kept telling Max how grateful she was for his help.

He played lots of tricks at home too. 'An old boy came to the house to change various locks,' he remembers. 'I deliberately walked into the kitchen where he was working wearing Liz's nightdress and a pair of my knickers on my head. I said, "Good morning." From the look on his face he obviously thought I was a pervert.

'Another stunt came about because we thought we'd lost Liz's wedding ring. She put it on the top of the washing machine but it vanished. We looked everywhere and decided it had fallen into the dog's bowl and he'd eaten it with his food. So for the next day or two when I took him for a walk over the common, I used a fork to check through his deposits. A couple came along and looked rather strangely at me as I was crouching on the ground mashing up dog's muck. I looked back at them and said, "Please excuse me. These are hard times." To this day they must talk about this nicely dressed bloke who was eating yuk. Luckily we found the ring underneath the washing machine a couple of days later.'

Max's friend Mac McCormick remembers Max getting up to mischief when they were on holiday on the Algarve, Portugal. 'We went swimming in the sea and Max came out of the water carrying a large dead fish,' he recalls. 'We walked back along the beach to our sun beds, passing the deserted loungers of a rather po-faced couple who we assumed had gone off for lunch.

'Max quietly slipped the dead fish into the woman's beach bag that she'd left behind. When she returned she put her hand into her bag to get something, and pulled out the fish. She then went completely hysterical and blamed her husband. Max had trouble keeping a straight face.'

Bernard disapproves of his youngest brother's behaviour. 'Max likes to tease everyone, but it can be hurtful and a little unkind,' he says. 'My wife Iris and I were in a Madrid restaurant with Max and Liz when Max started chatting to a striking slim young Brazilian model eating close by. After a while Max pointed to me and said, "My brother is a cross-dresser. I wonder if you have any spare clothes he could borrow." She was obviously desperately embarrassed, not I think because I was a cross-dresser, which I certainly am not, but because Max thought she wore clothes large enough to fit someone as bulky as me. I wasn't too annoyed. I still think of him as my little brother and I can't take such things seriously.'

Max equally enjoys a laddish dare. One friend had a bet with him that he couldn't pick up the next woman who walked down the street, persuade her to come up to his office and get her to agree to have some revealing pictures taken. Max took him on. 'The next woman we saw was a solidly built traffic warden of about thirty,' he recalls. 'She could have been quite a challenge. I went downstairs and started talking to her trying to work out the best way to break down the barriers between us.

'After a brief opening I asked, "When you go down the street giving people tickets what do you think about?" She replied, "That I'd like to be on TV." I couldn't believe my luck. We'd only been talking a few minutes and I knew I'd win the bet. I continued, "Perhaps I could help. I know several television directors and I'm sure I could put in a good word for you."

'Within ten minutes she was upstairs in my office. I then told her she had lovely legs and if she let me take some photographs, I was sure there would be an offer. She agreed. Then before I started snapping I told her I needed something a bit sexy to get people interested and that I knew comic Freddie Starr was looking for a sexy person to play a traffic warden in one of his TV specials.'

Almost immediately she took her top off. 'I took a few Polaroids and told her to come back the following week. She did and I kept my promise. I got her a walk-on part in one of Freddie's shows. It was a good game, and so easy I played it several times, but she was the only traffic warden who succumbed.'

On another occasion the joke rebounded on him. Alan Fields arranged a meeting with Ernest Maxin at Max's office at 6 p.m. Maxin was the successful TV producer of comedy shows for stars including Eric Morecambe and Ernie Wise, Norman Wisdom and Jack Benny, and was highly regarded.

'Max and I decided to have a bit of fun with him,' Alan recalls. 'I invited two models to come to the office and when we saw Ernest walking down the street we gave the girls a nod, they stripped naked and sat bolt upright on their chairs. Max went to sit behind his desk and when Ernest arrived, complete with a carnation in his jacket buttonhole, Max said, "Good evening."

'Ernest walked over to Max, shook his hand, then went up to each girl, bowed slightly, kissed their hand and didn't bat an eyelid. He then sat down and we got on with our meeting, leaving all of us lost for words.'

Occasionally Max used his story-telling skills to scare one of the stars he worked with. 'It was useful if the celebrity was arrogant and horrible,' he says. 'I once phoned Solomon King on a direct line immediately after one of his shows and, using one of my voices, claimed I was a reporter called Colin and worked for the *Daily Express*.' The conversation went like this:

'Your show was wonderful tonight.'

'Thank you, yes, everyone said I was brilliant.'

'I was wondering . . . Before the show a young lad came into your dressing room and stayed for quite a long time.'

There was a long pause. King's tone of voice completely changed.

'What are you saying?'

'Well, when he came out he looked rather dishevelled.'

'What are you insinuating?'

'Nothing. Just that he was in your changing room for rather a long time.'

Max continues: 'He terminated the conversation abruptly and moments later rang my phone to ask me to stop a story he thought would reveal that he was a homosexual. I said, "But you are homosexual." "Yes," he admitted. "But the public don't know."

'I waited until the following morning to get back to him and to say that everything was OK. I also said I had to go to an awful lot of trouble to stop it. To his credit he was eternally grateful.'

Pranks add an extra splash of colour to Max's hectic life. But although he has a modern outlook in many areas of life, he ran his office as if he was living in the Dark Ages. He didn't, for example, get an answer phone until the mid-90s, and only then because an Australian journalist who he'd let use a desk for a few months bought it for him as a thank-you present.

Clare Ellison, who worked as Max's PA from June 1991 for nine years, clearly remembers his work habits. 'In spite of the fact that Max was a technophobe and a Luddite his sense of humour overrode those little idiosyncrasies,' she says. 'He also insisted that everything was kept clean and tidy and one quiet day decided to tidy up all the wires in the office.

'It wasn't until a few hours later, when we'd remarked it was exceptionally quiet, that I discovered all the phones were dead. Max's way of tidying up had been to cut all the wires, including the main phone cable. You couldn't help but love him.'

For some years she worked on a typewriter rather than a computer. 'I had to use old-fashioned carbon paper between two sheets, which made typing difficult. After a couple of years I persuaded Max to get a fax machine. Just before I sent the first fax Max reminded me to get him a copy of the document. Perhaps he thought I was going to send the original down the phone line!'

He was also reluctant to have a mobile. When he was at meetings, lunch or away on holiday, he would leave a list of phone numbers for his secretary to call. Nowadays his mobile is rarely out of his hand, although he has yet to learn how to send text messages.

In the early 90s Max's list of clients covered consumer items and personalities. Clare joined just as he turned down doing PR for Paul Gascoigne. Gazza had become a national hero after his breath-taking performance in the 1990 World Cup and his then manager Mel Stein approached Max to do his PR. Most PRs, especially football fans like Max, would have jumped at the chance.

Stein, however, wanted Max to work for nothing. 'He told me to think of the prestige of having such a huge star on my books,' Max recalls. 'I replied, "I think a few people have heard of the Beatles and Frank Sinatra." I admired his cheek, but refused the offer.'

He did, however, take on Australian tennis player Pat Cash. He was coming to the end of his tennis career and had become so frustrated by his various injuries that he was throwing his racket around and getting a reputation for being difficult. His father got in touch with Max and asked if he could help. He explained Pat was living in the UK and wanted to move out of the tennis circuit and develop a different image. Max got him on various quiz and entertainment shows, one of which was with entertainer Bruce Forsyth. Pat also produced a record with fellow tennis player John McEnroe called 'Full Metal Rackets' but it was too heavy rock to be mainstream and didn't sell particularly well.

Another client was the Chinese restaurant called Mann's in Raynes Park where Max had taken Marlon Brando and later Muhammad Ali. It was astonishing publicity for a small local restaurant and they were naturally thrilled with him.

He also worked for Joe Bloggs, who made baggy jeans. They sent in boxes of jeans and sweatshirts that were intended for celebrities to wear, but Max gave them to the local kids at home. The association didn't last long, not because of what happened to the goods, but because the owner wanted to pay Max on a results basis, which he didn't like, rather than on the monthly retainer that he insisted on.

Clare loved her job, but after she'd been in the office for a while she began to realise that Max had a totally confidential side to his work. 'I remember picking up the phone one day and a man called Jack asked for Max. I asked, "Jack who?" He said, "Nicholson." I put him through and afterwards I asked Max if he had really been *the* Jack Nicholson. He said he was. I was so excited that I told all my friends, but Max didn't tell me what the phone call had been about. I was intrigued, but I accepted it was private.'

'Jack was fun and very lecherous,' Max remembers. 'Just like he is on screen. He didn't take himself seriously and had a magical way with women. They seemed almost hypnotised by him. I looked out for him occasionally. One fun episode took place with a girl on my party circuit. She was worried about being too naughty and asked my advice about what she should do.

'I suggested she saw a sex therapist and she came up to my office to discuss it further. I chose a day when Jack was around. She didn't recognise him and assumed he was there to help her. He didn't tell her to the contrary and she started telling him all the things she liked to do. He talked to her for ages and thoroughly enjoyed himself.'

One of Max's more hilarious PR jaunts involved Scottish wrestler Andy Robbins, who with his wife Maggie owned a 6ft 6in 54-stone grizzly bear called Hercules. In 1980 Hercules went missing while making a TV commercial on the Outer Hebridean island of Benbecula.

Although Andy actually found him quite quickly, word had already got out that he was on the loose and there was a tremendous amount of media interest in him. Max instantly saw the potential in terms of publicity and told Andy to keep Hercules hidden and not to tell anyone he'd found him. The subsequent 'hunt' turned Hercules into a household name. It wasn't until almost three weeks later that his unmistakable frame was 'found' in a field near Marrival on the neighbouring island of north Uist, 'playing' with some baby lambs.

All the papers covered the story and as a result Hercules and Andy were asked to go on the *Russell Harty* TV chat show. Max went along too. 'My leg was in plaster at the time, because I'd broken it playing football,' he says. 'But I hobbled along to make sure everything went OK. We did a rehearsal in the afternoon and Hercules was fine. The show itself went out live in the evening in front of a large audience. When everything was ready Andy and Hercules walked into the studio. I followed and the safety door shut behind us.

'The orchestra began playing. There hadn't been any music at the rehearsal and it gave Hercules a huge shock. He stopped, then started to move backwards at a tremendous pace. I was behind him on my crutches and panicked that he was going to crush me to death. Fortunately there was some scaffolding at the back of the studio and I managed to pull myself up out of his way moments before all 54 stone of him went wallop against the back door.

'It was so nearly the end of me and the headline flashed through my head: "Clifford comes to a grizzly end." There have been a lot of people who have wanted to bump me off, but that encounter was possibly the nearest I have come to it.'

It was around this time that celebrity manager Alan Fields asked Max to do PR for his client, comedian Lennie Bennett. Lennie, along with Jerry Stevens, had just been given his first TV series, *The Lennie and Jerry Show* by the BBC, who hoped it would fill the slot left by Eric Morecambe and Ernie Wise, who had moved to ITV.

The series was reasonably successful, but after a couple of years Lennie decided he no longer wanted to be part of a double act and moved to London Weekend Television to host a celebrity-based game show called *Punchline*.

Lennie, who now lives in Spain, found Max 'infinitely efficient'. 'I enjoyed his highly developed, individual sense of humour and his wide-eyed look of outraged innocence. He was obviously a very driven man, who liked to be in control. I always thought he'd succeed because he had a natural ability to come up with an angle to make a story work. He can be both quite cold and incredibly kind and we had one minor falling out when he was annoyed that in an interview with journalist Andrew Neil I made a jokey reference to his ruthlessness.'

Their professional relationship ended in 1985 when Lennie began presenting a daytime show called *Lucky Ladders* and decided he no longer wanted personal publicity. He had by then, though, introduced Max to comedian Freddie Starr.

Freddie's career was going downhill fast. He wanted someone to help him revive it and had asked Lennie for a recommendation. Lennie told him about Max. They met, Max agreed to take him on, and quite quickly got him spots on various TV shows including with Des O'Connor.

In retrospect, the liaison was always unlikely to last long. Max only works on an equal footing to his clients and expects them to take his advice. 'I found Freddie to be unpredictable and, as time went on, difficult to handle. He could be charming one minute and totally different the next. I knew he could be difficult, but initially he was fine. It helped that I found him hilariously funny and it was easy to get him publicity because he was such an over-the-top character.'

Neither man could have foreseen that their association would lead to one of the most remembered newspaper headlines in the annals of Fleet Street. It was also one through which Max redefined his role in the world of PR, which later changed the industry itself. Instead of him trying to persuade tabloid editors to write about his clients, they started to come to him for gift-wrapped stories. The change in balance made it a seller's market. Max had the goods that editors needed not just to enhance their reputation but because their jobs relied on the circulation figures of their newspapers.

The Freddie Starr story began in March 1986. Freddie, then forty-two, had agreed to have his life story written by his old friend, writer Vincent McCaffrey, but some way through the project he got bored and stopped co-operating. After a great deal of effort, Vincent persuaded Freddie to spend a few days with him and his 23-year-old girlfriend Lea La Salle, an actress and model, to continue working on the book.

Lea was fed up with Freddie for messing her boyfriend about, thought he was behaving like a spoiled child and decided to teach him a lesson. She, not Max, as legend has it, contacted a friend who was working on the *Sun* newspaper and, in a moment of inspiration or spite, offered him the fabricated story that Freddie had eaten her hamster.

The then editor Kelvin McKenzie rang Max out of courtesy to tell him he wanted to run the story, and also asked for a comment from Freddie and his manager. The two men denied the story and were desperate to stop it appearing in the paper. They thought the animal-loving British public would be so repulsed by what they read that it would terminally damage Freddie's already declining career.

Max, on the other hand, was keen it should run. In what was to become a characteristic operating technique, he saw potential in a situation that would have had most PRs wringing their hands in horror. 'I thought it was fantastic publicity,' he says. 'I also reckoned that most of Freddie's fans probably couldn't read or write, and the few who could wouldn't care what he ate.

'Instead I defended him tongue in cheek, saying I had seen him put some very funny things in his mouth over the years, but never a hamster. I also made sure Freddie's denial appeared in the paper, saying he'd hidden it not eaten it.'

The front-page splash appeared on 13 March 1986, with the unforgettable headline, FREDDIE STARR ATE MY HAMSTER. It's a date that's forever imprinted on Max's memory. 'It was my first huge story. Until then I was pulling off all kinds of nonsense but that was the first one that publicly put me apart from other PRs.'

The story quoted Lea saying that Freddie had put the hamster called Supersonic between two slices of bread and started eating it, that she felt 'sickened and horrified' by his actions, and that instead of being sorry for killing her much-loved pet he 'fell about laughing'. To add fuel to the story, she also alleged that Freddie had smashed the hamster's plastic-ball home against the kitchen wall while he was in it. As a result she had kicked Freddie out of the house and told him she never wanted to see him again.

Freddie's version was quite different. He was quoted as saying: 'This story is pathetic, stupid and garbage, absolute garbage. I love animals and I'm a vegetarian. I would never do anything to hurt a defenceless creature.' Nonetheless it seemed the damage was done.

Max, however, had a follow-up story ready, which he organised in suitably swashbuckling form. He instinctively has the ability to boldly spin stories that no man has spun before.

'The next day I arranged for a reporter to be flown by helicopter from the *Sun*'s offices in Wapping to Freddie's home in Waltham St Lawrence in Berkshire. The paper bought a hamster, which I named Sandwich, to take down with us. It gave us a few hairy moments when we dropped him in the cockpit and we all had to scrabble around on the floor until we found the wretched thing. I warned the reporter that, if it died, I'd make sure he'd be on tomorrow's front-page of the *Daily Mirror* for murdering a hamster in midair.

'At home Freddie talked about how much he loved animals and how he would never hurt them. He was then photographed with Sandwich on his shoulder. The *Sun* used his response on its front page the next day.'

Every paper ran with the story and the legend of Freddie and the hamster was born. As Max had predicted, Freddie's lacklustre career subsequently took off in spectacular fashion.

He was about to start a tour, which had looked as if it was going to be a terrible flop as so few tickets had been sold. But after the hamster story it sold out immediately. Another twelve dates were added to cope with the demand, bringing in an estimated extra £1million. Freddie altered the show too, so that at a prearranged time a butler came on stage with a silver dish, which he opened to reveal a mock hamster on a sandwich. Freddie lived on the back of the story for years and it undoubtedly made him a fortune.

It was classic Max: a quickly executed inspired idea combined with an ability to turn something extremely damaging into a huge success. FREDDIE STARR ATE MY HAMSTER is a headline that people still remember almost two decades later.

'I've always been able to come up with ideas,' Max says. 'I don't have brainstorming sessions and no one's ever trained or coached me. I just make it up as I go along. The *Sun* didn't pay me for the story, but Freddie did.'

Ironically, a few weeks later Freddie claimed the whole thing was his idea. Max didn't care. 'Everyone knew it had come from me. Stars are often like that. If an idea works it's theirs. If it doesn't they find someone to blame. I don't mind. It just shows how insecure they are.'

After the success of the hamster story the relationship between the two men began to deteriorate. 'As Freddie became more successful the worst side of him began to come out,' Max remembers. 'I thought he could be overbearing, talking appallingly about people the minute their back was turned. He ceased to have time for anyone but himself. I've seen it happen so many times when someone becomes successful. His behaviour didn't affect me directly but I was furious when, after I'd made arrangements for him to go to a children's hospital, he just didn't turn up. Although he was talented, he wasn't someone I wanted to be around and soon after the *Sun* story I decided I'd had enough.

'As I worked on my usual month-by-month basis it was easy to extricate myself. I rang his manager and told him I wasn't going to do his PR any more. Two days later Freddie rang to say he was sacking me. It was fine, I realised he needed to be top dog.'

Years later Freddie, who now lives in Spain, was in trouble again. His career was in tatters, he admitted beating his son, and his wife Sandie was divorcing him. 'When I heard about the stories that he'd been threatening his family I did absolutely nothing to stop them because I wanted to make sure everyone knew what he had been up to,' he says.

If style queens Trinny Woodall and Susannah Constantine can help change a person's life by altering what they wear, Max is the long-reigning king of the image make-over. Derek Hatton was the first in a long line of high-profile clients whose public face has been redefined in his skilful hands.

Derek Hatton was a left-wing Labour militant who in the late 80s was the highly controversial deputy leader of Liverpool council. He had a negative image with the public and was vilified for his strong views, alleged incompetence in handling the council's finances and his cocksure manner.

Hatton contacted Max in 1987 soon after he'd been sacked from his post for bringing Liverpool to the brink of financial disaster and was subsequently expelled by Neil Kinnock from the Labour Party. He had no alternative but to leave politics and find another career, but he realised that wasn't going to be easy.

'Everyone knew me for one thing and one thing only, which was left-wing politics,' Hatton admits. 'I wanted to change that. The manager of a Liverpudlian hypnotist I knew suggested I try a fellow called Max Clifford, who few had heard of at the time and, as I didn't have any alternative, I called him. I told him who I was and he invited me down to London to see him. I climbed the innumerable winding stairs to his office and we started chatting. To my surprise we immediately got on well. I found it very reassuring that he was an ordinary person, and not a London luvvie.

'He told me it might need something pretty spectacular to change my image and make people see me in a different light. It didn't take him long to come up with an idea and before I left he told me to come to a Piccadilly nightclub called Xenon, which not entirely by chance happened to be on his books, the following Wednesday night.'

Max was already waiting for Derek at the nightclub the following week. He introduced him to several waiting photographers and a beautiful young woman called Katie. He told the two of them to sit together in a corner. He ordered an elaborately decorated cocktail from the bar and two straws, put the drink on a table in front of them and told them to sip the drink through the straws.

'The photographers clicked away and then disappeared,' Hatton recalls. 'When they'd gone he told me Katie was in fact a member of the fabulously wealthy Barings banking family and related to Princess Diana, and was doing him a favour coming along. He said he wanted to build it up as 'a thing' between us and advised me to warn my wife Shirley when I got home.

'The picture was on the front page of the *Sun* the next day with the headline DI'S COUSIN DATES DEGSY. The article went on to say we'd both just come back from a luxury holiday in Barbados, which reassured Shirley as she knew I hadn't been away. Its effect was immediate and everyone started talking about me in a totally nonpolitical way. Because of my high profile at the time, it wasn't a difficult story to sell, but it was a brilliant ruse to come up with, an absolute cracker, and I knew that this man Max Clifford could do the business.

'We became mates and went to functions, openings and parties together where I was often photographed. Max barely charged me anything for his work, because I think our relationship helped both of us.' In fact, Max didn't need to charge Hatton. He was already being paid handsomely by the venues Derek was seen and photographed in.

'At the time,' Hatton adds, 'people kept saying, "Who is that man with Derek Hatton?" So he got some publicity out of it. Whereas now it would be the other way round. I also remember that whatever party we went to, he'd always leave to get home by 10 p.m. so that he could carry Louise, who was then about fourteen and wheelchair-bound, up to bed.'

Hatton, who is now a businessman and a presenter for Century Radio in Manchester, was also, inevitably, on the receiving end of Max's roguish sense of humour.

'One day he told me there was a young woman he'd like me to meet. I went along to his office and he introduced me to an elegant, rather beautiful female who was about six foot tall. We chatted for a while and then she started getting rather touchy-feely. I went along with it for a bit, but then out of the corner of my eye, spotted Max laughing his head off. Somehow it made me look more intently at the woman he introduced me too and I suddenly realised "she" was a man. I turned to Max, but he'd caught my expression and quickly left his office. I chased him down the road. I wanted to kill him, but he was too fast.'

Max may be quick on his feet, but he's even faster at seeing opportunities. And his quick thinking over a young woman who oozed sexuality had an unanticipated long-term effect on his life.

10. HOW SCANDAL CHANGED MY LIFE

Pamella Bordes was a call girl with social ambitions, who hit the front pages in 1989 with a juicy scandal. The hullabaloo about Freddie Starr had put Max centre stage and was a fitting prelude for his first big story. But this wasn't a kiss-and-tell, nor was Bordes his client.

'Contrary to what most people thought at the time, Pamella never came to see me. Nor have I ever spoken to her,' he confesses. Instead Max cunningly manipulated the story to make a smoke screen for another story he didn't want published.

Pamella Bordes, a stunning Asian beauty, was born in India, and slept her way round New York and Paris before arriving in London in the late 80s determined to find a rich husband and become a member of the Establishment.

She managed to flirt her way into getting a day job as a researcher in the House of Commons while at night keeping her links with the call-girl network. She exercised her practised charms on a host of lustful men including two newspaper editors, a politician and, so it was alleged, a tyrant, a wealthy tycoon and a member of the royal family.

She also became the sacrificial lamb Max used to protect a friend. It was the first time he was both poacher and gamekeeper, selling one story and keeping another under wraps.

'A madam who ran a high-class escort agency and was an old friend asked to see me,' he says. 'She was obviously very worried and after a cup of tea told me she thought she'd been rumbled and was about to be exposed by the *News of the World*. She'd discovered that Stuart White, one of the paper's top reporters, had been put on the story and feared that, once it came out, she might be arrested for running a brothel and put in jail. I wanted to help her because I liked her and because she looked after many rich and famous people including clients of mine and members of various royal families.

'I asked her to tell me everything about how she operated and the girls on her books. After a lengthy conversation she mentioned that one of her girls was called Pamella and was working as a House of Commons researcher. She was going out with Andrew Neil, who was then editor of the *Sunday Times*, Donald Trelford, then editor of the *Observer* and the then Minister for Sport Colin Moynihan, but the madam believed none of them knew she was a hooker.'

Max's heart beat fast. He instantly recognised the huge opportunity the Pamella story offered and how it could be moulded to suit his purpose. 'This was not only a big story but one that would enable me to turn the spotlight away from the madam herself. I said, "Stop worrying. You've just got yourself out of jail." I asked to see some pictures of Pamella, then rang Patsy Chapman, the editor of the *News of the World* at the time. I told her I had a great story about a call girl who worked in the House of Commons and could be a spy.

'She was very enthusiastic. I also asked if Stuart White could work on it, because I knew he'd have to be taken off following the madam, although of course I didn't say so. She agreed. Then over the next few weeks I drip fed Stuart bits of information about Pamella before finally giving him her name.'

As a result, in March 1989 the front page of the *News of the World* carried the headline CALL GIRL WORKS IN COMMONS, and detailed her conquests, which were alleged to also include arms dealer Adnan Khashoggi.

The scandalous, sensational revelations threw Fleet Street into a frenzy and Pamella's extracurricular activities monopolised the newspapers for weeks. It triggered a tidal wave of indignation too, especially from Prime Minister Margaret Thatcher, who ordered a top-level Scotland Yard investigation. She feared key government figures were vulnerable to blackmail, particularly as Pamella had been given a sensitive House of Commons security pass that allowed her to wander unsupervised through parliament.

Pamella was even spoken of as the next Christine Keeler, the call girl at the centre of the 60s Profumo affair, who slept with a cabinet minister and a Russian spy.

In the end no state secrets were spilled and, unlike the Profumo affair, no careers were ruined. It had all centred on lust. Max received a hefty payment from the *News of the World* without the editor suspecting his real motive; as for Pamella, she subsequently earned a sum said to be about £300,000 by selling her life story to the *Daily Mail*. She then left London for Africa where she spent some time living alone in the desert and was last heard of wandering around India taking photographs and asking, Greta Garbo-style, to be left in peace.

The good news for Max was that by the time all the juice had been squeezed out of the Pamella story, he had been able to remove any evidence of the madam's activities. The lady in question has long since retired and lives in luxurious comfort in Surrey.

More significantly the story changed the direction and nature of Max's working life. It was the giant leap that helped make Max become the multimillionaire symbol of our celebrity-crazed age and one of its most controversial characters.

'It opened the world of kiss-and-tell,' he explains. 'Even though she was never my client, my name was associated with the story and people started to call me and say, "You're the guy who sold the Pamella Bordes story. Are you interested in this . . .?" It significantly changed my PR business and many aspects of my life. It put me even closer to the centre of the media game and gave me greater impact and influence in dealing with its movers and shakers.'

Three years later, as a direct result of Pamella Bordes' story, another story of sex and scandal emerged that positively catapulted Max into the limelight. It was Tory politician David Mellor's alleged affair with Antonia de Sancha in 1992.

Forty-three-year-old Mellor, a married man with two children, was at the time National Heritage Minister and a close friend of

Prime Minister John Major. Thirty-year-old Antonia de Sancha was a 6ft-tall Spanish-born bit-part actress and part-time model who had once played a one-legged prostitute in a film in which she had simulated sex with a pizza delivery man.

As occasionally happens, Max had nothing to do with breaking the original story, but was involved in the follow-up, which allowed Antonia, the 'underdog', to give her side and set the record straight.

Their alleged affair was said to have begun in April, following a dinner with a mutual friend Paul Halloran, a journalist for satirical magazine *Private Eye*, but their trysts didn't stay secret for long. It was claimed that they used a flat belonging to one of Antonia's friends for sex and he spilled the beans to photographer Lez Chudzicki, who offered it to the *People* for £30,000. Phil Hall, who was then news editor, didn't have that kind of budget, but offered to buy it for less. Lez then tried the *News of the World*, but they couldn't decide whether or not to run it on matters of taste, so he returned to the *People*.

It is indicative of how times have changed and how little respect politicians now command, that today few papers, let alone a tabloid, would think twice about exposing the alleged sexual misadventure of a senior politician.

Lez told Phil where the couple used to meet and a photographer was secretly dispatched from the paper to take their picture and prove their clandestine liaison. He didn't have to wait long. When they arrived at the meeting place it was claimed that the couple fell into each other's arms and kissed passionately. Antonia's friend then bugged his own phone, which he was legally entitled to do, to get a recording of the alleged lovebirds talking together, and gave the tapes to the *People*. They splashed the story on 19 July, ironically Mellor's eighteenth wedding anniversary. The paper sold an extra 80,000 copies.

The revelation came at a great time for the papers and a terrible time for the government – John Major had not only launched his 'Back to Basics' campaign to restore family values, but was also considering tough new privacy laws to block reports of the private lives of public figures.

The scandal turned Antonia into a household name overnight and prompted a statement from Mellor admitting he had marital problems. He also offered to resign. Major initially turned his request down. What no one realised at the time was that Major's desire to keep his friend on board was no doubt influenced by his own affair with former MP and cabinet minister Edwina Currie, which had lasted from 1984 to 1988, ending two years before he succeeded Margaret Thatcher as Tory Party leader (the affair was divulged in Currie's 2002 autobiography).

Antonia rang Max nearly two weeks after the story appeared. 'She said so much had been written about her that was wrong and she asked me to help her put the record straight,' he recalls. 'She was also being attacked for selling her story, which she had not done. She had in fact been totally shocked about the newspaper exposé. She had known nothing about it in advance and wasn't paid anything.

'I told her it wouldn't help her get any more work as a serious actress and that the media would continue to attack her. So in my view she should make the best out of a bad situation, fight back and get some money out of it. At least that way she would have a few hundred thousand pounds in her bank, pay off any debts and buy a place for herself.'

Meanwhile his phones started ringing off the hook with media people asking what he thought Antonia should do. It was the beginning of his long-running and productive role as media pundit and commentator.

The story of alleged sexual shenanigans was right up Max's street, particularly as he'd always mistrusted Tories. 'I was glad it was damaging,' he says, 'but I didn't put an advert in one of the papers saying, "Do you have any sleazy stories about Tories? Contact this number." It just happened.'

A fascinating, slightly surreal battle then developed between the streetwise Max Clifford representing Antonia and another PR, Tim, now Lord, Bell, an establishment figure and former media adviser to Margaret Thatcher, who represented his close friend Mellor.

In one corner, five days after the story broke there was a cringe-making photo call of Mellor, with his wife Judith, and two sons, twelve-year-old son Anthony and eight-year-old Freddy, plus Mellor's in-laws, who had reportedly denounced him over the affair, leaning over a garden gate staring at the camera with frozen grins. This brazen, misconceived and contrived act of togetherness served only to further damage his image. Meanwhile, so-called 'friends' of Antonia were gossiping about her – for a fee – to the press.

In the other, Max sold Antonia's story to the *Sun* for £20,000 soon afterwards. Her version of their alleged relationship, some details of which she was later to deny, was told largely through the device of supportive 'friends'. He apparently told her that there was nothing left in his marriage, and broke her heart when he dropped her like a hot stone once their secret was out.

After the story was published, Max arranged for Antonia to make her first public appearance at the royal premiere of the Tom Cruise film *Far and Away* on 30 July. Antonia was so nervous she shook like a leaf and gripped Max's arm. As Diana, Princess of Wales, and John and Norma Major were at the premiere, so were the press and Antonia's appearance guaranteed headlines in the following morning's papers and brought Max another wave of publicity.

Three days later she made her television debut on *This Morning With Richard And Judy*. Max accompanied her to the TV studios.

Max then launched what he calls his 'wheels within wheels' operation, when he promotes as many other clients as possible within a running story. The Cheerleaders Club in Manchester, an establishment he looked after, was the backcloth for Antonia to do a sexy photo shoot. She modelled Aids Awareness T-shirts for the Terrence Higgins Trust because Max likes his high-profile clients to promote a charity. He also had her photographed with a 'new' boyfriend who supported Arsenal as David Mellor was known to be a Chelsea supporter.

Tim Bell's campaign to re-establish Mellor's reputation as a responsible minister and family man seemed, by contrast, in tatters.

Coincidentally, at just the wrong time for Mellor, Mona Bauwens, whose father was chairman of the Palestinian Liberation Organisation's financial body, appeared in the High Court. In the course of a defamation action it was revealed that Mellor had accepted a free holiday from the Bauwens in 1990. Newspapers, by now hungry for any details that would keep the story hot, also discovered that he had allegedly accepted another holiday from the ruler of Abu Dhabi. Though neither holiday breached ministerial or parliamentary rules, they added fuel to the newspapers' fire.

Mellor subsequently made an appearance on *News at Ten* and *Newsnight* and tried to blame the press for his predicament. If the over-the-gate picture of his harassed family stabbed himself in the back, his TV appearance was the equivalent of shooting himself in the foot.

Following a hastily arranged meeting of the Tory backbench 1922 Committee to discuss his position, its chairman Sir Marcus Fox told Mellor that the backbenchers wanted him to resign as a minister. He did so – nine long weeks after his alleged affair first became public.

Max earned well from the story, and was hugely entertained by its impact. But, he insists, 'It wasn't Antonia who brought him down, it was the freebie holiday paid for by Mona Bauwens that the newspapers felt was the final straw.

'I was very happy with my involvement with Antonia de Sancha, which led to David Mellor being shown to be the kind of man I believe he really is. I didn't approve of his behaviour, but contrary to what a lot of people think I don't actually hate him. I don't hate anybody.'

Judith Mellor divorced her husband in 1995 after his later affair with Lady Penelope Cobham. David Mellor now runs his own international business consultancy, and is a broadcaster and journalist.

As a result of the Mellor scandal, Max began to be described as 'the purveyor of sleaze' and a 'muckraker', both by Mellor and his Tory cronies. He was heavily criticised for instigating and then profiting from chequebook journalism. But sleazy or not, what had started as a trickle, soon became a flood and more and more people contacted Max with stories of the rich, powerful and famous. Kiss-and-tell stories are now seen as a fast-track route to celebrity status, albeit one that barely lasts fifteen minutes. Many blame Max for creating and stoking up this dubious market.

Yet even those who shake their heads in disapproval can't resist reading about what the great and not-at-all-good have been up to. And the insatiable public appetite for intimate details about well-known individuals has, following a kiss-and-tell, resulted in a steep increase in newspaper circulation figures.

'Basically girls kiss and tell for money and/or revenge. I've helped create the market and continue to get them huge deals because I believe they should choose whether or not to exploit themselves rather than be passively exploited by the media, who then waltz off with the entire profit from their stories.

'I understand David Mellor calls me a "sleaze-ball" because he believes I fed false allegations relating to him to the media. After all, I believe that he got away with it before I came along.

'Like everyone else, I don't enjoy being criticised. I sometimes get angry, but luckily my life has always been so full of good things that ten minutes later I'm laughing. When the attacks come from people I don't respect, it's water off a duck's back and doesn't bother me at all.

'I know there are plenty of people out there who really don't like me or what I stand for. If people don't know me personally and their views are based on what they think I am about, then that causes me absolutely no problem. If they are critical because of something damaging I brought out about them then obviously I wouldn't expect them to feel anything other than animosity towards me. However, if someone really knows me and is genuinely upset or offended by something I've said or done then that's when it really matters. Fortunately for me that doesn't happen very often.

'By and large the reaction I get when I'm out and about from the public is really warm and friendly and it's seldom that I experience a hostile reaction. I'm very much a people person, I'm always stopping to talk to people, be it in supermarkets, restaurants or anywhere else. It's a sure way of finding out, in a very real way, how people perceive me.

'Sometimes it's a bit like being a football manager; one week you're wonderful and the next terrible, and you can't let it all get to you. I don't have a thick skin. I have a healthy skin. I know what I'm about, as do the people who know me. I want to help people and when necessary fight their battles, and the greater the challenge the more I want to do it.

'I remember making an after-dinner speech at a charity evening in Manchester some years ago and during the question-and-answer session one woman stood up in front of the five hundred guests and said, "What about that poor David Mellor? You destroyed him." I replied, referring to the alleged affair, "I don't think so. He did a very good job on his own. I don't remember lifting him on to Antonia de Sancha."

'Everyone started laughing. Then another woman stood up and said, "I know you are being paid ten thousand pounds to speak tonight. Well, I think you should be ashamed." I managed to stay calm and replied, "If you speak to the organiser you will find that the entire amount is going to a children's hospice in Guildford. How about putting your money where your mouth is." She didn't say another word, but several of the other guests congratulated me afterwards.

Left My debut: Me on my mother Lillian's knee with, from right to left, Bernard, father Frank, Harold known as Cliff and Eleanor.

Below At the age of 16 on the roof of Hulton Press overlooking Fleet Street. (Peter Shrubb)

Left My move from journalism to PR happened in October 1962, when I joined EMI's press office.

Below Early days in the music business. Me with 60s pop star Donovan.

Right I was 19 when I met Liz, and quickly fell in love with her.

Below We married at St Barnabas Church, in Wandsworth on 3 June 1967, and my parents Frank and Lillian (left) and hers Richie and Etta (right) joined in the celebrations.

Right Liz and me during one of our first holidays in Spain.

Top Our daughter Louise was born in June 1971.

Above Louise at eighteen months, playing on the beach.

Right One of the proudest moments in my life was when Louise gained her degree. Liz and I cried with happiness at such a wonderful achievement after all her health problems.

Left One of the big scandals of the early 90s was the alleged affair of Antonia de Sancha and David Mellor. Here I am taking her to a film premiere.

Above Wife of Sir Anthony Buck, Bienvenida, who seduced chief of defence Sir Peter Harding

Right Rebecca Loos after her alleged affair with England football superstar David Beckham, and Cheryl Barrymore, who became her manager.

Right Paul Hudson with Mandy Allwood, when she was expecting octuplets.

Below A night to remember. OJ Simpson addresses the Oxford Union Debating Society, after one of the biggest murder trials of the twentieth century. (© Mike Jones)

Right Together with Louis Theroux during the filming of *When Louis Met …*

(PA/Anwar Hussein Collection/Getty Images)

Above James Hewitt and Prince Harry as young army officers. I can understand from the resemblance why there's been so much speculation.

Above Simon Cowell is a client and a good friend and his mum Julia is a lovely lady.

Left Me with Kerry Katona at the Christopher's Children's Hospice.

Left Boyband Westlife at one of their many visits to the Royal Marsden's Children's Unit in recent years.

Left Good actor, lively writer, dreadful footballer, the glamorous Tom Watt with equally glamorous Joan Collins. (Richard Young)

Below left Muhammad Ali, one of the true greats.

Below right Together with the extremely secretive magician David Copperfield in Las Vegas.

Right I've always loved football and have wanted to be midfield in everything. Here I am in my mid-twenties with my mates in the Dynamo Football Club (middle row, right).

Left With comedian Lennie Bennett. Running a half marathon without any preparation is not to be recommended.

Below I swim nearly every day, but swimming butterfly gets harder as I get older.

'Also, one evening soon after I bought my first Bentley in 2002, I was giving a friend a lift home following a meal in Southwark when we stopped at some traffic lights. A person in the car next to me, seeing the Bentley, wound down his window and spat at my car. I opened my window and asked, "Was that necessary?" The guy looked at me, then said, "You're Max Clifford aren't you?" I said I was. "Good on you, Max," he said. "Look, I'm really very sorry about that. I think you're great."

'And when I walk down the street cab drivers often shout out to me, "You're one of us, mate," or go thumbs up. They don't see me as a celebrity.

'It's why I compare accusations of being sleazy to mosquito bites. They prick and then they're gone. They don't penetrate deeply. What would upset me is if someone who knew me well thought I was sleazy, but so far it's never happened. I don't think that handling stories about people I believe to be sleazy makes me sleazy.

'Nor do I accept the criticism that I have wrecked people's lives. If you are having an affair and you are in a position of power, influence or fame you should be fully aware of the risk you are taking.'

Max is, however, happy to take the credit for firmly linking the Tory party with the word 'sleaze'. 'I helped get them out of power in the 1997 election, when Mellor also lost his Putney seat. It destroyed them and happily, even though it happened so long ago, it's a tag I believe they still haven't fully recovered from.'

He maintains he is not by nature a political person. 'Although I'm a natural socialist, I've probably voted only two or three times in my life. From an early age I've felt everybody should be looked after and I've wanted as good a quality of life as possible for all, not just the rich and powerful. In the 90s the Tories were looking after those who were already well looked after, often at the expense of those who weren't.

'But I've never relied on governments, councils or politicians to look after me. I've always taken care of myself and at the same time tried in a small way to help other people, by giving money to charity, influencing the media and offering the needy support. Perhaps it's a naively simple way of living a socialist life, but that's what I do.'

Antonia de Sancha, meanwhile, disliked life in the spotlight, nor did she want to carry on acting. Following a broken marriage, which she blames on the after effects of the Mellor scandal, she now imports Indian textiles for private clients. She turns her nose up at sleazy stories and adopts a high-minded attitude to her own experience.

'It was an emotional rape,' she says. 'But I don't think it has affected me long-term. The past is the past and I've moved so far from it all. I don't even know if Max's advice was sound. I've put the entire experience into a metal container and thrown it out. But I do think it's nonsense to use a kiss-and-tell story as a career stepping stone. It's not the way to go forward. I also think sleaze is disgusting. It's ridiculous to be obsessed with the details of other people's lives. There are so many more important things going on in the world.' 'At the time,' says Max, 'and for a long while afterwards, she was extremely grateful and appreciative that I helped her make the best of a bad situation.'

As far as Max was concerned, the whole episode resulted in more work, more people to protect and more stories to sell.

Perhaps encouraged by what they read about Antonia or seeing her at the A-list celebrity events she attended during that period, Max was contacted by several women over the subsequent months proffering stories of sexual misconduct by politicians. Max didn't take any of them on. Instead he used his considerable skills to protect those same men the women had set out to destroy. 'I often turn things down on instinct,' he says. 'Sometimes because I don't like the person who comes to me, or they can't justify their claims, or it would do too much damage to a family, or the person concerned is not pretending to be something he or she is not. And I don't think they deserve it. I couldn't look at myself in the mirror if I didn't. I have never wanted to take on a moral crusade.'

One example involved Ken Livingstone, the outspoken and anti-Establishment figure who was leader of the long-abolished Greater London Council and became Mayor of London.

'In the 90s a friend of Ken's who was a politician and very jealous of his success tried to sell me a story about Ken and a particular lady,' Max recalls. 'I spoke to her, but I didn't think she was trustworthy, or that her allegations were justified, or that Ken had led her astray. So I told her I wasn't interested in helping her.

'I then rang Ken, who came to see me in my office. I explained to him who she was and advised him how to avoid being trapped. I said if she rang him and started talking about the alleged affair, it was likely the conversation was being taped as proof for whichever tabloid was interested. He should keep saying he had no idea what she was talking about. She did ring and he talked to her along the lines I'd advised and the story never appeared. To this day I don't know if the allegations were true or not. I wasn't interested. I just didn't think Ken deserved it. He was single, he wasn't lecturing us on family values and telling us all not to have affairs, while having one himself. I didn't take a penny from him either.

'It's one of the ways I build up relationships with people. I'm keen to earn money, but only when I feel comfortable doing so. I wouldn't feel right watching someone being destroyed by a story of mine, when they didn't merit it. And this includes a few Tories.

'Kenneth Clarke was one. A female teacher at a private school came to me with a story about Clarke when he was a senior cabinet minister. I didn't like her, checked her out and found there were several skeletons in her own cupboard. So I stopped the story at source by telling her that once her story was out, her other affairs would be exposed plus the fact that she was a lesbian. I asked her if she could face all that. She admitted she couldn't and I didn't hear another word from her.'

Max also turned down Geoffrey Boycott's former mistress Margaret Moore, who rang him in 1996 with a story alleging the legendary cricketer had beaten her black-and-blue. 'We met shortly after the alleged attack at Claridges hotel in central London,' he recalls. 'She told me he'd punched her about twenty times on the face, and banged her head on the marble floor. I looked at her and asked, "Apart from a couple of bruises, where's the damage?" She smiled and replied, "It's his word against mine." I knew not to get involved. If a cricketer like Boycott with such upper-arm strength had punched her as she claimed, her face would have been swollen and black-and-blue beyond recognition. Or she would be dead.

'A few days later Boycott himself called me asking for my help and I looked after him instead and made sure no one believed her tale.'

Max did, however, in the run-up to the 1997 general election, expose two other married Tory MPs whose private lives in Max's view fell well short of their public image. They were Jerry Hayes, who had an alleged homosexual affair with a nineteen-year-old, and Piers Merchant, who was allegedly involved with a nineteen-year-old blonde, Anna Cox, a one-time Soho nightclub hostess. Merchant was first said to have fondled her on a park bench, but initially denied having an affair. Months later he was caught again with Anna and was forced to resign his Beckenham seat.

'The ironic thing was,' remembers Max, 'that Piers and I were speaking on opposite sides in a debate about press freedom at Durham University, where he'd been an undergraduate, just before the second exposé broke. The debate took place on the Friday. He insisted he was innocent, that he had been totally misrepresented by the press and that everything had been blown up out of all proportion.

'Unbeknown to him, but known to me, the *Sunday Mirror* had put a hidden camera in his hotel room which caught him with Anna. Then on the Sunday the *Mirror* exposed his affair with her and he was out.'

The following year Max exposed Labour MP Ron Davies, who was accused of having an encounter with another man on Clapham Common. He too resigned.

'For every story I break, there's probably about twenty I could have broken and didn't. People come to me all the time with all sorts of stories. More often than not, I say, "If I were you, I wouldn't break the story, because you won't be able to handle the publicity, or how you'll be treated by the media. Go away and think about it. You can make a lot of money, but it'll destroy your life. Unless you've got a very broad back, don't do it."

'I don't have hard-and-fast rules about what stories I take up or turn down. I see life in my own way and speak as I find. It may be right or wrong but that's how I am.' Max is just as instinctive when it comes to personal friendships and at his happiest when they exist on his terms.

11. MY FRIENDS AND I

S ocially, Max has always been a Pied Piper. When he was
younger he took groups of children swimming. Nowadays he
likes to invite friends and favourite clients out for meals, or fly them
by private plane to his home in Marbella. He leads, they follow and
even when he accepts invitations he usually brings along a small
entourage of trusted companions.

He has an enormous number of acquaintances but few close
friends, and he prefers to spend time with several people rather than
just one. His older brother Bernard calls him a 'social grasshopper'.
Even those friends who have known him a long time admit he is an
enigma. They enthuse about his sense of fun and say he is a true
friend when they are in need. But they find him hard to get to know
and confess to feeling wary of getting on his wrong side.

Max admits that socially he can be quick-tempered, intolerant
and impatient. 'I don't suffer fools gladly,' he says, 'and I'm a
difficult person to spend much time with. If people come to
Marbella, I put them up in premises close by. They don't stay with
me and even then, after a day or so, I'm likely to be bored and quite
irritated. It's partly because I'm so busy, my spare time is so

precious and I'm always so inundated with people wanting things from me, that I find it hard to be easy-going when I'm trying to relax. But I'm better than I was.'

One of Max's long-term friends whose company he did enjoy was Adam Faith. Max originally met the pop singer turned actor turned financial journalist when he worked at EMI. Max had just started out on his working life, while Adam's recording career was beginning to stall. He'd had his first number one with 'What Do You Want' in 1959 and another hit a year later with 'Poor Me', but by the mid-60s none of his releases were reaching the charts.

Personally the two men had much in common. 'Adam was three years older than me but we came from similar backgrounds,' Max explains. 'We both left school at fifteen. Both our dads were gamblers and both our mums were terrible gigglers, but also held everything together. There could be sixteen people lying dead outside the front door, but our mums' sole concern would be to check that we were well wrapped and left home in time for school.

'I had a lot of time for Adam and we shared a similar attitude to life. This was that you should try to make each week as good as you can, because you don't know what will happen next week.

'Adam married Jackie Irving, a dancer, in 1967 and they later had a daughter called Katya, but he always loved the ladies. No matter how deeply he was involved in a conversation, if a stunning woman walked past him, he'd stop and say, "Look at that!" Then he'd somehow get them involved in a conversation. Although he was small and not your standard sex symbol, he had amazing charisma with women and nearly always got a positive response. We had more than a few laughs over the years and often went to parties together.

'After his open-heart surgery in 1986 he used to say to me, "Max I've got to cram in as much as I can while I can." In 2001 a proposal came to Max to do a TV drama based on himself. Max remembers, 'Adam was determined to play me. Unfortunately, for various reasons it didn't work out, and sadly he died a couple of years later aged 62, following a heart attack.'

Another of Max's friends is Tom Watt, the actor who has ghosted David Beckham's autobiography. Tom was given the starring role of Lofty Holloway, a weedy barman with a heart of gold, in *EastEnders* when the soap started in February 1985. Once the series got under way – at its peak it had about 25 million viewers – Tom set about organising a charity football team, which was largely made up of other actors from the soap.

They played most Sundays and gave any money they raised to various charities. As they often played against ex-professional footballers, their matches were always packed with spectators. Max heard about the team and got in touch with Tom.

'He said that one of his then clients, Laing Homes, a home building and land development company, would like to help sponsor the team,' Tom remembers. 'So we agreed to play about ten games over the year that would be designated Laing Homes games. In return the company agreed to cover all our costs, including transport, advertising posters, programmes and hospitality. Max even got them to pay for new kit for us. All I had to do was get the actors from the series along. I was delighted as it meant that without expenses everything we made could go straight to our chosen charity.

'The arrangement lasted about two years, during which time we raised about two million pounds for charity. Laing Homes benefited too, because we played matches where they had property developments. I got to know Max quite well during that time. He'd often come along and train with us and although we teased him that he was useless and overweight, we'd sometimes let him play in midfield. The matches were one of the few show-business-type events Liz agreed to come to. She and Louise often turned up to watch. I got on really well with both of them and often went round to their home.'

Max also began inviting Tom and his team to come along to club openings, or a premiere party after the match. It was here they found something else in common other than football. Tom, like Max, enjoyed practical jokes. 'We started to invent identities for some of the team who didn't have recognisable faces and non-actor friends, when we went to these parties,' Tom remembers. 'We'd pretend one of them was a famous footballer, journalist, or film producer and make up outrageous stories about them and they'd play along. We had enormous fun watching how it panned out during the evening, especially amongst the girls who were there.

'Usually, the more outrageous the story we invented, the friendlier the girls became, particularly when they thought there could be a film part for them. Max and I tried to outdo each other in how preposterous we could get.'

Tom and Max often met for meals and it was at a Chinese restaurant in 1988 that Max introduced Tom to one of his guests, Ann Jackson, a one-time Miss Great Britain finalist. She has since become his wife and mother of his son.

The two men see less of each other now, but when they do, they have just as much fun. 'Max is incorrigible,' he says. 'When we last met one of his friends asked me what I was doing. Before I had time to reply Max had launched into a whole saga about me moving to the depths of the country and becoming a dairy farmer making cottage cheese and yoghurt. Not one word was true.'

Alan Fields, who has known Max for thirty years, says Max will do almost anything for a laugh, just to prove he can get away with it. 'One evening in May 2004 a group of us were having dinner before he was going to be interviewed on BBC2's *Newsnight* by Kirsty Wark. He was going to talk about model Naomi Campbell, who had just won her court case against the *Mirror* for invasion of privacy.'

'They dared me to say a sentence during the interview made up of any words they gave me,' remembers Max. 'I agreed to take up the challenge as long as each of them gave a hundred pounds to charity. They then went round the table giving me a random word to put in the sentence. The words were "cupboard", "chocolate", "Tiddles" and "fatty".

'I then went off to the studios and my mates went home to watch me. Kirsty asked me something about Naomi's case. I replied, "It's a bit like Fatty Arbuckle when he was in the cupboard eating chocolate with Tiddles." Arbuckle was a great comedian in the early part of the twentieth century who was accused of raping a young actress. Kirsty didn't respond as she was checking her papers for the next question, but a fellow guest on the programme looked at me as if to say, "What the hell are you talking about?"

'I don't suppose any viewers took on board what I said either, but I'd got away with it and five minutes after I left the studio Alan rang me and we had a good laugh. The charities benefited too.'

On other occasions Alan admits he's been hurt by Max's sharp tongue. 'He's very honest and says it as he sees it, at times a little too harshly. He often criticises me for allowing people to get away with things and for being too soft. Sometimes he's also too forthright about what he wants to do and can't be cajoled to change his mind. But it's not something he's acquired with success or fame, he's been like it throughout the thirty years I've known him.'

Sometimes Max's honesty is a godsend. In the mid-80s he told Barry Ryan that he no longer wanted to do public relations for him or even be his friend. It was a bold, dramatic, even desperate gesture to try to shock Barry into getting a grip on his life that was spiralling out of control due to his alcoholism. It worked and Barry – along with others of Max's friends – credits Max with saving his life.

Barry remembers: 'At the time I was absolutely livid, nor could I believe it. After all, Max was one of my oldest friends and we had done so much together.

'But he was right. I was drinking very heavily and throughout the previous couple of years Max kept telling me it was a problem, but I was in such a terrible state I didn't want to listen. Bad as I was, his dramatic action got through to me, which is just what he wanted. I sought help and was taken into The Charter private psychiatric clinic in Chelsea where I stayed for a couple of months to dry out.

'It's no exaggeration to say he saved my life. If I had carried on behaving as I was, I wouldn't be here today. Instead I haven't touched a drop of alcohol for twenty years. I've since become a photographer, remarried and have two children. I consider myself a lucky man and am very grateful to him. Honesty is the most generous thing you can give a friend when they're in a mess. I know people think he's hard-edged, but I think he's terribly kind.

'A lot of men, for example, couldn't have coped with what he has gone through with Louise. Not only has he always been there for her, but when I asked him if it's been a difficult sacrifice he just shrugged and said, "Of course not. She's my child." '

Max's robust attitude is typical of the man and was developed in childhood. Whilst he is very happy for his friends to lean on him and will do countless favours for them, he never leans on them in return. 'I believe I can take care of everything myself,' he says.

TV agony aunt Denise Robertson, who first met Max in the mid-80s, says, 'Although I wouldn't claim that we are very close, if I was in trouble, I'm confident I could pick up the phone to him and he'd pull out all the stops for me. I equally know he couldn't let himself beg for help from someone else. It would kill him. He holds on tightly to his ability to control things and won't let himself crumble, something we all need to do at times. He has iron willpower, but no valve for letting off steam. He has been almost paternal to me, even though I am older than him.

'He doesn't tolerate bullshitters in any shape or form. When we meet at social situations I notice he stands on the fringes, looking and analysing everyone in the room. He seldom betrays emotion. You never know whether he is pleased or vexed, but behind that implacable face all sorts of things are going on. Overall he is a benevolent man, but I wouldn't want to be his enemy. He can be quite fearsome if he takes against someone.'

Former tabloid editor Phil Hall believes the only people who need to be afraid of Max are those who have crossed him in some way. 'The one time I got on the wrong side of him was over a complete misunderstanding over a story. He kept accusing me of stitching him up. I kept telling him I hadn't. He didn't actually lose his temper but it was obvious he was furious. We sorted it out but it made me think I never want to fall out with him.'

There have been no such difficulties with Max's neighbours. Ann Pritchard, who with her husband John and three children lived next door but one to Max when he and Liz lived in Raynes Park, describes him as 'a diamond. You can't fault Max as a neighbour,' she says.

They have had a lot of fun together and even their first encounter had an amusing twist. 'It was when I'd broken my leg,' Max remembers. 'The only thing I could wear over my cast was tracksuit bottoms. At the time I was doing PR for Slazenger, the sports goods company, and they'd given me lots of white tracksuits. So I went to work in a pair of white tracksuit bottoms and a smart navy Tommy Nutter blazer with brass buttons. Because it was too awkward to go by train, a car came to pick me up each morning. Apparently she thought I was an admiral.'

They soon realised he was much too mischievous. 'Max loved playing tricks,' Ann remembers. 'One summer, while the neighbours who lived between us went on their summer holiday, he bought dozens and dozens of plastic daffodils and tulips to plant in their front garden as a surprise when they came back. Their faces were a picture when they arrived.

'On another occasion, when Louise was still small, he and Liz decided to clear out their loft on a Sunday afternoon. They found Liz's wedding dress, headdress and shoes. Max persuaded her to try them on again, just, he said, to see if they would fit. She did and they both went downstairs to show Louise. All of a sudden Max shoved Liz out of the front door and closed it, leaving her alone in the street in a wedding dress, with lots of people passing by and staring at her strangely. She came running down to us laughing her head off and stayed with us until he agreed to let her back in.'

Sometimes Max was funny without meaning to be. 'I remember when they wanted to have their kitchen redone,' Ann continues. 'They didn't have much money at the time and the builder told Max it would be cheaper if he removed the old kitchen tiles himself. He agreed, but found it such a struggle he came down the road to ask my husband, who is a builder, to help. He didn't bother changing and turned up covered in dust, wearing a pair of swimming trunks and goggles and holding a Philips screwdriver and a hammer, which he'd used to try to prise off the tiles. John went round with the proper gear and removed them all in no time.'

Max more than repaid their kindness. 'For years and years,' she says, 'he'd take one or more of my three sons and several other local children out for treats on a Saturday. They'd go swimming, then on to the local workman's café for lunch of egg and chips and after that to the sweetshop where Max would pay for whatever sweets they wanted. Sometimes he'd also take them to Hamleys and tell them to choose any toy they wanted.

'They loved going out with him so much that, on most Saturdays, you'd see a row of children sitting on their garden wall waiting for him. It wasn't just because he bought them things, but because they found him such fun to be with and thought of him as their friend. My sons used to knock on his front door and ask Liz if he could come out to play. He often did and would run around playing football with them for hours.

'When my youngest son was five and had to write an essay at school about what he had done over the weekend he wrote about playing with his good friend Max. I'm sure the teacher had no idea he was writing about Max Clifford and assumed he was another little boy.'

Russ Kane, former voice of London's Capital Radio's Flying Eye, met Max soon after Liz died. At the time his own wife Sally was seriously ill with cancer. 'Max was incredibly kind, helpful and supportive to me when Sally died,' he says. 'He is far more complicated than he lets people believe. He has a strong sense of what is right and wrong and feels he has a moral right to expose others who are duplicitous and hypocritical.

'On a personal level he is very private, but he doesn't take himself seriously, just what he does seriously. Since Sally has died he has kept closely in touch with me and helps me stay positive and upbeat. I think of him as Obi-Wan Kenobi.'

Max has recently developed a firm friendship with singer and TV presenter Des O'Connor. Although the two men have known each other since the 70s, it's only in the last couple of years that their relationship has grown. Des explains: 'Max used to bring along a variety of guests to be on my shows in the 70s. We were polite to each other, but I used to look at him out of the corner of my eye and even though on the surface he seemed pleasant enough, I decided he was someone to steer well clear of, particularly as I thought he was instigating all the scandals I read about in the Sunday papers. I was wrong. He is the complete opposite of what I thought. He is warm, quietly spoken and very caring and only gets stories in the papers if people approach him and ask for help.

'We now have a great deal of fun together and more recently we are talking about the possibility of doing some business in Spain. I much appreciated how friendly and warm he was when my baby son Adam was born in September 2004. I've also come to see that he does a wonderful job looking after and protecting people who have problems. He is a decent human being and a bit of a pussycat.'

Max was always much more gregarious and outgoing than Liz, so it was perhaps inevitable that, particularly as they married so young, there would be irresistible temptations in his life. 'Although I always loved Liz there were two women I would put in that special category,' he admits. 'One was a French girl who I used to see on a casual basis for several years. The other was someone I met when I was in my late thirties. Her name was Ria and she was a gorgeous dark-haired model a few years younger than me.

'I first saw her when I went to the south coast for a show-business client who was performing down there. We hit it off immediately and we were close for five years. She was very special to me and if I hadn't been married I would have married her. As it was I couldn't have left Liz. I'd have felt ashamed of myself, especially as we were going through so much with Louise.

'Although I can sometimes be economical with the truth, I was very honest with Ria and told her that our relationship couldn't go anywhere. But she was such an important part of my life that I even took her to visit Louise during one of her spells in hospital. I know it sounds strange, but I loved my daughter and I loved Ria and I wanted them to meet.'

Most daughters would have found a get-together with their father's lover intolerable, but Max and Louise's relationship is unusual as well as close. Louise remembers the occasion clearly. 'I was fourteen and although Dad didn't exactly say she was his girlfriend and I didn't exactly ask, it was obvious to me that she was very important to him. I wasn't shocked or upset. I'd always thought of Dad as strong, virile, clever and good-looking, so it made sense to me that women would fancy him.

'He talked to me at length about Ria when I was seventeen. I'd just heard I needed to have an operation on my back and knee and told him his timing was very bad, but he explained he wanted me to know the truth about his relationship with her. Part of me felt upset that he'd put me in a difficult position as regards my mother, but another part understood.'

Max and Ria's relationship altered when she became pregnant. 'We'd been together for about four years by then and I don't know if she got pregnant deliberately or if it was an accident,' he says. 'I'd always left contraception up to her because I felt using a condom made sex too clinical. It was both stupid and risky of me. We talked about whether or not she should have the child and I told her it had to be her decision but that I loved kids and if she wanted to keep the baby, I would support him or her.

'It was the beginning of the end for us unfortunately, and some time afterwards she told me she'd met someone else and finished it between us.

'It was the first time in my life I'd been rejected by a woman I cared about and I was very upset, but on the other hand I knew it had been my choice not to leave Liz and that it was right that Ria built a life of her own. By chance I bumped into her at a gym in 2000. She'd married and had four children and looked marvellous, but our conversation was awkward, not least because her kids were running around. I would have loved to have taken her out for a meal to explain that I didn't use her and that I did really love her, but I could tell it wouldn't have been appropriate.'

Louise felt confident her father would never split up the family. 'Despite the fact Dad said he loved Ria, he always told me he'd never leave us. He explained that Ria was very demonstrative, whereas Mum, who we both knew was very self-contained, seldom expressed her emotions.'

The pressures of work and his double life meant Max needed another outlet. He had it in playing sport, a hobby that revealed more about him than any straightforward social or business encounter.

12. MUHAMMAD ALI AND OTHER TALES

Entertainer Tommy Steele introduced Max to squash. It was the perfect aggressive, competitive type of ball game he liked. Tommy was a terrific player and found the game a good way to let off steam and relax. He had a private squash court at his luxury home in Richmond and regularly played with comedian Lennie Bennett.

He rang Lennie one day in the early 80s to ask if he fancied a game. By chance Lennie had arranged to see Max that evening and on impulse asked Tommy if Max could come too. 'Although he was personally very shy and didn't like strangers, to my surprise, he agreed,' Lennie says. 'Tommy and I had a few games, and then Tommy asked Max if he'd like to play too. Despite the fact that Max had never played squash before he said he would, then ran himself giddy for an hour and a half trying to beat Tommy.

'He couldn't, of course, but he'd tried so hard that afterwards both of his feet were covered in blisters. He was so angry that Tommy was better than him, particularly as Tommy was seven years older, that Max decided there and then to take up the sport. He became brilliant at it and I don't think Tommy ever beat him again.'

In addition to swimming, a day rarely goes by without Max taking some form of exercise. One of his regular tennis partners is David Rouse, an old school friend, who has since become a builder and does all the decorating work Max needs.

'Max is a good player and usually beats me because he is so fit,' he says. 'It's just as well as he hates losing and gets very aggressive when things don't go right for him. He reminds me of John McEnroe when he plays; he shouts at himself and at me if things aren't going well and we have lots of rows about whether or not a ball is out.'

'I can't help it,' Max admits. 'I'm very competitive. I recently got so wound up when my opponent hit a few freak shots that skimmed the net and went in, that when he disputed an "out" call I made, I overreacted and yelled that he was cheating. It was terribly unfair because he's not the sort to ever cheat, but at the time I was too angry to care. I apologised after I'd showered because I knew I was in the wrong. In a way it's not a bad thing. It gets my feelings out and clears the air.'

Max particularly enjoys the company of sportsmen too. 'I've found them to be more honest than most. They take the knocks life gives and don't blame everybody else for their own misfortunes.' He particularly admires Muhammad Ali. 'Ali claimed to be the best and he was,' he says. 'He also has a humility and warmth and shows a genuine interest in people, even when there are no cameras or journalists about.'

The two men were introduced in the late 70s by Ali's photographer Howard Bingham.

'We began to get friendly and he sent me some signed pictures of himself and some boxing gloves to auction for charity. He was still fighting then and when he came over to the UK, I arranged various charity events for him and did some PR. Ali often phoned me to ask how he was perceived in England and I'd always tell him he was probably the most popular American ever with the British people.'

In the mid-80s Max asked Ali if he'd visit patients at the Royal Marsden in Surrey, then rang Professor Powles to check if it would be OK. 'At the time,' Powles remembers, 'the hospital unit I ran was a tense environment. Although I was beginning to be successful with bone-marrow transplants, it was still early days and three out of five cancer patients I operated on died. Each patient had to be kept in isolation for weeks at a time and there was strict barrier nursing.

'I told Max I couldn't imagine anything better for the psychology of my patients than having Muhammad Ali talk to them through the window of their room.

We set a day and Max arranged for several of us, including Ali, his wife Lonnie, and twin daughters Jamilla and Rasheeda, to have lunch together beforehand at Mann's Chinese restaurant in Raynes Park.

'Although Ali had Parkinson's disease, his brain was still incredibly quick. It was also touching to see how protective his wife and daughters were of him. It was a warm, relaxing and easy-going lunch and afterwards we all went on to the Marsden together. His visit was extraordinary. He went to each room and communicated through the glass to each of my sixteen desperately ill patients. It was amazing to watch their reaction. Initially each one looked startled to see him, but somehow through his simple gestures and words, he managed to communicate with them at a profound level and the change in their demeanour and morale was visible.

'Princess Diana had previously visited my unit. She had made a good impression, but Ali's impact was far greater. I could tell that in some indefinable way he'd given each patient hope and encouragement in their personal fight for life. Equally interesting was that Max, in typical fashion, stayed right back and didn't try to grab any of the limelight for himself. It helped make the communication between Ali and the patient both more private and powerful.'

Max adds: 'We were scheduled to be at the hospital for one and a half hours, but Ali stayed for four. He wouldn't leave until he'd seen every patient, both adult and child. He also spoke to the nursing and cleaning staff. When we left I thanked him so much. But he said, "No, thank *you*. I enjoyed it." He meant it too.'

In 1993 Howard Bingham published his photographic book *Muhammad Ali: A Thirty Year Journey*. Ali had agreed to go on a book tour and do several signings. One of the destinations was Manchester, where he'd also accepted an invitation to open a bar. 'The owners had paid him a lot of money,' Max remembers, 'but they hadn't realised until shortly before he was due to arrive that, as a Muslim, he didn't drink alcohol. We were all very worried that if he discovered he was promoting alcohol he'd walk out.

'So there was a mad rush to hide everything remotely alcoholic and redo the display to imply the bar was only selling healthy fruit drinks. The major transformation was completed just in time. Ali arrived, everything passed off well and I don't think he has ever discovered the truth.'

Afterwards Max arranged a dinner party for twenty in one of the hotel suites where Ali and his entourage were staying overnight. 'At the end of the evening an elderly lady started clearing up. To everyone's surprise, Ali and Bingham rolled up their shirtsleeves and helped her do the washing up in the suite's kitchen. We discovered it was her birthday and when she'd finished Ali insisted she sat down and had a drink with him.'

Derek Hatton was one of the lucky guests. 'It was great of Max to invite me as Ali was one of my all-time heroes,' he remembers. 'Ali was surrounded by his own people from the States, but when anyone discussed future plans, he always turned to Max and asked him what he thought. I said to myself, "This fellow Max has it, and not just for me."'

When Ali came back to the UK in 1999 Max suggested another visit. 'I knew that a couple of brain-damaged boxers used to meet regularly at 2 p.m. on a Monday in The Eatwell transport café in Raynes Park, Surrey. I asked Ali if he'd pop in briefly and say hello, chancing my luck that they would be there as usual. They were and they couldn't believe their eyes when they saw their hero walk in. Ali sat and talked to them for quite a while. It was an experience of a lifetime.'

Meanwhile, back at the office, Max's professional reputation was continuing to grow.

In November 1992 Claire Latimer, the Downing Street caterer for John Major, contacted Max because she was worried about the circulating rumours that she and the prime minister were having an affair. The rumours had begun about four years earlier when Major was chancellor, and, although unknown at the time, just months after his four-year affair with Edwina Currie ended. They then died down, but by the end of 1992 seemed to be gathering steam again.

At the time Norma Major tended to stay tucked away at the constituency home in Huntingdon rather than reside at Number 10, and when Major's dinner guests went home, Major and Claire would sit together chatting way into the night. Perhaps, so it was whispered, they weren't confining their activities to the washing up.

'Claire wanted my advice about what to do,' remembers Max. 'I told her to say nothing and do nothing.'

A couple of months later in January 1993, the left-wing *New Statesman* magazine and a scandal sheet, *Scallywag*, published the story that she and Major were having an affair. Major took legal action, causing *Scallywag* to fold and emptying the coffers of the *New Statesman*.

Although Max had done very little work for Claire, his name became associated with the story. He denied he was involved, but the more he did, the less he was believed. Soon after the rumours were published, there was a break-in at his New Bond Street offices, in which the front door was broken down, some papers were rifled, but nothing was stolen.

'I was sure it had been organised by Conservative Central Office, who were worried I might know all kinds of things that could embarrass John Major and damage the party, and wanted to look through my files,' he says.

'The police came round but as nothing had been stolen, they didn't get involved. It then crossed my mind that my office phones might be being tapped, so I asked a friend who was an expert in that area to check them out for me. They were, so I decided to have a bit of fun.

'I rang a trustworthy contact and told him that I had amazing information on Michael Heseltine, who was then Trade and Industry Minister in the Tory government. I said he'd been up to all kinds of mischief that would put David Mellor's alleged antics in the shade. It was complete nonsense, but I just wanted to see what would happen.

'Two days later I had a call from a so-called 'freelance' journalist who said he'd heard on the grapevine that I had a Michael Heseltine story coming up and he'd like to talk to me about it. I knew my contact wouldn't say anything, so I'm sure that whoever bugged my phone passed on the information. The Tories must have been desperate to find out what I knew.

'Over the following few months I made several more calls mentioning almost all the names in the cabinet and hinting how I could expose them. I hope I led them on a merry dance.'

Someone was certainly eavesdropping on his calls in 1997 when Max was asked to do some public relations work for General Abacha, Nigeria's military strongman.

'Some of Abacha's intermediaries phoned then came over to negotiate a deal. They offered me a million pounds a year to do PR for them, but I wasn't interested in helping put a tyrant in a good light. So I said, knowing they'd never agree, that the only way I'd get involved would be if I could take any journalist anywhere in Nigeria and they would be free to talk to anyone, however critical they'd been of his regime.

'Shortly afterwards I had a call from someone in the foreign office saying in a friendly, not at all threatening manner that they didn't think it was a good idea for me to get involved with him. Abacha died shortly afterwards, so nothing happened.'

Max also turned down the chance to help rebuild Michael Jackson's reputation a couple of months after a television documentary by Martin Bashir in February 2003 during which the superstar singer revealed he shared his bed with young boys.

'Even though I'd helped launch the Jackson Five in the 60s when I worked for EMI I said I wasn't interested. I had previously been contacted by one of Jackson's lawyers who asked me whether he should agree to be interviewed by Martin Bashir. I told them he shouldn't, as I believed Bashir would only be interested in trying to shock. But they went ahead anyway.

'After the programme was broadcast I told them I didn't want to get involved. I didn't think Jackson had the personality to win the media over. I felt he had gone from weird and wonderful to being seen by some as just weird. I wasn't comfortable with a middle-aged man sleeping with young children whatever the circumstances. I believe it has got to be an abuse of power and influence. If he wasn't Michael Jackson, the boys or their parents wouldn't have let it happen. I felt the public could accept people having affairs but what he was up to leaves a very uneasy feeling with most people.

'Also over the years I'd had people coming to see me, including a young English boy and an American couple, complaining about Jackson's behaviour towards them. For various reasons they decided not to take their complaints any further, but I hadn't liked what I had heard.

'Though he was cleared on ten counts of child molestation in June 2005, I thought reinventing him would be the hardest job in PR after representing Saddam Hussein or Neil and Christine Hamilton. Jackson might convince himself he is Peter Pan, but he doesn't convince me.'

The year 1994 was a bumper one for Max, with a phenomenal run of front-page stories: the romance between a magician and a model, the politician's wife's affair with the chief of defence, and a former minister's affair with a deputy judge's wife and daughters. It was also a year when Max was particularly vilified in the press. The London *Evening Standard* called him the 'feral face of PR' while the Tory-supporting *Daily Mail* declared he was 'the publicist without whom no tawdry political scandal would be complete'.

Early in 1994 Max was asked to do PR for a proposed European tour by magician David Copperfield, who, at the time, was earning an estimated staggering $26million (£15million) a year. Max organised a press conference to promote the tour and Claudia Schiffer was one of the guests. The supermodel was introduced to the superstar and the pair immediately hit it off. Shortly afterwards David was quoted as saying, 'We didn't mean to fall in love, it just happened.'

Max was delighted. 'It was a tremendous bonus that she happened to be in the right place at the right time. The relationship created hundreds of thousands of pounds' worth of press coverage for David. It put him on the front pages in Europe where she was well known, while getting her on the front pages of the American papers where he was a superstar.

The relationship between the two men was, however, at best uneasy. Max found Copperfield 'full of himself'. He didn't like him and couldn't resist conjuring up a few tricks of his own.

In the early 90s Copperfield regularly did two shows a day in 5,000-seater theatres in the States. 'Before the tour started I organised a jamboree for about a dozen European journalists to travel to San Francisco to meet him and watch him perform. Amongst the group was Jack Tinker, the *Daily Mail*'s late theatre critic and freelance writer Chrissie Iley.

'The show we watched was great, but I got fed up with him after a couple of days and particularly with the sycophants who surrounded him. One evening when we were all about to have a meal together one of his staff declared breathlessly, "David is going to join us for dinner. Isn't that wonderful?" I replied that when he arrived we should all get up and clap. I meant it sarcastically but he took me seriously and when Copperfield joined us, he jumped up and started clapping. The rest of us followed. Copperfield waved to us as if he was the queen. Copperfield, like many stars I've met, was a legend in his own mind and such a wonderful caricature you couldn't have made him up.

'Later during the dinner another member of his staff said to him, "David, you have the most beautiful eyes. I can see why women fall in love with you." That did it. I had to have a laugh at his expense. So when it was Jack Tinker's turn to interview Copperfield, I told Copperfield's minders that Tinker was a violent alcoholic with a terrible temper and that I was relying on them not to put any drink near him.

'In fact Jack, who was barely five feet tall, and a brilliant journalist, was the calmest, nicest man. When he went in to see Copperfield he must have been extremely surprised to find two heavies, well over six foot, standing on either side of Copperfield, and a large table separating the two of them. I did a similar thing with Chrissie Iley. I told the minders she was a raving nympho-maniac, so when she came to do her interview this time there were two enormous female bodyguards on either side of Copperfield. I confessed to both of them afterwards and we all laughed.'

David bought Claudia a huge $1.5million diamond engagement ring. Some commentators called the whole thing a Max set-up, others that they both became disillusioned. Whichever was believed, after three years the magic went out of the relationship and the wedding was cancelled.

There was no mistaking the dulcet tones of a racy woman when Bienvenida Buck rang Max's office early in 1994.

'She sounded nervous and asked if I'd consider taking on a story that involved someone high up in the Ministry of Defence,' Max recalls. 'We arranged to meet at Claridges. It was hilarious. I realised she'd done a lot of escort work, because there were a couple of old boys in the restaurant having lunch with their wives who went white and almost fell off their chairs when she walked in with me. She even went up to say hello to them. I've never seen anyone eat their meal so fast and leave.'

Bienvenida was the daughter of a Spanish watch repairer; her mother had abandoned her when she was a toddler. Her father died when she was still a child and she was subsequently placed with abusive foster parents. Despite her bad background she was a social climber, an outrageous *femme fatale*, and very good at making a man feel good about himself.

She married Sir Anthony Buck, a man old enough to be her father, in 1990 and shortly afterwards seduced the chief of defence, Sir Peter Harding. He was so smitten he'd unwisely put his feelings in writing: 'Nothing has ever happened to me like this ... your mind is agile, deep and challenging. Your body is incomparable and your face utterly beautiful,' he wrote. She claimed he also talked to her about troop movements in Yugoslavia, then in the middle of a civil war.

Max knew the story was a winner, but didn't try to persuade her to go to the papers. 'Most of the women who come and see me with a kiss-and-tell end up not telling. I did what I always do and asked her to think carefully how she would live with herself afterwards. I then said she should go away and think about it.

'She came back to talk it through several more times, always dressed up to the nines. Unlike most people who arrived panting after they climbed the three flights of stairs to the office, she'd be cool and calm. Apparently she paused halfway up.'

Bienvenida chose to go ahead and Max contacted Phil Hall, then deputy editor of the *News of the World*.

'I told him about the story and he said he'd probably take it for about £20,000, but that he'd first have to check with Piers Morgan, who had just taken over as editor. We agreed to speak the following day. By chance I heard Piers' voice as he walked into his office. They started discussing the story and as Phil didn't put the phone down properly I heard their entire conversation.

' "Piers," Phil said. "It's Christmas. We have a story about an affair between Lady Buck and the chief of defence and Max only wants £20,000 for it. It's the only time I've known him to have incorrectly judged the real worth of a story, which must be about £70,000 of anyone's money."

'Piers agreed it was brilliant.

'I kept my cool, waited until the following day, then called Phil.

' "So, what was said?"

' "Yes, we are very keen. We just need to sort out a deal."

' "Well, it must be worth £75,000 of anyone's money, but what do I know, I'm thick."

'There was a long silence, then I added, "You need to be more careful next time so that when you want to put the phone down, it really is down." '

'Max had his deal,' laughs Phil. 'It cost £55,000 more than I expected, but it was one of the most hilarious stories of our time.'

News of the World photographers snapped the two unlikely lovebirds kissing outside the Dorchester hotel. The paper's reporter then whisked Bienvenida off to the South of France to get their scoop in peace.

It went fairly smoothly until Bienvenida tried to seduce the reporter. She proved so tricky that he rang Max and asked him to tell her to concentrate her energies on the story.

It was a cracking yarn and kept the nation's eyes glued to the papers for weeks, particularly as, until then, Sir Peter had seemed the epitome of a strait-laced Tory Establishment figure, when in fact it appeared that he had been gullible. 'I didn't have a conscience. If the Chief of Defence is shagging a prostitute and talking to her about troop movements, he shouldn't be in that job.'

Sir Peter resigned almost immediately, and the already tarnished image of the Tory Party took another knock. Bienvenida's brief unhappy marriage ended and she went on to make about £175,000 from her story.

Once Max had fulfilled his initial role as agent for the story, he moved on to provide his own brand of after-sales service. This can best be described as a combination of agony uncle and father hen. He happily offers clients advice on everything from job choices to relationships with men, and many become part of his extended family.

'Unlike Antonia, who couldn't bear the limelight, Bienvenida adored it. She was as good as gold about all the publicity and very grateful for all I'd done for her. Once the story was out, Piers, Phil, Bienvenida and I went to the Savoy for a celebratory lunch. She wore a revealing purple dress and incredibly high heels. Bernard Ingham, Margaret Thatcher's former spokesman, was dining at a table near to us and had a few days previously attacked what he called her disgusting behaviour in the press.

'I remembered how the old boys had behaved when I first met Bienvenida at Claridges and whispered in her ear that she should go and say hello to Ingham. She stood up, swept over to his table, smiled and said as loudly as she could, "Bernard, how lovely to see you again. It's been such a long time." He turned puce with rage. "What?" he shouted. "We've never met." She took no notice. Instead she bent down and kissed him quickly on the cheek, pausing dramatically afterwards to make sure as many people as possible had seen her. She then walked slowly back to our table. We barely contained ourselves.

'Bienvenida went on to make a career out of being a *femme*

fatale. She set up a website and wrote a book about seduction and romancing the rich.'

Max was interviewed many times about Bienvenida for both radio and television. The exposure on this and many other stories boosted his profile even further. Countless ordinary people realised he was the man to go to when they had a story to sell, a grievance to air, or they needed someone to right a wrong.

One of the people who watched Max discuss Bienvenida on television was James Harkess, a retired deputy circuit judge living in South Africa. He was so impressed with Max that he rang him to ask for help in dealing with former Tory minister Alan Clark, who had published a sexually explicit diary.

It was to become one of Max's all-time favourite stories.

Harkess told Max he was beside himself with anxiety because multimillionaire Clark, a close confidant of Margaret Thatcher, had broken what was supposed to be a gentlemanly agreement by referring to his sexual exploits with Harkess's wife Valerie and two daughters in his diary. To add insult to injury he had called them 'the coven'.

As a result the family faced humiliation and rejection from tight-laced South African white society. He was particularly concerned about his 34-year-old daughter Josephine, who had just become the third wife of Anton van der Spuys, a rich architect. As Harkess felt their reputations had already been ruined, he wondered if Max could at least help them to get their own back.

Four days later Valerie, then 57, James and Josephine flew from Cape Town to London steaming with indignation and ready to put their side of the story. Valerie's other daughter Alison, 36, however, remained tight-lipped at home.

'It was as if the circus had come to town,' Max laughs. 'I organised a press conference so journalists could meet them, then sold Josephine's story to the *News of the World* and Valerie's to the *Sun*. Afterwards I continued to get them as much exposure as possible. They were on Sky News, *This Morning with Richard and Judy* and gave interviews to other papers. They made over £100,000, and the story on top of publication of the diary delivered yet another knock to the government's Back to Basics campaign.'

Valerie confessed she and Clark, an obsessive philanderer, had been lovers for fourteen years; then she discovered he'd also seduced

Josephine and Alison. She didn't immediately stop seeing him, but had now done so and called him 'a depraved animal'.

Josephine claimed Clark exposed himself by showing his erect penis to her and Alison when he collected them from school in his car. She also said he rubbed himself up against them throughout their teenage years.

Clark's loyal wife Jane rounded on the family. 'If you bed people of below-stairs class, they will go to the papers,' she said snottily. Clark immersed himself in self-pity and said he felt wronged and 'bitterly traduced by people whom, many years ago, I held in affection and trust'.

'It was a win–win situation, and a wonderful Whitehall farce,' Max comments. 'The Harkesses loved it, I loved it and, whatever Clark said, he loved the publicity and being called a loveable scoundrel. I made a lot of money out of it too.'

After two weeks the Harkesses returned home with their reputation still in tatters, but their heads held high. They had achieved what they'd wanted. A decade on and Valerie and James Harkess remain delighted with Max's efforts on their behalf and have no regrets about going public with their story. 'When Alan Clark told me in 1992 that he was publishing his diaries he promised he wouldn't mention anything about the family,' Valerie explains. 'So it was an absolute bombshell to discover he'd broken his word. We had to do something. I don't think a man of any calibre should use a liaison to make money.

'We wanted to have our say, but we were fish out of water as far as dealing with the press was concerned. Max was the bridge between us suing Clark – which would have been costly and unpredictable – and giving us the opportunity to be heard. He is the only person in the world capable of fulfilling that role and the only person to go to if you have a true cause for feeling wretched.

'It was a horrifying time but Max pulled me through. He was so tender and kind. He is a true man of the people, a charismatic person who understands the human condition and doesn't make judgments. He is also a man of courage and integrity with a cool, decisive way of looking after people who are in deep trouble.

'Despite all the papers putting our lives under the spotlight, I think going to Max was the right thing to do. What other way was there of dealing with Clark's effrontery and lack of honour? I didn't feel ashamed. I'm not the only woman in the world who has had an extramarital affair. Nor did I talk just for the money. If I'd only been interested in money I'd have sold the story while Clark was still a Tory minister.

'He was a man who had known my daughters since they were twelve and had become a family friend. It was appalling to take advantage of them both, but particularly Josephine. He had a one-night stand with her when he knew that she had drink and drug problems. When I accused Clark of exposing himself to my daughters and one of their friends he initially denied it, but later quietly told me he had to deny it because it was virtually a criminal offence. He said he hoped I didn't mind.

'If Max hadn't been there for us, I think my relationship with my husband and children would have disintegrated as a result of all we went through. Instead James and I became Catholics and remain close.'

James Harkess admits he was initially very shocked when his wife told him of her affair with Clark, just before the diaries were published, but that he quickly forgave her. 'I didn't have any doubts about supporting her and agree that Max did a wonderful job,' he says. 'As a Catholic I forgave Clark too. Not one of us is perfect.'

Clark quickly got over his feelings of being traduced and being known as a cad. Nor did he bear a long-term grudge against the *News of the World* for printing the story. He joined them shortly afterwards as a columnist.

The one thing that never recovered was the government's Back to Basics campaign.

Meanwhile, Max's skill at looking after someone in deep trouble was about to be tested to its limit.

13. SUPPORTING THE UNDERDOG

Cheryl Barrymore and Max were delighted to bump into each other again at a TV studio in 1974, the first time they'd met since Max left EMI. Cheryl's husband Michael was acting as the BBC's warm-up man for the extremely popular *Little and Large* show while Max had brought along a client who was doing a spot on another programme.

'We caught up on old times,' Cheryl recalled, shortly before she died. 'I told him I'd stopped performing, but had instead become Michael's manager because I knew he had the talent to be a major star. Max told me he'd set up on his own and that a lot of his work involved keeping people out of the papers when they'd done something wrong. I remember saying to him, "You don't have to worry about us. We're as good as gold and adore one another." Little did I know how wrong I was.'

Cheryl was, however, right about Michael. He became hugely successful as an entertainer and TV presenter, but the more famous he became, the more tormented he felt. He became addicted to drink and drugs, and in 1994 declared he was gay. Slowly and inexorably, he ripped their lives to pieces and totally crushed the woman who had devoted her life to him.

'After twenty happy years together Michael suddenly changed from being the nicest man you could meet into a monster, and I was struggling to cope with his abuse,' she said. 'You can only count on a few friends when you're really in trouble and when Max, who'd read about his appalling behaviour in the papers, rang and offered help, I was very grateful.'

Cheryl and Michael separated in 1997 and divorced a year later. Cheryl was so traumatised that her health rapidly deteriorated. 'I couldn't keep any food down and my weight plummeted to five stone. Max kept in touch, gave me lots of moral support, visited me continually and kept saying, "I'm going to help you get through this." And he did. I have no doubt that at the time he saved my life. I wouldn't have survived if he hadn't been there for me. Even just talking to him made such a difference.

'When I began to recover he tried to encourage me to work, because he knew that's what I liked to do. I'd written and produced so many of Michael's shows that when we divorced I lost both my husband and my career. I was physically and emotionally too ill to do anything immediately after our divorce, but Max kept gently encouraging me.

'One day he asked me to help him out by taking one of his clients to and from a TV studio. It doesn't sound much, but at the time I could barely get out of bed. I took some persuading, but looking back it was the best thing for me, because I had to make myself look reasonable, leave my house, which I hadn't done for months, and interact with people. It helped give me back some self-respect and I began going out again.

'Months later, when he felt I was ready, he suggested I write a book putting my side of our relationship. I was initially reluctant but I gradually began to feel that it was cowardly not to say anything.'

Before the book came out, Michael's career, which had already begun to flounder badly, virtually disintegrated. He had given a party in March 2001 at which Stuart Lubbock, one of the guests, was found dead in his swimming pool. At the inquest Michael said he hadn't jumped into the pool to try to save Lubbock because he couldn't swim, but in Cheryl's book *Catch a Falling Star*, published at the end of 2002, she'd innocently written that Michael had learned to swim when they bought their house in Roydon. This created a huge stir and for weeks people suggested that Michael could be accused of perjury. In the end he escaped all charges.

Cheryl also alleged in the book that Michael had drugged her on three occasions without her knowledge, went on hideous sexual expeditions with young men, was often violent and once nearly killed her. Max sold the serialisation deal to the *Daily Mail* for £175,000. Once the book was out, Cheryl gradually began putting her life back together. It was hard. She was very private and socially shy.

'Max was very fatherly towards me and invited me to anything and everything; balls, parties and charity dos to try to get me to meet new people and some hand-picked friends from the past who thought highly of me. I rarely went, which I know upset him. He once made me go on a blind date with one of his friends. My stomach was in knots the entire evening. I could have killed him.'

Working with Rebecca Loos was, however, a great step forward for her, and she successfully negotiated several TV shows on her behalf. 'Max kept encouraging me and never took a penny of the agent's fees for himself,' she said. 'He's a wonderful friend, and if you are his friend you'll be his friend for life.'

Their relationship is another example of how Max likes to care for the underdog. He took Cheryl under his wing and she never forgot his kindness. 'I felt very sorry for Cheryl,' he explains. 'Asking her to look after Rebecca was a way of giving her something to do, earn some money and build up her self-esteem. Michael treated her appallingly. He is yet another star who is only interested in himself and doesn't care who he uses or what he does if he will benefit. Ironically, at the height of his drug-taking, one of his staff asked me if I'd do some public relations work for him. I made it clear I wasn't interested.

'When Cheryl was told she had terminal brain cancer early in 2005, she refused all treatment and asked me not to tell anyone and particularly not Michael. She wanted to make the most of the short time she had left and go on her terms. Four days before her death in April she said that she didn't want him to come to her funeral. But the reality was she never got over him and I think she'd have taken him back at any time.

'She should have been able to walk away and put the relationship behind her, but she couldn't. I can cut myself off from anything that's bad and move on, and find it hard to understand that other people can't even when whatever it is, is obviously destroying them.'

Cheryl's terrible plight had evoked much public sympathy, but that is not necessarily why Max supports a person or a cause. He's just as likely to back individuals who have been vilified by the public.

OJ Simpson was one of the most famous American football stars in history, and a legend in his own lifetime. But he is most remembered for being acquitted of the murder of his ex-wife Nicole and her friend Ronald L Goldman. Simpson's arrest and nine-month trial, which was televised live to vast audiences, was one of the most sensational of the twentieth century.

Nicole had often complained to friends that OJ beat her during their stormy short-lived marriage, and when she was found brutally murdered on 12 June 1994 at her home in Los Angeles, suspicion immediately fell on Simpson. He was arrested a few days later after a televised car chase when he fled his house in a car driven by a friend.

Max had done some PR for OJ several years previously and a few days before the trial began he received a phone call from a friend in the States, who was a fan of OJ's. 'He said he thought OJ had already been found guilty by the media and asked if I could help redress the balance. By chance I'd already talked to friends in Los Angeles and I believed he didn't do it. One can never be completely certain, but I'd known him for many years and backed my instincts, as I almost always do.

'He was such a brilliant player that each time he went out on the pitch he was a prime target for the opposing team. He'd be spat at, insulted and physically attacked, but he didn't retaliate. I reasoned that if he could exercise that sort of control on the pitch, as well as handle the intense pressure of his fame, he'd be equally controlled off the pitch.

'I also knew a lot about Nicole. She was mixing with all sorts of dodgy people and taking every kind of drug. I knew too that she would sometimes complain to the police that he was beating her up when he wasn't even in the city, let alone at home. I said as much publicly.

'I also had a contact in the Los Angeles Police Department who played me over the phone a tape of OJ's arresting officer Detective Mark Fuhrman calling black people "vermin" and saying, "The only good nigger is a dead nigger and if we don't find evidence we'll plant it."

'My contact was appalled but it was difficult for him to do anything about it as he couldn't be seen to work against his own officers, so I used other contacts to make sure the tape was brought to the attention of OJ's defence lawyers. The tape was heard in court and the obvious racism raised grave doubts about the validity of OJ's arrest. As a result he was sensationally acquitted on 3 October 1995, but he has remained convicted in the minds of millions.'

The following May OJ came to the UK for a few days and asked Max to handle the publicity. 'I was pleased to do so, but I was aware that some of my staff might not want to have anything to do with him, and said whoever had a problem didn't have to get involved.'

Max's PA Clare felt relieved. 'I didn't want to deal with him and was grateful to Max. Other employers wouldn't have given their staff the option.'

Meanwhile Max's phones rang off the hook with requests for interviews with OJ from papers, TV and radio both in the UK and in Europe. Max had plans of his own. 'I thought the best way to try to re-establish his reputation was to find him the right platform to speak from. I thought carefully and settled on the prestigious Oxford Union debating society, where I'd also spoken several times previously. Students are less influenced by publicity than the rest of society and prefer to make up their own minds.

'I set it up and OJ spoke on the motion: "The Oxford Union believes first and foremost in freedom of speech: nothing more, nothing less." It provided a golden opportunity for him to discuss racial injustice in America and, apart from a smattering of protests, he won over his audience of nine hundred with his smooth, composed delivery.'

Even Clare's attitude softened. 'I decided to go along to hear him and wasn't surprised he won the debate. I've never met anyone with such magnetism.'

Max had also arranged for OJ to appear on *This Morning With Richard and Judy*. 'This was largely a waste of time,' he says. 'They were so determined to interrogate him that as soon as he began to answer one question, they hurled another at him. But overall I felt his visit helped shift the hard-line public attitude towards him.'

As a result of working with OJ Max received several threatening letters and phone calls. 'My support for him didn't win me any popularity points. Instead I got death threats from Neo-Nazis. One caller said, "OJ Simpson is a dead man. How can you stand up for that black murderer? You won't be standing up for much longer." I reported it to the police and they put a monitor on my calls.

'OJ and I keep in touch. He's still grateful for my support and says he knows how nasty it was for me at the time. But I've always been comfortable backing my own judgment, even when it goes against the public view.'

A year later Max received another batch of death threats as a result of his name being linked with the five white men accused of murdering the black teenager Stephen Lawrence in April 1993.

'They rang me and we met. I didn't like them but I knew they'd been found guilty by the media rather than by any court and deserved to be heard. They were never my clients. I just gave them some free advice. I said if they wanted to change public perception of them they should do *live* TV and radio, but no press.

'For example, I told them not to be interviewed by Martin Bashir on the ITV *Tonight with Trevor MacDonald* programme unless it was live. When an interview is live, people hear it exactly as it is and make up their own minds. Anything recorded or in newspapers will be given an angle or slant. They went ahead anyway and appeared in a recorded edition of the programme in April 1999. They answered questions about the fatal stabbing, but they didn't end up endearing themselves in any way to the public.'

Max doesn't regret helping the men but this time the racist calls came from the black rather than the white community. 'One caller said, "You want to stand up for white trash? Well, we're going to make sure you're not going to stay around." I told them to fuck off and then told the police, who again monitored my calls.'

Another batch of death threats came in the wake of him giving free advice in November 2003 to the families of the Guantanamo Bay detainees who were being held at the American naval base in Cuba without trial under suspicion of being terrorists. Again Max believed that they, as much as anyone else, had a right to be heard. He helped them get their views into the papers and threats swiftly followed. 'One caller threatened both me and Louise. He said, "We know where you live and how important your daughter is to you." I told the police, because I was concerned for Louise and they had people keeping an eye on my office and home for weeks.'

Not all the abusive calls are anonymous. In September 2003 someone sounding like George Best made a threatening telephone call to Max's employee Nicola Phillips. One of his lovers, Gina Devivo, had approached Max to sell the story of her affair with the ex-footballing legend and Max asked Nicola, who had been working with him for some time and who he trusted to handle the story, to deal with her.

Gina initially tore into George, but then pulled back from doing the story and went back to him. A day or so later Nicola received the following message on her mobile: 'Don't you fucking bug me, you c**t. Get the message? Leave us alone you piece of shit. Don't fucking call here again and don't bug me because if you do I'll beat the shit out of you, you c**t.' The voice sounded to Nicola like George's and the call was apparently made from Gina's mobile.

The police were informed and the incident remains on their records.

Max was both concerned for Nicola and ashamed at the depths to which he felt Best had sunk. 'I thought that, as a footballer, George Best was a superstar, but that, as a man, he wouldn't even make the substitutes' bench,' he says.

Max insists he doesn't deliberately court controversy, but he won't be intimidated by threats. 'I still occasionally receive death threats when I get involved in controversial issues. They aren't pleasant but I've come to anticipate them and I'm not frightened. I accept you can't do what I do and expect to get off scot-free. Of course at one level it's stupid to give my enemies fuel to attack me, particularly as there's no commercial gain from helping society's outsiders. I do it for a variety of reasons and it gives me a feeling of satisfaction. But I know it's a risk and that it only needs to go wrong once.'

Out of all the people he's helped and all the stories he's dealt with, however, there is just one he regrets getting involved in.

14. STORIES BEHIND THE HEADLINES

M ax's intuition rarely lets him down, but he admits he made a mistake over Mandy Allwood. A 31-year-old woman with a five-year-old son, Allwood had, after a series of miscarriages, undergone hormone fertility treatment without telling her partner. In the spring of 1996 she discovered that she was pregnant with eight babies.

It was inevitable that she wouldn't be able to keep her multiple pregnancy under wraps and the lawyer acting for her and her boyfriend Paul Hudson rang Max on Tuesday 6 August to ask for help.

'He said a major story was about to break about his client who was physically very delicate and asked if I could protect her from the media and negotiate the best deal for her story.'

Mandy's situation had all the controversial and moving elements to make it a gripping read. It was the type of human-interest story every paper would desperately want. Max moved fast to maximise the story's potential. He met Mandy, Paul and the lawyer in a café in Wimbledon Village the following day to explain how he worked, what he charged and how the story was likely to pan out. He also explained that the papers that didn't get the story were likely to give her a hard time.

His first impression of Mandy was positive. 'She seemed delightful, co-operative and understood the position she was in,' he says. But he didn't have much time for her boyfriend Paul, something he now admits he didn't take sufficiently into account.

He offered the story to Phil Hall, then editor of the *News of the World*, who tied up the deal with an offer of £50,000. At that time big stories were worth less than they are today, normally only about £30–£40,000. Max, who usually takes his twenty per cent commission from the client, negotiated for the *News of the World* to pay his commission instead. It meant Mandy could keep the full £50,000.

The story of her eight-baby pregnancy filled the August edition of the paper and ricocheted around the world. It also, as Max had predicted, ignited a firestorm of criticism. Newspapers, radio and TV programmes unleashed wave after wave of attack on the risks of attempting to bring eight babies to term. How could a mother jeopardise her own and her babies' health?

Why should an unmarried mother get free fertility treatment on the NHS, especially when the 37-year-old father was out of work and supported by the state? The *News of the World* was also criticised for making a morally questionable financial deal.

'It was reported at the time that medical experts advised her to reduce the number of foetuses to give others more of a chance to live,' Max says, 'but she'd just point to her vast stomach and say, "Which one should I kill?" I reminded some of the editors who were saying how disgusting it all was that they had enthusiastically bid for the same story. But that's the hypocrisy of the industry.'

Phil felt he had neither the time nor the expertise to put the paper's case to the world's media, and asked Max to represent the *News of the World* for a fee of £15,000. 'I knew that anything I said publicly would be treated cynically,' Phil says, 'but that people would take Max at his word. He handled an extremely difficult situation very well.' Neither man predicted at the time how this fee would later cause so much trouble.

Max stayed on full alert after the initial story was broken. Every media outlet, even those who called Mandy selfish and self-serving, wanted to speak to her. Max handled the flack and made countless appearances on TV insisting that Mandy's primary concern was delivering eight healthy children, 'even if there's not a penny involved'. He also constantly reassured her so that she didn't feel too much under siege.

Mandy took heart when Dr Kypros Nicolaides, an expert on foetal medicine, told her there was a possibility that she could have all the babies. He reminded her that the famous Walton sextuplets who were born in 1983 had all thrived and that with the huge medical advances and the total care and protection he promised to give her, there was a chance.

Meanwhile the other papers launched investigations into the backgrounds of both Mandy and Paul, not least to have something original to say on their own pages. 'I'd warned them it would happen,' says Max, 'and as I do with all my clients asked them to tell me anything bad that they might have got involved with, so I could anticipate what might come out and try to protect them.

'Paul said there was nothing, but once the story broke, I began to get county court judgments addressed to him at my office from people he owed money to but who hadn't known where to find him. He didn't even tell me that he went bankrupt in 1995. I was furious that he had misrepresented himself to me. I advised them that once they had their money from the *News of the World*, they should pay their debts as quickly as possible, to curb the bad publicity.'

Although Max still warmed to Mandy, his original wariness of Paul had developed into dislike. 'He was one of those cocky dudes who thinks he knows everything and that everyone else is a fool. I thought he was a bad influence on Mandy, but she was obsessed with him and would do anything for him.'

Tragically Mandy went into premature labour at 22 weeks and lost all her babies at the beginning of October. This led to the heart-rending sight of eight tiny coffins and another spate of stories.

Two months later Paul told Max they no longer wanted him to represent them. Max was OK with that. 'I had by then arranged various interviews and appearances for her in Europe as well as in the UK that had earned her about £190,000 after commission. I felt the story had run its course and told Paul it was a wise decision.

'Almost immediately afterwards, however, I started getting calls from journalists telling me that Paul was trying to sell them further stories directly. They told him they couldn't bypass me. I think it made him angry and was probably a trigger in his decision to accuse me of breach of trust. I had a letter from their lawyer claiming I'd turned down £250,000 for an interview with German TV. It was nonsense. I was on twenty per cent commission so the more money they made the better it was for me.'

Their case was heard at the High Court in London in June 2001. It was the first time Max had been taken to court by a client. The judge, Mr Justice Park, threw out eleven out of the twelve charges against him, those that basically claimed Max had 'made a secret profit' while selling Mandy's story. Justice Park also called their evidence 'unreliable'. He did, however, consider their allegation that the *News of the World* payment to Max was a backhander – that working for the *News of the World* was a conflict of interests – and that the money should have come to them.

Max insisted he'd told Mandy and Paul about his arrangement. He also counterclaimed for unpaid commission. In the end Mandy and Paul won on a technicality. Max had no written proof he'd spoken to them about his arrangement and had to pay them his £15,000 fee. But the judge added that Max had 'no intention of behaving dishonestly or corruptly towards his client'. They in turn were told to pay Max the £4,970 they owed him in unpaid commission, an amount that was only finally settled three years later in the summer of 2004.

'I was very angry at the time because I'd really tried to look after them,' Max says. 'I'd stopped nasty stories about Paul coming out and, among other things, got them free use of a London gym near where the *News of the World* temporarily housed them. In retrospect I regret taking them on, but luckily I have a natural instinct to move on and it no longer niggles. What mattered is that it was a tragic story where all the babies died.'

Mandy went on to have three daughters naturally. Ironically Max received a phone call from her out of the blue in April 2005. 'I was wary of talking to her,' he says, 'but she said she just wanted to thank me for all I did for her and that she was sorry about what happened. I told her life was too short to bear grudges.'

Max's web of contacts in high places is wide and intricate. He plays a long game, is happy to build up relationships with people slowly, give them free advice and tip them off when contacts tell him about stories circulating about them. He likes doing people favours, knowing that in return there might come a time when they will have a story for him.

This was the basis of how he discovered that Cherie Blair was pregnant with her fourth child at the age of 45, a secret that was only known to a small circle of trusted friends and family.

'In the late 90s a woman came to me wanting to sell her story about a brief affair with a senior Labour politician,' he begins. 'The man in question is someone I both like and admire. I wasn't impressed with her and I told her I didn't want to take her on. When she left I rang him and we had a chat. It soon became obvious that he'd briefly been swept off his feet by her, was basically happily married and that if it came out it would have completely devastated his wife and family.

'I said I thought she might now go directly to a Sunday tabloid and advised him, just as I had warned Ken Livingstone years previously, how to avoid being caught out. I added that any paper would be unlikely to go ahead just on her word. Instead they would get her to phone him and bring the subject up so they could record the call.

'She did phone and, as I suggested, he kept the conversation short and told her he didn't know what she was talking about. It killed the story. He was grateful and told me he'd never forget it. In October 1999 he rang to say he'd been waiting to do something to thank me and told me that Cherie was pregnant.

'I checked it out with my own contacts and heard the plan was to announce it in two weeks' time. I then phoned Piers Morgan at the Mirror. He was very keen on the story but rang Alastair Campbell, Number 10's chief spin doctor, to check if it was true. Alastair said it was, then tipped off the *Sun*, so both papers ran with the 'exclusive' on 1 November 1999. Piers was furious – if he hadn't called Alastair he'd have had the story for himself.'

Although Max has always supported the Labour party, he thinks both Tony and Cherie Blair are often badly advised. A prime example occurred in 2002 when Peter Foster, a convicted Australian conman, negotiated a discount on two Bristol flats for Cherie. Though buying the discounted flats was not in itself illegal, or even big news, Cherie Blair's association with Peter Foster was embarrassing for the Blairs and for the government and became a big story in the media. The episode became known as Cheriegate.

Max had been aware of the close relationship between Foster and Cherie for some time. 'I was contacted by a couple of his employees. We met in a pub in Cobham. They told me he'd been boasting about his increasing influence over Cherie and asked me to help expose him. I agreed and was about to put together a deal when they got cold feet and disappeared.

'I'm amazed Cherie did any business with him. From a PR perspective it was a disaster waiting to happen. Foster was at the time involved with Cherie's close friend and 'lifestyle guru' Carole Caplin, something that put him very close to the most powerful man in the country. Not surprisingly, the friendship provoked a wave of criticism in the press. I don't blame Alastair Campbell. He may well have told Cherie not to have anything to do with him, and she might have told him in no uncertain terms that she'd choose her own friends.'

Max first met Campbell decades ago when he was a journalist on the *Daily Mirror* and they have since met occasionally at various social and political occasions.

'Campbell is a man who, like myself, has been in the right place at the right time. He left the *Mirror* and had just got involved with Blair in 1994 as his press secretary when Blair was elected Labour leader. Blair then went on to win the 1997 election and became a superstar. Initially the new prime minister was all things to all people. Even the right-wing *Daily Mail* wasn't hostile to him.

'So although it was a wonderful time to be Blair's right-hand man, Campbell was thrown in at the deep end with no experience of public relations. Being a journalist requires totally different skills. Despite that, overall he did a good job.

'However, he was in such a strong position when Blair first came to power, that he should have used it to build good relationships with his enemies, help a lot of people, and get powerful and influential people in the media on his side. That way when the going gets rough, as it inevitably does in politics, he'd have had such a powerful PR foundation, he could have asked key journalists to go easy both on the party and the prime minister.

'It seems that either his position went to his head, or he didn't understand the fundamentals of PR, because instead he upset a lot of people and only fed stories to his friends, which anyone can do and requires absolutely no skill. I believe it was a fundamental mistake and as a result he made a lot of enemies for himself and possibly also for Tony Blair.'

Max is also critical of Peter Mandelson, now European Commissioner in Brussels. 'The public views him as slimy and he only has himself to blame,' he says. The two men have met a few times, but the occasion Max remembers most is when Mandelson was Tony Blair's campaign manager for the 1997 election.

'We saw each other at a fundraising do at the Reform Club in Pall Mall shortly before the election,' he says. 'I'd obviously been a great help to the Labour Party because the exposés of Tory sleaze I'd got into the papers had obviously damaged them. The room was crowded but he made a special effort to come over to talk to me. He said that what I was doing was much appreciated, but he hoped I understood that nobody could say so officially. I replied that that was fine because I was doing it for my own reasons not for him or the Labour party.

'However, there is an important part for someone like Mandelson in politics. Someone who flits in and out of the shadows and will be all things to all people in order to find out what is going on.

'There have been comments in the papers that there was a sexual *frisson* between Blair and Mandelson. But I think it was more a case of two people who are not natural bedfellows using each other and finding it works well for both of them. Knowledge is power and Blair always wants to know as much as possible about what is going on. Mandelson could tell him who said what and when.

'On the other hand, Mandelson and people like him enjoy being around powerful people. They feed off the power and it makes them feel powerful too. I don't know why Tony Blair let him stay in his inner circle for so long and kept bringing him back, firstly after he resigned after he took out a secret loan to buy a house and then after allegations of misconduct over passport applications. I can only assume he has some embarrassing information or a lot of political talent.

'But I wouldn't trust him. I'd feel his loyalties would lie with whoever was most likely to benefit him at the time. In fact there are very few people I've met in politics that I've warmed to. I find them cold and calculating, but that's the nature of the beast. Politics is an artificial world full of artificial people and in many ways reminds me of the entertainment industry and PR.

'You don't get many what I would call "real" people in politics, or those with charisma, and it's become increasingly difficult for a politician to be an individual. Politics now attracts "grey" people who won't stand up and say when something is wrong. As a politician, you have to conform and stick to party lines or risk being destroyed by your own party. It's why most intelligent people don't go into politics nowadays. They can make a much better living in other areas.

'But I admire Tony Blair. He's a genuine politician and backs his own judgment even when it's unpopular. I think the May 2005 election, even with his reduced majority, demonstrates how success- ful he is. Despite the unpopularity of the Iraq war and although his own popularity was at an all-time low, he was still more popular than either of the Tory or Liberal Democrat leaders and led the party to victory.

'I also admire Gordon Brown. His economic achievement since 1997 speaks for itself.'

Although Max is the most broad-minded of men, he takes a dim view of the lack of discipline in today's society. 'Although I think the Labour party is far better for this country than the Tories, it's far from perfect. I hate the filth I find in hospitals nowadays and the fact that discipline has gone in schools. Teachers are now frightened to tell pupils off for fear of how their parents will react. When I was a kid and got into trouble at school, I'd be in a lot more hot water with my mum and dad when I got home. But nowadays too many fathers storm up to the school and threaten to punch the teacher for daring to punish their child.'

The lack of discipline has also put him off going to see live football matches, despite his huge love for the game, and he now watches them on television instead. 'I can't bear the obscenities of the mindless few at matches,' he explains. 'During one of the last games I went to, a Leeds United *v.* Chelsea game, I heard a father telling his young child to spit at someone. I also worry about the increasing violence in society that means more and more people particularly the elderly and vulnerable are frightened to go out.'

He has his own solution. 'I'd bring back compulsory national service if only for a six-month period. I'm sure it would be a big step forward in teaching a lot of young guys discipline and respect.'

The year 1999 was a particularly special one for stories. Apart from the Cherie Blair scoop, Max also helped expose both another Tory politician, Jeffrey Archer – in one of the major political stories of the decade – and glam-rock star Gary Glitter.

Jeffrey Archer was a confident Goliath on the Tory Party landscape and a bestselling novelist. The mild-mannered David, Ted Francis, was a TV producer and acquaintance of Archer's, and went to Max for help because he'd been to school with Max's brother Bernard and had known Max all his life. It was a curious coincidence and yet another reason why Max feels he was born lucky. 'Things just come to me from all sorts of sources,' he says.

It all began when Archer, then deputy chairman of the Tory Party, phoned Ted Francis to ask him to agree they had dined together on a specific September evening in 1986 when he has later admitted he was dining with a close female friend. 'I wrote a letter, agreeing that we had,' Francis recalls. 'I did it as a favour to make sure he didn't get into trouble with his wife, Mary, because I thought that's why he needed it.' Francis thought no more about it.

In fact, Archer needed the alibi for an entirely different reason. Shortly afterwards the *Daily Star*, following the *News of the World* scoop, sensationally accused Lord Archer of Weston-super-Mare of giving £2,000 to prostitute Monica Coghlan and spending the night with her. It was one of the great tabloid shockers of the age and Archer sued for libel. The resulting court case was more exciting and absorbing than an Archer thriller and had everything: sex, politics, a 'fragrant' wife, furious confrontations and lashings of raw passion.

Archer's victory hung on the truth of his alibis for two dates – 8 and 9 September. He could prove that on the eighth he'd dined at one of his favourite restaurants, Le Caprice, in St James's Place with a film agent. He also had Francis's letter confirming they had dinner together at Sambuca, an Italian restaurant in Knightsbridge, on the ninth. Francis was furious with him. 'It wasn't until the trial started that I realised Jeffrey had manipulated me and intended to use my letter for his defence. As it happens, I wouldn't have testified.' The alibi wasn't needed in the end as the *Star* crucially changed the date they alleged he was with Coghlan from the ninth to the eighth.

The case ended sensationally in victory for Archer and a record £500,000 in damages. Nonetheless, Francis's lie gnawed away at his conscience and a decade on, when in October 1999 Archer stood for London Mayor and, more significantly, looked as if he could win, Francis decided to talk to Max about telling his story.

Max spoke gently to his brother's friend. 'I said, "Ted, I know how quiet and shy you are. Think about it carefully as you will be in the middle of a huge media minefield."' Francis decided he couldn't go through with it. But after a couple of months he called Max again.

'I had to do it,' he recalls. 'It looked as if Archer might become mayor. Candidates Frank Dobson (official Labour) and Ken Livingstone (independent) were splitting the Labour vote and he might have crept through the middle. I found that totally inappropriate. Max didn't put any pressure on me. He kept saying; "If you don't want to then don't." But I had to stop Archer.'

Max sold the exposé to the *News of the World* and Francis was a little disappointed. 'I would have preferred the story to go to the *Observer*. I felt the *News of the World* would add a tacky aspect to the sensation. But Max said it was the right paper and that all the other papers would follow.'

The paper naturally wanted to avoid being sued by Archer, so before they printed their scoop, Francis phoned Archer to discuss the false dinner date. This call was recorded and provided the evidence that what Francis said was true.

'I wasn't interested in getting any money, but Max persuaded me that I should get something out of it. At the time I was working voluntarily as a domiciliary carer for the aged and disabled. My car was clapped out, which made it difficult to do their shopping, so I asked for about £14,000 to buy a second-hand Audi.'

Just before the story came out in November 1999, the *News of the World* whisked Francis and his wife away. 'We went on the run and stayed in various hotels, which we kept changing to avoid being recognised. I felt completely bewildered but remembered to ring my neighbours every day to apologise for all the reporters hanging around our door.'

The Tory Party was stunned by the revelations and a totally discredited Archer resigned as mayoral candidate. As Max predicted, following the News of the World exclusive and for the next couple of days it was front page in every other newspaper both tabloid and broadsheet.

Max then arranged for Francis to do a radio interview with Derek Hatton at Talk Radio offices in Oxford Street, followed by a press conference. Max, the media juggler-in-chief, chose the venue deliberately as it gave him the opportunity to promote Hatton and the radio station, both his clients, on the back of this huge story.

Francis gave a few more interviews after the trial. 'Max didn't put any pressure on me to do them and I made an extra £5,000, which I gave to charity.'

It wasn't, however, the end of the story. A year or so later the police asked Francis for a statement about the letter and his alibi for possible charges of perjury. 'I phoned Max and told him I wanted to be indemnified against libel because I didn't want Jeffrey to sue me. It hadn't registered with me at the time that by asking me to give him a false alibi he'd committed a criminal offence and that I might be in trouble too.' Max asked the *News of the World* to send a solicitor to advise him.

Shortly afterwards Archer was accused of five charges of perverting the course of justice and perjury. This sensational six-week trial began at the Old Bailey in June 2001.

Max was called as a witness. 'I expected the defence to do everything possible to discredit me, but they obviously wanted me out of the witness box as soon as possible and didn't ask a single question. I just gave some straightforward details to the prosecutor. Archer didn't even look at me.'

Although the Tory peer had bounced back time and again from scandal and financial ruin, nothing protected him this time and he was sentenced to four years' imprisonment. Ted Francis was charged with perverting the course of justice but was found not guilty.

Surprisingly Max wasn't pleased that Archer was sent to prison. 'I wanted him to have his comeuppance and to be shown up for who and what he was,' he says. 'I was also glad he didn't become mayor. But a year's community service would have been better than jail. It might have taught him some humility if he'd been given the job of scrubbing floors for old age pensioners or cleaning public toilets.'

In retrospect Francis has mixed feelings about what he did. 'I'm neither pleased nor sorry. I felt I'd achieved my objective, but I also felt diminished by the experience. I hated being hurled into the spotlight. It was more terrifying than being shot at during the civil war in Nigeria. I am not a wannabe celebrity.'

He has no problems with Max's involvement, however. 'I know some people think badly of Max, but I believe he's fundamentally a sincere and honest man. Sometimes his way of behaving is a little too direct for me, but I remain very fond of him. I have no interest in Jeffrey any more. I used to go to his champagne and shepherd's pie parties, but now we don't even exchange Christmas cards. I don't think he is capable of change. I think that his actions showed an amoral side to him and that he enjoys risk for its own sake, whereas I don't think Max is without morals. He's just a pragmatist.'

Archer was released in 2003 and has since launched an appeal against his conviction.

Max has been pivotal to many people's lives in both good and bad ways. His increasing power has given individuals a voice, saved their reputation or highlighted their actions. He is particularly proud of his hard work behind the scenes to expose paedophile rock star Gary Glitter.

'I'd heard about him abusing young girls for many years but no one could get sufficient proof to pin him down,' he says. 'Then in the late 90s I was approached on behalf of a young girl who alleged that she had been abused by Glitter, and who would talk in order to encourage other child-abuse victims not to remain silent.'

Max sold the traumatic story to the *News of the World* for £10,000. The police didn't follow it up. Nor did Glitter issue a writ for libel.

It was only when Glitter, whose real name is Paul Gadd, took his computer to PC World for repair in November 1997 that the full extent of his depravity came to light. Four thousand horrific pornographic images of young children as young as two were found on the hard disc. The police were informed and he was arrested.

'Initially many people refused to believe he'd done anything wrong,' remembers Max. 'They wanted to keep him as their rock and roll hero.'

His trial took place in November 1999. The young girl was a witness and movingly told how Glitter, then 35, first ingratiated himself with her parents, who were flattered that a famous pop star took such an interest in their daughter. She also revealed he had sex with her from the age of fourteen.

Though the jury rejected her claims, partly because she had sold her story, hours later Glitter was jailed for four months for having a vast computer library of child pornography. It was the end of his rock career. Stores throughout the UK withdrew his records from the shelves and concerts were cancelled overnight. Max punched the air in triumph when he was sent down. 'It meant he was known for the vile sick person he is and that wherever he went parents would watch out for him.'

There was a domino effect from this conviction, too. It was only after Gary Glitter had been jailed that one of pop impresario

Jonathan King's victims, Kirk McIntyre, found the courage to go to the police.

As in the Glitter case, Max knew that the pop impresario was a paedophile long before he was arrested. 'Two of his victims came to see me several years before he was caught. They were both tall, well-built adults who physically looked as if they could cope with anything. But once they began to tell me what he'd done to them when they were young boys, they each broke down in tears. It was the first time they'd spoken about it and it was very emotional for them and for me. I subsequently spent a great deal of time with them. They could confide in me but, as often happens, they couldn't face talking publicly. Instead I passed on their names to the police. Nothing happened. It was only much later, after the court case, that I brought out their stories in the press.'

King's depravity eventually came to light when a victim complained to the police about one of King's friends and the investigation implicated King. In his arrogance King protested his innocence on TV, following which 22 of his victims came forward. At his trial in 2001 the jury heard he'd 'got away with it for years'. Like Glitter, King drew his proposed victim's family into his net, allowing them to believe that their child was safe in his company. He would also pick up star-struck young boys at a youth disco in Walton-on-Thames or in his white Rolls-Royce. He'd then use the tried and tested paedophile grooming techniques. He first flattered the boys, then lured them to his home on the pretext of seeking their views on music. He was convicted of six offences of indecently assaulting boys aged between fourteen and sixteen during the 1980s and sentenced to seven years' imprisonment. He was also put on the sex offenders' register and banned from working with children.

'I'm delighted to have played a small part in his arrest and trial,' Max says. 'I even have a letter from the Surrey chief of police thanking me for my help in bringing him to justice. King and Glitter are typical paedophiles, manipulative and arrogant. Their arrogance is necessary for them to squash their guilty conscience. And they need to be manipulative to undermine the victims. The only difference between them and other paedophiles is that they like the spotlight, whereas most prefer to stay hidden away.'

King was released on parole at the end of March 2005, marching out of jail as arrogant and unrepentant as ever. He declared he would press ahead with appeals against his convictions, and blamed Max for what he called his 'trial by media'.

Max is immune to his personal attack and scathing about his behaviour. 'His denials ring hollow. Paedophiles always try to justify themselves and rarely show remorse. King might be deceiving himself but he isn't fooling anyone else.

'Inevitably, if you are in the public spotlight there's going to be an element of trial by media, but that doesn't take away from what he did. His personality is overbearing for an adult, so how much more so for a star-struck child who dreams of fame? They just wouldn't be able to cope. His victims came to me; I didn't go looking for them. What he did to them was unforgivable. I feel nothing but revulsion for the man.'

Max also helped paedophile victim Shy Keenan, a young woman who had been horrifically sexually abused by her stepfather Stanley Claridge throughout her childhood.

'I had heard of Max Clifford and admired him for unveiling the sleaze in the Tory Party. He sounded like a no-nonsense Rottweiler and I thought he could help me expose my stepfather.

'When I met him I thought he was lovely. He told me how he admired me for being brave and strong and would indeed help.' Max thought up a media plan to prove beyond doubt that Claridge had done those terrible things. This involved the BBC *Newsnight* team making a documentary in which Shy bravely confronted Claridge and got him to admit that he and many others who were part of his paedophile ring had used her for sex. The award-winning programme, called 'A Family Affair', was broadcast in November 2000. As a result, he and several other paedophiles were subsequently arrested, tried and, in 2002, given hefty jail sentences.

Shy was enormously relieved. Understandably, though, she did find it difficult when, as a result of the exposure, the world's media flocked to her door. 'Fortunately Max continued to be involved. He protected me from the bombardment by dealing with the press for me and then arranged for me and other victims to get our story published. None of us wanted money. Instead he arranged for the papers who talked to us to give a donation to help victims of child abuse get psychological support.

'He may be a tough nut to some people but he was very gentle with me. It's a squishy side few people see. One particularly good thing about him is that he doesn't feel sorry for you. He empathises and makes you feel empowered rather than pitied.'

Max was pleased to help Shy. 'But,' he says, 'despite the tightening up on the law relating to paedophiles, it remains very difficult to get victims to testify. Many paedophiles are rich and powerful, which sometimes wrongly helps them get away with it.

'Shy bravely gave up her anonymity, but often when victims come to see me they don't realise that they will be identified, or how the press and public will react. I am one of the few people who can explain exactly what it will be like so they can decide whether or not to go through with it. It is a valuable position to be in and I think it was meant to be. It's part of me being gamekeeper rather than poacher. I love the caring side, because I can expose those who deserve to be exposed and protect those who are desperately in need of protection.'

And those who need protection aren't always those you would expect – one of them was one of the most beautiful and popular, and yet most needy, women of the late twentieth century.

15. THE PRINCESS OF WALES AND THE ROYAL FAMILY

Max first came into the magnetic orbit of Diana, Princess of Wales in the late 80s, when one of her close friends phoned him on her behalf to find out if he knew whether the rumours that Prince Charles was still having an affair with old flame Camilla Parker-Bowles were true. He confirmed they were. From then onwards until Diana's death in 1997 he was intermittently involved in her life. He gave lots of advice privately behind the scenes and was regularly asked by the media to comment publicly about her, and other members of the royal family.

'After I'd been on radio or television, people close to Diana would often call me for follow-up advice. I was always willing to help as I had a lot of time for Diana, even though she was neurotic. She handled an impossible situation extremely well. Once she realised her beauty was her power, she used it as a way of beating the royals and restoring the balance between them and her. Becoming the most popular woman on the planet put them firmly in their place.

'In the early days I advised that she should be seen to be of the people rather than stay at a distance from them, that she should pick up a baby rather than shake an adult's hand.'

Max, like almost every man on the planet, was susceptible to Diana's beauty and charm. He also felt very sorry for her. 'She'd been so young and naive when she married Charles and thought of him as her Prince Charming. But as the years went by she realised that she was being used by the royal family. Her role was to have Prince Charles' children, attend royal functions when required, and the rest of the time stay quietly out of the way. But she wasn't prepared to play their game.'

A far-reaching link with the Princess that had unimagined consequences began when Max received a telephone call in 1984 from James Hewitt asking for help over a clandestine relationship with a VIP. The memory of the call is ingrained on Hewitt's brain.

'Max agreed to see me and, soon afterwards, I was climbing the flights of narrow stairs to his New Bond Street office wondering how we would get on and what he would be like.

'I didn't really want to be there, but I desperately needed help and advice, because there were all sorts of rumours doing the rounds about my relationship with Princess Diana. So I asked a friend, without going into details, if he could recommend someone trustworthy who could tell me how the press operated. He recommended Max.

'Max instantly impressed me. Although I initially hedged around identifying the woman I was involved with, it was obvious he immediately understood who I was talking about. We seemed to hit it off personally. I found him straightforward, pragmatic, intuitive and I trusted him.'

Max also warmed to Hewitt. 'He arrived looking extremely smart, but his manner was unassuming. We talked for a long time and he gradually opened up. I was pleased he felt I could keep his massive secret.'

Hewitt first saw Diana at a polo match at Tidworth, Hampshire, on a sunny June day in 1981, shortly before she and Charles were married. Hewitt, then a dashing young captain in the Life Guards, was 23. Diana was a shy, blushing 19 year old.

'I was playing for the army and Prince Charles was playing for the navy in the Rundle Cup,' he remembers. 'Unfortunately I fouled him in the last few minutes and his team scored. If I recollect accurately they won by just one goal, so I was very annoyed. I spoke to Diana at the end of the match and found her to be a very attractive woman.'

Max sat quietly as he recounted his story. 'I've always been a good listener, which is possibly one reason why so many people have felt able to confide in me.

'James told me that, although he instantly felt very drawn to Diana, he didn't think it was appropriate to do anything about it, but that she instigated the friendship by telephoning soon afterwards and inviting him to join her and some mutual friends for dinner in London. Apparently Charles wasn't there. They got on well and soon became friends, but initially friendship was all it was. James could see that she was very much in love with Charles.

'He went on to say that, soon after her marriage in July, the dynamic of their relationship changed. He became a shoulder for her to cry on. She would ring him and they would meet to talk. She told him how she was devastated because she realised Charles didn't love her and how she desperately wanted him to.'

'We became increasingly close,' Hewitt adds, 'and I like to think I helped her cope.'

Prince William was born in June 1982 and, a few months after that, Diana invited Hewitt to come and see her at her home at Kensington Palace.

'James lowered his voice as he continued his story,' Max recalls. 'He said they talked for a while, that the atmosphere between them grew very thick and that she came to sit very close to him. They then made love for the first time. He said he hadn't known it was going to happen, but didn't resist her. He rapidly fell in love with her and said he hoped he made her happy too.'

In those early days their secret trysts were never easy to arrange in terms of time, but the location wasn't a problem. They often met at Kensington Palace. Nor, strange as it may seem, did they try to hide the fact. Hewitt would drive in through the police barrier at the Palace, park right outside and knock on the front door. 'It was amazing,' he says, 'how we managed to meet in those early days without anything appearing in the papers.'

They talked endlessly and she confided in him that she was bulimic: a terrible psychological eating disorder that involves binge-eating then making yourself sick. Girls who suffer from it are usually under severe stress and have low self-esteem. 'I didn't have a clue what bulimia was,' he admits, 'but Diana always seemed fine when she was with me.'

Max continues, 'He told me that, a few months into the affair, she rang and asked him to come round to the Palace as soon as he could. Almost immediately after he arrived, she told him, part anxiously and part matter of fact, that she was pregnant. He asked if she was happy about being pregnant. She told him she was and that she hoped the baby was a girl.

'Once she was pregnant, he said they stopped having a full sexual relationship, as it seemed more respectful, but that they continued to see each other regularly. He stayed close to her throughout, to give her support, and wouldn't let himself think too deeply about the ramifications.'

Prince Harry was born on 15 September 1984, and Diana rang Hewitt soon after the birth to tell him she'd had a baby boy. 'I told her that it was wonderful, absolutely lovely and happy news,' he says.

Their affair picked up again very shortly afterwards. They met about twice a week, mainly at Kensington Palace, but also at Highgrove, the royal home of the Prince of Wales near Tetbury in Gloucestershire, and in Devon at his mother's house. It was about then that he began to get rather anxious that they might be discovered and went to see Max.

'He was absolutely certain at that time that he didn't want anything to come out and I agreed to help him,' continues Max. 'I asked who knew about the extent of the relationship and he said a footman, some ladies in waiting, and the police who guarded Kensington Palace.

'I told him to keep quiet and not to say anything to anyone. I explained that, in these kind of situations, the papers might speculate, but that there were only two people whose word would be taken as cast-iron evidence: his and the woman he was involved with. If they didn't provide that evidence, then their relationship could never be absolutely confirmed.'

James took Max's advice. 'The only people I talked to were my parents, who I obviously completely trusted. I wanted additional guidance from my father, and he told me to be very careful.

'Max didn't charge me for his advice following our first meeting. Nor has he charged me since.'

Diana and Hewitt were so in love that he confessed to Max that he believed she would leave Charles for him.

'But his confidence didn't last,' adds Max. 'By the end of 1985 he realised he was never going to have her. It was around the time she danced with Wayne Sleep at the Royal Ballet and gave Charles a video of her performance for his birthday. It proved to him that she still wanted to win Charles's heart back. He confessed he felt very jealous that she still loved Charles, particularly as she knew Charles didn't love her.'

Meanwhile, Princess Diana was increasingly involving Hewitt in her life. He saw a lot of the two small princes and they got on very well together. Diana also spent as much time as she could with Hewitt in the Devon countryside where his mother lived. Despite the fact that she had the reputation for only wanting to go shopping and for not liking country pursuits – particularly not riding, which she was supposed to be very nervous about – she and James went on many long rides together and he thought she seemed happy and content in the countryside.

Throughout this time Hewitt was regularly on the phone to Max, keeping him up to date with what was happening in his own life and asking about any rumours Max might have heard. 'I told him that the rumours about him and Diana were growing all the time. He felt very anxious, so I came up with the idea that he should present himself as the young princes' riding instructor as it would provide some justification for them being seen together.

'James thought it was an inspired idea. It helped take a lot of pressure off him, and he told me he felt even more reassured when the papers began describing him as riding instructor to Diana, as well as William and Harry. In fact he only gave them the occasional lesson, or helped out when they all went to a gymkhana, but it did mean the two of them had more opportunities to meet and share some aspects of their lives.

'He left all the arrangements for their own rendezvous up to Diana, because her diary was so much busier. He confessed that sometimes he longed to see her, but couldn't because she was occupied. But he never complained, as he felt that she was under such strain in her marriage and so much pressure generally. He didn't want to be another problem in her life. Instead he wanted to be her solution.

'By contrast, Diana could sometimes be impulsive and indiscreet. In 1989 she invited James to stay at Highgrove for the weekend because Prince Charles was away, but he couldn't go because he was playing polo. Coincidentally the match was between Captains and Subalterns – the team James was playing for – and 13th/15th Royal Hussars. Diana had become Colonel-in-Chief of the Hussars that same year, so she immediately rang them to find out why she hadn't been invited. Naturally they asked her to come along and she took William and Harry with her.

'Apparently the Hussars were given a grand lunch in the pavilion while the Captains and Subalterns team had curled-up sandwiches on a picnic rug behind the parked cars. They were in the middle of their picnic when Diana suddenly turned up, with both her sons in tow, and sat down to join them. James was worried about stoking the fuel of the rumours about them, and asked in a whisper why she'd come and whether she thought it was a bit obvious. She whispered back that she'd been bored and had wanted to find him, so had told her hosts – the Hussars – that she was going for a walk. Everyone loved Diana so she got away with it, without looking as if she was being rude.'

Diana was particularly vulnerable at the time. It was not just because of Prince Charles's ongoing affair with Camilla, but also partly because extracts of tapes of lovey-dovey telephone calls between her and close friend James Gilbey had recently been published in the papers. The tapes recorded her saying, among other things, that she clothed Hewitt 'from head to toe'.

'James told me it wasn't true,' remembers Max. 'He said she didn't buy him suits, because he always had his made-to-measure, but that she did occasionally give him shirts and ties, which he thought had been largely donated to her by various clothing companies. Her presents did include a tie pin with a fox's head in diamonds, a gold fob watch with the words "I will love you always" inscribed on it, and a gold cross that bore the message "I shall love you forever". They meant a great deal to him but were sadly all stolen from the boot of his car when he moved from Devon to London.'

'I was generous too,' Hewitt insists. 'Diana had a habit of biting her nails and I promised to buy her a present if she stopped. She did, and I sold a horse for £6,000 so I could buy her a pair of beautiful emerald earrings.'

The relationship faltered when Hewitt told Diana towards the end of 1988 that he had to go to Germany with his regiment. 'She felt I was abandoning her,' he says. 'But the reality was that I had no choice in the matter.'

It was around this time that Hewitt received a letter from writer Andrew Morton asking for help on a book he was writing on Diana to be called *Diana: Her True Story*. Hewitt was unsure what to do, so turned to Max. 'I told him to stay clear of it, especially as nothing specific had yet come out in the press about them,' Max recalls. 'Hewitt also spoke to Diana and said she told him to do what he thought was right. He thought about it and subsequently replied saying he couldn't help.' The book revealed, among other things, that Diana was trapped in a loveless marriage, and it became a worldwide bestseller.

Not long afterwards Hewitt was sent to serve in the first Gulf War. It was a nerve-wracking time and, shortly before battle commenced in January 1991, he managed to borrow a satellite phone from a journalist and rang Diana.

'He told me later that he had been very frightened of what might happen to him,' says Max. 'He felt much better once he'd spoken to her, and revealed that Diana had sounded elated to hear from him. Not surprisingly, it was a very emotional conversation and he told me that, at one point, he said, "I think I'm going to be killed, but, if I get out of this mess, will you marry me?" Apparently she hardly paused before answering, "Yes." '

The clandestine lovers wrote passionate letters to each other every day. These letters have since become the source of much controversy and there has been continual speculation that Hewitt will sell the letters Diana sent to him. He has discussed the matter with Max on several occasions, but has not yet made a decision.

The Allies' victory in the Gulf War was quick and decisive, and Hewitt, who commanded A Squadron, Scots Guards, felt elated by the military operation . . . until a fellow officer showed him a copy of the *News of the World*, which accused him of having an affair with Princess Diana. 'He confessed he felt he'd been punched in the gut,' Max recalls. 'By the time the paper reached him, it was a couple of days after publication. He was desperate to speak to me and Diana, but communications were so bad – he was at the time in the middle of the desert – that he only managed to make one phone call, to Diana, on the Ptarmigan, which is a secure mobile battlefield phone system.

'He said Diana sounded quite calm about the allegations and told him that the Queen hadn't even mentioned them to her. James, however, was anything but calm, but luckily he was about to fly back home and rang me a day or so later from Bahrain, his first stopover.

'I told him I didn't think the newspaper story was that bad and told him to continue not to say anything to anyone and to keep his head down. I also congratulated him on doing a good job during the war. He told me he was going to fly back to England via Germany and was going straight to Highgrove to see Diana.

'He apparently stayed there a couple of days. Prince Charles was away again and James said they had a very emotional reunion. It was a romantic idyll that didn't last and he said shortly afterwards that their relationship began to fizzle out again. He wasn't sure why. The only reason he's come up with is that she felt he'd deserted her by going to Germany, but that her feelings for him were temporarily reawakened when she thought he was going to die.

'The relationship ended abruptly in 1992 when she refused to take his calls. He was hurt and upset, particularly as she didn't explain what he had done wrong. He said it was a small comfort to know he wasn't the first friend she'd dropped like a stone. He admitted he drowned his sorrows in drink,' Max adds, 'and that he's never got over it or let himself trust or fall in love with anyone else since.'

Despite his protestations, Hewitt developed a reputation as an inveterate ladies' man. He had other girlfriends during the time he was seeing Diana, although he insists that none was special, including a four-year relationship with Emma Stewardson. In spite of the fact that they became engaged, he insists, 'She loved me, but I didn't love her.'

Even once the relationship between Hewitt and Princess Diana was over, the rumour and gossip about them continued unabated. Hewitt, with Max's encouragement, continued to deny he and Diana had anything more than a platonic friendship, including in 1993, when he agreed to give an interview to writer Anna Pasternak for the *Daily Express*. 'Although he felt Diana had treated him badly, he still wanted to protect her,' Max says. 'So he denied there was anything romantic between them and continued to imply that they first met when Harry was a toddler.'

This was soon to change as Hewitt was increasingly feeling hard done by. It gnawed away at the loyalty he had, until then, felt he owed to the woman he loved. He decided he could no longer stay silent and arranged to see Max. He told him he wanted to sell his story.

Max recalls, 'He asked me how much it would be worth to the newspapers. I said he could get about £125,000 for the first exclusive and then lots more from newspapers abroad, but that he needed to be able to prove the relationship one hundred per cent. I then told him to go away and think about what he was intending to do. I warned him that, if he went ahead, he'd be regarded as a complete rat, particularly as Princess Diana was very vulnerable as well as much-loved at the time.

'He contacted me a few days later to ask if it was possible to sell the story without the public knowing it came from him. I explained that it could sometimes be done, using quotes from a "friend", but that, in this case, it wouldn't work because it was too big a story.

'A day or so later, he told me he definitely wanted to go ahead. I said that, although it was up to him, I thought he was making the wrong decision and wanted nothing to do with it. I wouldn't have felt comfortable with myself doing anything else.'

Hewitt didn't listen to Max. It is something he now regrets. 'I agreed to cooperate with Anna [Pasternak] on a book about my romance with Diana. She persuaded me, and I mistakenly felt it was right at the time. I didn't even mention the book to Max.'

Princess in Love, published in 1994, was a marshmallow version of Hewitt and Diana's romance, a kiss-and-tell in all but name. It provoked a vast amount of publicity and was roundly criticised. Princess Diana was quoted as being 'absolutely devastated'. Hewitt was vilified, and his behaviour was ripped to shreds; he earned the sobriquet of being Britain's most notorious 'love rat' and, as Max had warned, became one of the most-hated men in England. Hewitt also subsequently gave a badly received interview to the *News of the World* attempting to justify himself.

'Any fool could have seen it coming,' Max states. 'It was something that could so easily have been avoided. If he'd said nothing, everyone would have known the affair had happened, but they would have thought of him as being a hero rather than a villain. He would have been respected for keeping quiet and seen as a man you could trust. All sorts of doors would have opened for him to do anything he wanted to.'

Diana then hurled the equivalent of a burning torch into a vat of pure alcohol by admitting to the adultery in her now-famous doe-eyed *Panorama* interview with Martin Bashir in November 1995. Max's view was sought about whether she should do the interview. 'I said the pluses would outweigh the minuses, and it was important for her to get her view across.'

When she was asked directly whether she had been unfaithful with Hewitt, Diana replied, 'Yes, I adored him. Yes, I was in love with him. But I was very let down.'

Hewitt was astonished by her frankness and wanted to telephone her straight away, but thought better of it. 'He told me he decided she probably didn't want to speak to him,' recalls Max, 'and couldn't face the rejection. He did, however, call her after her divorce came through on 20 December 1995. He didn't try her direct line as he suspected she might not answer if she knew it was him, so he went through her butler Paul Burrell. In fact she took his call. He was delighted and wanted to say he hoped they'd remain friends after all they'd been through, but instead simply told her he was glad she'd got her divorce.'

Hewitt has since mainly lived off the liaison in one form or another, and, in 1999, two years after Diana's death, published his autobiography *Love and War* to give his side of the story. 'I thought it was a good idea so that people could see what he was about rather than read what journalists wrote about him,' Max adds. In the book, he revealed intimate details of the affair, but not the true date the relationship began. 'I didn't feel it was appropriate at the time,' Hewitt explains, 'but you cannot hide the truth forever. Nor should you.'

James Hewitt hasn't had any connection with either Prince William or Prince Harry for many years. But the rumours over the similarities between himself and Harry haven't let up. 'He's told me that people often remark on how much Harry looks like him,' adds Max, 'but I know that his view is that Prince Charles is Harry's father and that he blocks his mind to anything else. He obviously recognises that they have the same colour hair, but I believe they have a lot of other things – the army, polo, drinking, girls – in common too. When you look at the two of them, anyone can understand why there has been so much speculation for so long.'

In November 1993 Max was asked to come to the rescue of Bryce Taylor, who then owned LA Fitness. Bryce and Max used to meet at charity squash tournaments and when Bryce found himself in very hot water, he got straight on the phone.

'He asked to see me urgently and confessed he'd planted a hidden camera in a false ceiling above a leg machine Princess Diana used at the Isleworth, west London branch of LA Fitness. It had taken pictures of her working out wearing a leotard and cycling shorts and with her legs apart. He'd sold them to the *Sunday* and *Daily Mirror* and they were about to be published.

'But he'd got cold feet and said he'd pay me anything to help him. I thought the whole thing was rather funny and agreed to try a damage-limitation exercise. Contrary to what some people think, the original story idea wasn't mine.' Max went through his normal routine – part sleuth, part investigating reporter – to extract as many details as possible from Bryce, looking for the clue that could help him give advice. He was both patient and persistent.

'What machines does she like best?'

'The leg machine. She regularly uses it.'

'Where is it?'

'By the window.'

'Is there another one in the gym?'

'Yes. Right at the back.'

'That's all I need to know. Leave it to me.'

The photographs in the *Sunday Mirror* on 7 November caused ructions. Diana could do no wrong with the adoring British public at the time and Bryce, like Hewitt, was labelled a 'ratbag'. Diana's friends said she felt 'violated' and 'utterly betrayed'. Diana's lawyers immediately issued writs banning publication of the pictures permanently, the first time the royal family had used the law to hit back at the press. This led to the general view that the *Mirror* had showed a disastrous breach of faith and judgment, and, what's more, threatened press freedom.

Some large companies withdrew their advertising from the Mirror Group newspapers, but the newspaper's sales still rose by more than 100,000.

Max didn't feel any guilt, since he was only involved once the pictures had been sold. 'I think it was wrong that Bryce took the pictures in a sneaky way. Naughty, but understandable.

'I said that Diana was no shrinking violet. She went to the gym carefully dressed and made up. If she regularly worked out on a piece of machinery right in front of a window that looked out on to a forecourt, instead of the one right at the back, she knew full well that everyone could stand there and look at her. Plus, as the most photographed woman in the world, she couldn't be too upset by pictures that showed what a great figure she had.

'I also tried to boost the image of LA Fitness in every interview I gave. Despite the fact that I'd never been near the place I said it was a great gym with terrific equipment and I could understand why she and so many stars went there all the time. LA Fitness lost lots of members after the pictures were published, but gained roughly the same amount, no doubt because of all the publicity.'

A pre-court settlement of the writs followed. Mirror Group Newspapers were believed to have paid Princess Diana's legal costs of about £1million and they gave about £200,000 to charities of her choice. Bryce Taylor apologised to the princess and gave up the £300,000 he'd reportedly made from selling the pictures to the *Mirror* and abroad. There were, however, strong hints that a member of the royal family helped funnel a large payment to Bryce in return for him settling out of court. He sold the club in 1996.

'I've often wondered just how much Diana knew about the pictures,' Max continues. 'Because in one particular photo that Bryce showed me that wasn't published it looked like she was actually waving at the camera and, in another, she appeared to be looking up at the camera and smiling. Most people tend not to smile when they are exercising vigorously. I think she was in on it and had the pictures taken as part of her overall plan to embarrass the royal family.

'I've also wondered if there was more to Bryce's relationship with Diana than we initially thought, and friends of both of them have shared my suspicions. He was an attractive and charismatic man. She was lonely. Also, Isleworth seems an unlikely venue for her to travel to, when there were more glamorous places close to Kensington Palace. It wouldn't surprise me if they were a lot closer than has so far emerged.'

Another huge Diana story followed in 1995. Hilary Ryan, who like so many had seen Max on television, rang his office to say she had a story about then England rugby captain Will Carling and the Princess. Max saw Hilary almost immediately. Hilary was Carling's PA, but felt totally disillusioned with her boss. She claimed she had played a very important part in helping develop his business, but the many financial incentives he promised her didn't materialise. She felt he had let her down very badly and was fed up.

She told Max that Will had met Diana at the gym and the two giggled together over a cup of coffee. Carling then installed a private phone line in his office specifically for Diana to use. Hilary was told she was not to answer it and that the number was private.

Max passed the story of the friendship to the *News of the World* and it appeared in August, a few months before Diana's interview with Martin Bashir. Carling never claimed to have had an affair with Diana, and nor did the paper, but his wife Julia left him shortly after the revelation. Max doesn't doubt that his relationship with the Princess was purely platonic.

'I don't think Diana fancied him. Will just ran round her like a puppy dog. The person she really loved was Pakistani heart surgeon Hasnat Khan. Realistically it was never going to work out, because he didn't want to be seen as merely part of the most famous woman in the world.

'She was, however, in the mid-90s also besotted with another medical man for almost two years. He was a medical student in his early twenties and they met in America at a big fundraising event Diana flew out to. She fell for him as soon as she saw him and he apparently fell hopelessly in love with her too. He was good-looking, bright and witty and wanted to become a surgeon. I heard about it because someone asked me to keep my eyes and ears open in case he wanted to sell his story. He never has. It cooled just before Dodi Al Fayed came on the scene.'

Diana met Dodi, son of Harrods owner Mohamed Al Fayed, in the summer of 1997 when she accepted an invitation for a ten-day Mediterranean cruise on his family yacht. Before her sun-tan oil had time to dry rumours were circulating that they were secretly engaged and they were photographed kissing on deck.

Max doesn't know if the engagement rumours were true, 'but,' he says, 'I was told by someone very close to her that for her the biggest part of Dodi's attraction was its effect on the royal family. She was pleased they hated the relationship and at that stage in her life it was more important to get back at them than be in love. On the other hand one of the stewardesses who worked on Mohamed's yacht said she believed they *were* totally in love.'

Nor does he have a firm view about whether Diana and Dodi were murdered but says, 'I know she was genuinely afraid the Palace was out to get her. Her worldwide popularity had become a constant thorn in their side.'

In February 2001 a young man who worked for Sophie, Countess of Wessex, and her company RJH came to see Max. 'He felt very disgruntled and told me that her partner in the business Murray Harkin was involved with cocaine and rent boys,' he recalls. 'Also that the company was taking advantage of its royal connections. When they pitched for business, they didn't mention they were a public relations company. Instead they would tell potential clients that the Countess of Wessex and Prince Edward would like whoever it was to join them for dinner.

'He had recorded telephone conversations to prove that what he said was true. I put him in touch with the *News of the World*, not so much because Sophie was taking advantage of her royal links, but because she wasn't honest about it. I also hated the fact that Harkin was offering clients young boys and sex tours to Asia.'

The *News of the World* sent their undercover reporter Mazher Mahmood to meet Sophie and Harkin posing as an assistant to a wealthy Arab sheikh who was a potential client. He was armed with a hidden camera and tape recorder and explained he wanted a PR company for a new leisure centre in Dubai.

Seduced by Mahmood's polished manner, Sophie was famously indiscreet. Her disparaging remarks recorded at the Dorchester Hotel on 14 March included commenting that Cherie Blair was 'horrid, horrid, horrid' and that Prince Charles and Camilla Parker-Bowles were 'number one on the top ten unpopular people. People don't want Camilla to be Queen.' She also called the Queen a 'poor old dear'.

The story was printed over ten pages and must have made excruciating reading over breakfast at Buckingham Palace. Sophie then tried to soften the worst of her comments by granting an interview to the *News of the World*. That interview only made matters worse for the royal family, saying that Prince Edward was not gay, that they didn't sleep in separate bedrooms and that she was having IVF treatment.

On 10 April she issued a statement regretting any embarrassment to the Queen and resigning from her position as chairman of RJH. Harkin now runs another PR company.

'It turned into a media circus,' says Max. 'As usual a tabloid broke the story, then the broadsheets condemned it while filling vast amounts of space with all the details. Whatever she would have said would have made matters worse. She had put herself in an impossible situation. The way she was running her company meant she was bound to be turned over one day. If she believed it wouldn't happen she was either incredibly naive or stupid, or both. The only thing she could have done by way of damage limitation would have been to put on record warnings to Harkin that she wouldn't tolerate his behaviour and that he had to change.'

Max had often talked to Paul Burrell, Diana's butler and right-hand man, on the phone and when Burrell decided to sell his story in the spring of 2001, he came straight to Max. He felt deeply bruised by the way he believed the royal family had treated him after Diana's death, and angry and humiliated when they accused him of stealing 342 items from her estate, an accusation on which he was charged in August 2001.

'He was absolutely determined to sell his story,' remembers Max. 'He said it was all very well for people to talk about how loyal he was but that he didn't have two pennies to rub together. I told him it would be wrong to sell his story to one paper and that if he did he'd be completely castigated by the rest of the media, because it was too big a story for them all to miss. I suggested that the best thing for him to do was to divide the story up in a deal between News International, Associated Newspapers and the Mirror Group. That way he would make a lot of money and have three big newspaper groups on his side.

'The deal didn't progress any further as a couple of days later Burrell's lawyer made it very clear to me that if he did do a deal with me two or three of his main witnesses wouldn't give evidence on his behalf. He was very distraught and said, "Max, what choice have I got? If I lose the case I might go to prison." I told him I totally understood. I'm very philosophical about these things, particularly as I always have so much going on. Although Paul believed the witness story, my instinct told me his lawyers could well have been in the middle of a newspaper deal and didn't want me involved.'

The trial sensationally collapsed in November 2002, when the Queen 'suddenly' remembered that Burrell had told her he was removing Diana's things to look after them. Burrell subsequently sold his story to the *Mirror* without Max's involvement and the other papers rose up against him.

The two men are still in touch, however. 'Each time we speak he says if only he'd done it my way, and that he was wrong to talk to just one paper. He earned more than ten years' money going with the *Mirror*, but if he'd taken my advice he could have earned more than twenty years' money and kept key journalists as friends.'

Max thinks the royals post-Diana are a sorry lot. 'But,' he admits, 'I'd rather we had a royal family than a republic. Overall they benefit the country, but as individuals they are much ado about nothing. The monarchy is at the heart of the class system and, although it's not as powerful as it used to be, I believe it still plays too big a part in this country. I also believe there are too many royal properties and that if they sold, as I think they should, all but two or three of them for the benefit of the nation, they could still live in splendour.

'One of the good things about having a free press is that we have been able to see the royals for what they are; a very dysfunctional family. Until thirty years ago you hardly read anything that wasn't positive about the royal family. Now it's the opposite and there's so much negative comment that's it's difficult for people to respect them.

'The media will continue to play an important part in the future of the monarchy; in order to survive the royal family has to adapt. William is their best chance. If he is his mother's son as I think he is, he will understand the media age and use it to his advantage. But I don't think it will be difficult for William and his generation to have a private life. I look after many well-known people who have wonderful private lives the press doesn't hear about, so it can be done.

'In the meantime nothing will change with Prince Charles. He's from a different age and I think he finds it difficult to be in tune with the people. His speech early in 2005 about ambitions and aspirations in which he said people shouldn't expect success and money if they didn't work hard was a perfect example. Coming from a man who has been given everything all his life, it was unbelievable. Not only is he out of touch, but the people around him seem just as bad. Didn't anyone dare say he was going to make himself look stupid? It's the blind leading the blind.

'At least they provide a lot of entertainment. Charles and Camilla certainly generated a lot of laughter in the build-up to their wedding, particularly when the wedding venue was changed from inside Windsor Castle to the local register office. People who go without to pay for their daughter's wedding or who struggle to make ends meet, saw that even people with all the money in the world, who are able to call on the finest constitutional and legal experts, can still get it hopelessly wrong. They had seven years to prepare for the wedding, which was always their target once Diana died, and they still couldn't get it right.

'Luckily on the day, in spite of the earlier disasters, everything went smoothly and Camilla looked lovely. But there is still a huge mountain to climb before the pair of them win the respect, admiration and love that Diana and indeed the Queen have achieved with ordinary people.

'I wasn't sure before but, ironically, the incompetent and shambolic way the wedding was sorted out has convinced me that there is no way the Palace could have organised the tragic car crash that killed Diana and Dodi.'

Mohamed Al Fayed remains convinced they did, however, and has taken every opportunity to accuse the Duke of Edinburgh of masterminding a secret-service plot to murder both Diana and Dodi.

Al Fayed got in touch with Max in the spring of 2000 because he wanted to change his image in the media. 'It's not something you can succeed in doing by just altering how you behave and what you do,' Al Fayed explains. 'I needed someone like Max to bring it to the public's attention.'

It was a juggernaut-sized challenge. On a personal level Al Fayed and Max are two strong-minded individuals who like to do things their own way and don't respond well to instructions.

On a professional front it was obviously difficult to put a positive spin on much that was going on in Al Fayed's life: there were criminal charges pending against him for allegedly paying £10,000 for advance information relating to his libel battle with disgraced former Tory minister Neil Hamilton; at the same time a former employee was claiming £3 million for wrongful dismissal, and at least six female employees had made claims of harassment against him. And as well as accusing the royal family of plotting murder, Al Fayed was also regularly accusing every major politician, including Tony Blair, of being 'dishonest bastards and crooks' at a time when the prime minister was still in his first term and enjoying a honeymoon with most of the British public.

It was the sort of impossible challenge Max finds irresistible. Rather than take on the battle to change the negative aspects of Al

Fayed's life, Max decided instead to concentrate on his good qualities. It is testament to his abilities that he managed to unearth a few gold threads with which to spin a different image from this most unlikely of sources.

He did, however, remain wary. Throughout the time he worked for Al Fayed he made sure he didn't commit himself for too long at a stretch. 'I agreed a monthly retainer with Mohamed and didn't have a contract, which meant either of us could pull out at any time. He was fine in small doses and being one of, rather than my only, client,' he says. 'I'd never work for him full time. It's a huge advantage that I always have so much work I can tell anyone to get lost.

'I decided the best way of changing his image was mainly through his football club Fulham, where he was chairman. Football is such a huge passion and media obsession in the UK that anyone who is seen to be involved in it immediately has a very good base.

'In addition I tried to build good relationships between him and various journalists and editors, and of course tried to stop him shooting himself in the foot. I personally enjoy the fact that he is his own worst enemy and fights battles he can't possibly win, but I had to watch how these came across in the media.

'One move we made was to take the then *Daily Mail* gossip columnist Nigel Dempster out for lunch and as a result his attacks on Mohamed stopped. We also took a couple of tabloid journalists to see the inside of Dodi's flat for a feature and another to see the shrine Mohamed had made for Dodi. It gave them something positive to write about and took the steam out of other more negative stories.'

As luck and hard work would have it, Fulham won the First Division in 2001 and were promoted into the Premier League. There was a victory party after the match at Harrods and Max was delighted to see that five national newspapers editors accepted invitations to join in the celebrations, something Max knew would result in a softening of their attitude against him.

'Mohamed is a showman,' he adds. 'Fulham was his London Palladium and Harrods his Royal Albert Hall. I don't know whether he bought Fulham because he thought it would make him a hero, but it did for a lot of people. He certainly didn't know anything about the game, although he pretended he did. I asked him once if he'd played football as a boy and he replied, "Of course." I then asked what position he played. He said, "Captain" – he didn't even know the positions on a football pitch. He also insisted he had supported Fulham for years and used to stand on the terrace and watch players he called "Jimmy" Haynes and Bobby "Robinson". He meant Johnny Haynes and Bobby Robson. In my opinion, that is not something a genuine football supporter would get wrong.'

Max also brought to the public's attention some of Al Fayed's work for charity. 'He gives very generously to several charities and always followed up my suggestions of places to visit like children's hospitals. There is a warm and compassionate side to him, which is rare in someone so rich, successful and powerful. I also encouraged him to do a certain number of media interviews, including one with comedian Ali G. He enjoyed it because he can laugh at himself.

'He is not an easy person to deal with and, if I'd let it, working with him could have become very difficult. Instead if I suggested something and he disagreed, I'd say, "If you're not going to do what I say don't blame me if this and this happens." It inevitably did and when he tried to blame me I'd laugh at him. He'd often, for example, complain about the government's attitude to him and I'd say what did he expect if he kept calling them "crooked bastards"?

'On the other hand, I had a lot of time for him personally. It was his flunkies who got up my nose. They sucked up to him and said anything he wanted to hear. It particularly annoyed me when they tried to bend my ear too. I'd go to watch a football match at Fulham and one by one they'd come up and whisper something, usually against each other. They were obviously trying to get to him through me.

'When he asked me to investigate some conspiracy story I thought was nonsense I'd refuse. Instead I said I didn't believe him and that if he wanted something done about it, he should tell one of his flunkies. He'd lose his temper and swear at me. I'd swear back and shortly afterwards we'd end up howling with laughter. Although he might not like it at the time, deep down he respects people who stand up for themselves.

'We often teased each other too. When I introduced him to a female friend of mine, almost the first thing he said to her was that I was gay. I instantly retorted that *he* was in fact gay and had been having an affair with the Duke of Edinburgh for years, which was why he was so bitchy about him. And not only did he lie about his age but that he was really ninety. He roared with laughter.'

Throughout Max's life lucky coincidences have occurred just when he's needed them. One happened after Max had been working with Mohamed Al Fayed for several months and had decided Al Fayed needed someone with newspaper experience almost permanently alongside him. Al Fayed had also gradually become more demanding on Max's time.

It was at this point that Phil Hall lost his position as editor of the *News of the World*. Max offered him a job and gave him Mohamed to look after. This meant he could do a favour for a pal and also shed some of the workload of looking after Mohamed. 'I've always thought someone up there likes me,' he says, 'because time after time everything falls into place.'

Nonetheless, after two years Max decided he'd had enough. 'The people around Mohamed were making what I was trying to do for him increasingly difficult. They kept telling him about conspiracy theories and contracts out on him, none of which I believed and which they probably made up to justify their existence. So we called it a day, but we still regularly meet for lunch.'

Mohamed remains one of Max's fans. 'He is a great public relations guy, efficient, communicative, human and sincere. He talks from his heart and I know he doesn't only take jobs for money. I was pleased with what he did for me and that he was always there twenty-four hours a day, seven days a week, if I wanted to contact him. I also liked the fact that he stood up to me. I still occasionally use him and often ask his opinion about a whole range of issues. I also leave him to talk to the press on my behalf.

'He did such a good job for me that, after the two years, I told him, "My life has become so boring now everyone likes me."'

Max doesn't expect everyone to like him. He's been described as hollow, sanctimonious and chippy and is loathed and feared, loved and respected, and trusted and mistrusted in almost equal measure. Some believe he walks on water. Others wish he'd drown. It's made him both a household name and one of society's most controversial characters. Along the way he's also developed unexpected secret powers.

16. POACHER AND GAMEKEEPER

By the mid-90s the young lad who always wanted to be at the centre of what was going on had become a powerful ringmaster with a jangling set of keys that could lock or unlock a multitude of secrets. Sometimes he would take the skeletons out from people's cupboards and rattle them around. Other times he would bury them for good, never to be found.

'From the time I was a child, I've always wanted to win, and getting the right results for a client is my definition of winning. I always set myself a mental target of what I want to achieve.

'Sometimes I want to build a client up, then at other times keep their activities quiet. When I take on a new client the media becomes both my ally and my enemy, so that if something comes out in the papers about him or her that I haven't wanted to appear, I feel I've lost. It's a competitive thing and the person I'm competing with is me. It's always been that way and I enjoy it.'

Newspaper editors prefer to be on his side, and there's barely a newspaper – and this includes the qualities as well as the tabloids – that Max hasn't given stories to and been given favours in return.

Although most newspaper executives are reluctant to reveal publicly the extent of Max's control and influence over what they publish, one senior woman journalist admits that he caused a seismic shift in the way her newspaper did business. 'In the 80s, before Max had made his impact, lawyers would contact my newspaper on behalf of their clients to sell a story. They usually had little knowledge of how to go about it, and often even less interest, as they rarely made much money out of it themselves. Alternatively an individual with a story to sell or grievance to air would phone the news desk direct.'

This was inevitably awkward. He or she had to disclose the facts quickly and concisely which, if they felt stressed or deeply traumatised, was both difficult and embarrassing. News-desk journalists are frantically busy people with little patience and less time to listen carefully to long, painful stories.

Max describes handling the media without knowing how it works as 'like walking in a minefield without a mine detector'. Him taking on the role of middleman took the strain away from both parties; it got the best financial deal for the client and helped the journalist get the best story.

By the mid-90s the name Max Clifford became synonymous with an exclusive story that newspapers would pay good money for. 'He was the power in the land for anyone who wanted to do what is called in the trade "buy-ups",' the senior journalist continues. 'Once he was on the scene the number of stories that came directly to us from individuals or lawyers dropped dramatically.'

Being a shrewd man, Max has turned his unique position to his advantage, persuading editors to keep one story out, with the promise of the next big exclusive to come.

Piers Morgan, former editor of the *Daily Mirror* and *News of the World*, has worked with Max for twenty years and knows him well. He readily acknowledges his talents. 'He is the greatest PR for acting in the best interests of his clients, both in how he deals with papers and getting stories. He could have been a brilliant newspaper editor. He is trustworthy, always looks after his mates and no tabloid editor worth his or her salt would cross him. It would be self-defeating because he's the one who has all the big stories.

'I left things out of the paper all the time for him. Quite regularly we'd have a B-grade scandal and Max would have something else up his sleeve, which was just as good if not better. So if he wanted to suppress one and publish the other, and the story he was giving us was better than the one I was suppressing, there was no problem doing the deal.

'On top of that, he always tried to get publicity for one of his many PR clients on the back of a scoop. If I thanked him for a great story and told him how well it had worked, he'd say something like, "How about doing this on the beauty page for me?" and I'd feel a duty to give him what he wanted. I don't think it was morally wrong that he often controlled my agenda. He understood, as I did, that the whole thing was a game. It might be a game with far-reaching consequences for some celebrities, but invariably the celebrities involved had made it their business to court the press for their own advantage, so I didn't have any moral problems saving one neck to hang another.

'It has also meant Max has brilliantly bought himself a lifetime's "get out of jail" card. Newspapers won't turn him over because why would they bite the hand that feeds them? Why kill your golden goose? Max is an honourable rogue. But so are the people who run and work in newspapers, so it's rogues dealing with rogues.'

Another former newspaper editor agrees that Max had some control over the editorial content of his newspaper too. 'Although I don't think I ever personally kept a big story out just because Max told me to, I would often do deals involving his commercial clients.

'It was a "sprat to catch a mackerel" situation whereby we would do stories about a product he wanted to promote to get an exclusive from him at a later date. But we wouldn't write just anything. If, for example, he rang to tell me he needed to promote a device to help people with bad backs, he'd have to prove that it was genuine and had been properly tested by a recognised medical organisation. It was something he was always happy to do.

'It was never a good idea to be on the opposite side to him. He knew all the tricks and, if he really didn't want a story in the paper, he could stop you from finding the evidence to prove whatever it was.'

Another journalist admits her paper would readily publish pictures of stars wearing or using a product Max was promoting. 'It never worried us, because we didn't plug anything that was morally wrong. Nor were the public duped. Newspapers are always promoting various products and you might as well publicise one that helps you get another story.'

Max has also proved to be a brilliant negotiator. 'He is very straightforward to deal with, but also very canny,' says Piers. 'If he has a story to sell he works out in his mind which paper he wants to sell it to. But once he's made the call he refuses to name his price. It's a brilliant tactic because you don't know what he thinks the story is worth. If you go low he laughs and says it's worth three times that, but if you go higher than he anticipates he's quids in. He can't lose. It's a simple but very effective bargaining technique.

'You also know that if you don't look after him and pay him well, he'll go somewhere else. He's quite honest about it and says, "I can't bring you stories at the moment because you're not paying enough." He says it to everyone so we all up the ante and he and his clients make loads more money. He is brilliant at creating a false marketplace in which he is the only person selling the goods.

'I was also very happy to give him a bonus as well as his twenty per cent commission if the story went really well. He'd work his socks off to make something come off. I've always found him easy to deal with too. His word is his bond. There is never loads of paperwork, detailed contracts or lawyers to deal with.'

Phil Hall doesn't see anything wrong in paying large sums for kiss-and-tell stories. 'The *News of the World* has been successfully running sleazy stories for over one hundred years,' he says. 'The difference Max has made is that the people on those pages, who help sell those papers, which in turn make huge sums of money for the proprietors, now share in the spoils. Newspaper proprietors who claim it is a disgrace are at the same time counting the millions that these stories make for them in a back room. I think it's fair that if you're getting a huge hike in your circulation others should share in the profits.

'Max likes simple, straightforward situations. He offers you a story and wants a quick answer – yes or no. He doesn't like people thinking about it for days on end and he can't bear being messed around.'

Max agrees with this assessment. 'I always have too much to do. I try to give things my best shot and do as well as I can in the shortest time possible. I don't have time to dwell on things.

'In the last ten years there's been a huge increase in girls going to celebrity parties to try to bed someone famous as a potential investment that they can sell at a suitable date. Of course, if they go to enough of them, they are bound to pull someone. Every situation is different, but it shows that if you are famous and treat someone badly he or she has a chance to get back at you. It also means even more work for me.'

Not surprisingly Max had, by the end of the 90s, outgrown his small office. Louise, who had worked for a short while for a small PR concern near the family home, also now wanted to join her father. As there was no lift in the building Max would carry her up and down the three flights of stairs on his shoulders, which was far from ideal.

So in March 2000 the company moved to fifth-floor offices a few yards down New Bond Street, which had a lift and a more secure entrance. It consists of a large, open-plan office where his seven or eight mainly twenty-something female staff, known in the industry as Max's Angels, sit, a small office for Max and a boardroom for meetings. Round the walls hang framed copies of a selection of the front-page stories he has brokered.

Max's own office is filled with both family photographs and photographs of him with many of the celebrities he's worked for. Unlike many offices there are no systems charts on the walls, regular staff assessments or complex planning meetings. Equally out of the ordinary is the large box of tissues kept on his desk – he has found that most new clients with a big story to tell will have a good cry.

His lack of structure always surprises his audience when he gives talks at business conferences, which he is often asked to do. 'I could give talks seven nights a week,' he says, 'but I keep it down to about twice a month. I charge a minimum of ten thousand pounds for a forty-minute presentation.'

During these events, he is always asked what his business plan has been. 'I inevitably reply, "I've never had one. I've always relied on my gut reaction."' Nor is he given to introspection. 'I'm not the type to overanalyse things. People worry too much about detail and as a result their lives are full of problems. I prefer to follow my instinct.

'In general, although it may sound arrogant, the things I can do, I can do better than anyone else. If, for example, someone tells me how to cook, I'll listen because I can't cook, but if someone tells me that I should or shouldn't take on a particular client, I don't take any notice. Public relations is an individual business dealing with individual people and I always back my judgment against anyone else's. Most of it is common sense anyway but which, fortunately for me, for some reason nowadays seems to be in very short supply.'

Nicola Phillips helps him with stories, while the others, including Louise, who doesn't like to get involved with kiss-and-tell projects, work on the PR accounts that span pasta sauces and property companies, to a cosmetic surgeon and mineral water.

Although the work that comes in varies month by month, about eighty per cent of his business is general public relations and creating images for clients. The other twenty per cent is divided between promoting and stopping stories, doing media interviews and public speaking.

Max usually works from home on Mondays and Wednesdays and rarely arrives before noon on the other three days, partly because he likes his sleep and partly because he prefers to deal with early-morning business from home, before taking his daily swim. Every day is different depending on who phones and what's in the newspapers.

Despite being a control freak, Max is a benign boss. He lets his staff get on with their work and merely keeps a paternal eye on what they are doing, interfering only if he feels he has to. He treats each one as part of his extended family. He often takes them out en masse for meals, brings in cakes for tea and gives them presents of the luxurious Crème de la Mer make-up when he comes back from trips to Spain.

All his staff are devoted to him. 'He is our father figure as well as our boss,' explains Lucy Murphy. 'I personally think of him as my guru and can't imagine anyone I'd rather work for.'

As much of his work is confidential he prefers to employ someone he knows or who comes to him through a personal recommendation. He is not particularly interested in qualifications but rates common sense, enthusiasm and being trustworthy very highly. He also prefers employing women to men and likes to be surrounded by pretty girls.

The office phones ring continually. One result of his regular appearances on television is that many see him as a combination of a modern day Robin Hood and Mr Fix-It. 'People ring all the time to ask for help but some requests are ridiculous,' says Dee Wilson, Max's office manager. 'A man once called to say the roof of his house needed rethatching and asked if Max could pay for it. And a woman rang to say someone had dug up her daffodil bulbs and wanted Max to find out who it was. Others ask him to pay their children's school fees.

'We are always polite and tell them that Max can't do everything. There are other people who contact us about problems with their local council, when they are facing eviction, or are waiting on a particular payment. Sometimes we tell them to say they've contacted Max Clifford and it's often enough to get the cheque they've been anxious about for months to arrive in the next post.

'There are also those who ring with tragic stories. We listen even when it's obvious we can't do much to help. Sometimes it's like working for the Citizens' Advice Bureau. We did some time ago help a grandmother who contacted us about her grandchild who had got involved with a cult group and believed she was being abused. Max managed to get a paper to write about them and get her granddaughter away. She was so grateful she kept asking Max what she owed him. He refused to charge and when pushed in the end replied, "Buy me a cup of tea."'

When a member of the public rings with what sounds like a good story, he or she first speaks to Nicola. She filters out time-wasters and asks for any evidence of what is being claimed. 'Sometimes,' she says, 'whoever calls has a ludicrous idea of what their story is worth and will ask for hundreds of thousands of pounds for something that is of no particular interest. I have to bring them down to earth.'

She deals with the more modest stories herself and hands over the bigger or more complex ones to Max. 'If someone has a story they want me to keep out of the papers, I go through it and take it from there,' he says. 'If it's a story they want me to sell, I ask for proof, and if they can't provide it I don't go ahead.

'When there's a nub of truth that I think stands up, I get on to a paper and leave it to them. They have the expertise, like lawyers and journalists, and the time to check everything thoroughly. I don't. Nor do I have the inclination. If they want to go ahead I then work out how much I'm going to sell the story for based on judgment and experience. I do the deal and move on.

'I don't tout for business. I decide who I want to take on. I've never wanted to deal with arrogant stars. I know they'll be on the phone all the time with constant demands. The only reason they employ a PR is to have someone constantly on hand to baby-sit them and that's not for me.' His deals with clients always work two ways. He is happy to advise them, but they have to listen to him, or risk being dropped, as with Freddie Starr.

He refuses to be paid on a results-only basis for his PR work, whether it is for his long-term clients or those who come to him with one big story. Nor will he accept an annual retainer. Instead he negotiates a lump sum or to be paid monthly in advance, preferably with a bonus at the end for a job well done.

Max works on the old-fashioned gentlemanly basis that his word is his bond, and his deals with both clients and newspapers are done verbally or on a handshake. 'By the time I'd set up on my own I'd seen so many contracts lead to confrontations and then a bad working relationship between client and PR that I decided it wasn't the way to get the best out of people. In any case, if either side is unhappy you can always get out of a contract, but it involves lawyers and arguments, which is too negative.'

He remains a technophobe. He hasn't yet mastered how to use a computer so he doesn't send emails. 'I just don't have the patience to learn,' he explains. 'Someone will start explaining how it works and within twenty seconds I'm bored. There are always so many different things I could be doing that stimulate me, I hate wasting even seconds on something that doesn't.'

Although the tabloids with large circulations and the deepest pockets are Max's most regular customers for his stories, they are not automatically his first choice. 'I sometimes offer a story to a paper for what it might lead to rather than what I might make financially,' he says. 'The goodwill an editor or journalist feels when I give them a top story can lead to features on twenty or thirty other clients. In other words, I do something for them because I need them to do something for me, or because they have done something for me in the past. It's a case of seeing the wider picture, wheeling and dealing, and treating people the way you like to be treated.

'Though I deal with all the papers, my best clients for stories are the Sundays: the *News of the World*, *Mail on Sunday*, *Sunday Mirror* and *Sunday People*. While my best dailies are the *Daily Mail*, *Daily Mirror* and the *Sun*. Once a story has appeared in a paper I often then sell it to magazines, like *OK*, *Hello!* and *NOW* and to TV.'

Sometimes Max spreads the story and the fee across several papers, giving each an exclusive angle. He might sell the main part exclusively to a Sunday paper for, say, £40,000 but hold back exclusive pictures for a daily to use the next day for £10,000.

He prides himself on his good long-term relationship with the majority of editors and senior journalists, something he says is 'based on mutual understanding and a professional attitude'. In return he will often provide journalists with information about a story when it doesn't benefit him at all financially, but does help build up a working relationship.

'Lots of journalists ring me for advice about a running story that hasn't necessarily originated from me. I correct them if I think they have wrong information, give them insights into what is really going on if I can, and suggest who they can contact to get at the truth. When I fill various editors in on certain aspects of a story I accrue lots of points. It means that if a few weeks later I ask them not to put another story in the paper because I want to protect another client, they'll do it. I can also get across a lot of plugs for other clients.'

Even PRs who work for other companies ring to ask how to handle a story about one of their clients when they feel out of their depth. 'Some of them have worked for me in the past, others have met me at a function or heard me speak. I'm always happy to help and never charge. And of course, if anyone wants to spark off a rumour, who is the best person to come to? Me. I can get it to all sorts of people.'

Max has expanded on the home front too. In 1996 he, Liz and Louise moved from their suburban semi to a large detached house in the exclusive residential estate of Burwood Park in Weybridge, Surrey, where he still lives. He paid £600,000 for the property, paying off the mortgage within a year. 'Because of my background, I don't like to owe any money to anybody,' he explains.

'I wanted something comfortable rather than a mansion and this house is perfect. I get a great deal of satisfaction from being able to afford it. When I wake up in the morning and the sun is shining I go out into the garden, read the papers, have a swim and watch my two cocker spaniels running around. It's lovely.'

There's a sweeping U-shaped drive at the front of the house and cream flagstones at the back that lead to a lawn edged with mature shrubs. The house itself has been decorated in soft neutral colours. The sitting room has comfy sofas in a rich Devon cream and a jukebox that Louise bought her father one birthday. There's a TV room with a creamy-yellow tiled floor, taupe corduroy comfy chairs and a sofa covered by a throw that is decorated with baby elephants and protects it from the dogs. In the centre of the room is a vast taupe ottoman. The sidelights are candle-shaped and the light switches and curtain rods gold. There are innumerable pictures of Liz and Louise beaming from identical dark-brown leather frames on almost every surface, and lots of porcelain ornaments of dancers and animals.

All the living rooms are filled with fresh and silk flowers. The kitchen is conventionally modern, rather than high tech. Max doesn't cook and usually eats out. In 2004 he had an extension built that added two bathrooms and two dressing rooms, a conservatory and a 50ft x 12ft swimming pool that has a special hoist so that Louise can ease herself in and out of the warm water.

Max is very house-proud and likes everything to be kept clean and tidy. When he arrives home from playing tennis, for example, he puts his white shorts and top straight into the washing machine. If he or any guests have a drink or some tea, when everyone is finished he will take the cups and glasses into the kitchen, rinse them and put them straight into the dishwasher.

He is also always buying things for his home. When he recently bought a new iron in the local shops, he paid over two hundred pounds for one with more options than a washing machine.

He thoroughly enjoys shopping locally in Cobham and every Saturday buys armfuls of fresh flowers for himself and friends. Being with him is a bit like accompanying Father Christmas on an out-of-season tour. Max doesn't have a goody bag to dispense presents, but everyone smiles at him and the majority who know him stop for a chat. Moving a hundred yards down the street can take almost an hour.

Max loves it and doesn't brush anyone aside. He seems to know everyone and always asks about their family, from how Great-aunt Sally is getting over her operation, to how young Susan is doing at school. He enjoys going to his local café and is as happy with a cheese-filled jacket potato and cup of tea as with a gourmet meal in a top London restaurant.

'My tastes are actually very simple. I like Scotch eggs, and nothing better than sitting in front of the television with a bowl of whelks watching football on a Saturday night.'

In 2000 he also bought a three-bedroom apartment in Marbella off plan through Majestic Real Estate, the company behind most of the lush developments along the coastline. It is one of a hundred luxury apartments in the exclusive Neuvo Andalucia area of Marbella. Swanky Puerto Banus is just three minutes' drive away. He bought the apartment for £555,000 without a mortgage, then spent £100,000 on furniture. 'I waited until I could afford to pay for it outright, so I wouldn't notice if the money wasn't there.'

There are three pools in the complex and Max swims daily. 'It's not leisure-time swimming, I really push myself and can do fifty lengths of butterfly, crawl and breaststroke.' Three golf courses border the development. Another is directly opposite his Surrey home, but Max dislikes golf and is never seen on any of them.

Buying the property was the accumulation of a forty-year love affair with Spain. 'Liz and I started visiting Spain by going to places like Torremolinos and Benidorm. I've loved Marbella for years because you don't need to speak Spanish, it's very secure and much more convenient than the Caribbean but most of all for its brilliant blue skies and its all-year warm sunshine. It's also very good for Louise. She swims a lot and there's a great hospital with good doctors nearby if we need it.'

He spends about three months in Marbella each year, broken up into one- or two-week slots, but he is not on holiday in the conventional sense. His mobile is never off and he wheels and deals almost as easily from Spain as he does from London. 'I'm always working. I can't go on holiday and forget everything.'

In Marbella too, everything is meticulously organised. He keeps a selection of clothes in the apartment and has Polaroids of all that is inside his wardrobe so he knows what he has and in what colour.

Almost inevitably, Max became professionally involved with Majestic. 'It is run by two Russians and a French financial controller. I started out promoting them as property developers but they now have their own television network, radio station and racetrack where they regularly hold big concerts. Elton John and Rod Stewart have performed there. I do all the PR and get Majestic a wide range of cover both in Europe and the UK on TV and radio, in newspapers and magazines, even when I'm talking about other stories.'

At the start of 2003 he treated himself to the ultimate status symbol of a Bentley. 'It cost £185,000 and I ordered it as a present to myself for my sixtieth birthday. It's the perfect car and owning one gives me an enormous sense of achievement, particularly as my dad's means of transport was a pushbike. However much hassle and bustle is going on in my life, I always feel better when I get into my car, with its air conditioning and beautiful sound system.'

Apart from his homes, though, Max has little interest in financial investments. 'Despite the fact that I've been lucky enough to make a very good living, I prefer to keep to the simple philosophy of sticking to what I'm good at. I'm always being asked to invest in the stock exchange or buy shares in other people's businesses, but I inevitably refuse. I don't think I have a natural instinct for business as such.

'Nor do I want to talk for hours about the ins and outs of a deal. Sometimes the investments I've been offered would have paid off, but mostly not. As someone who came from a family where there was no money, I prefer to keep my money in a current account. I know it's stupid and that I could earn a lot of interest if I put it elsewhere, but I like to be able to compare exactly what I made this year with last.

'Every Friday night as I'm about to go home, Dee gives me a print-out of how much money I have in the bank. I put it in my briefcase then once or twice a month when I go to bed I take it out and compare the figures. Here too, I'm in competition with myself and always want to do better. Then I forget all about it. I never think that the cheque I sent to charity could have made me even wealthier.'

One of the unexpected side effects of Max's success and subsequent reputation, however, is that some rich and powerful individuals are now using his name for their own purposes. 'It's got back to me that they've told people, particularly those they want to intimidate, that I'm working for them and could bring out vital information against them at any time, when it's totally untrue. The fact that I'm being used as a threat could become very dangerous if the people they want to frighten believe I'm genuinely trying to destroy them. It makes me the enemy of a total stranger.

'I've always said my downfall won't be due to something I'm involved with but something I know nothing about. I'm the least paranoid person in the world but I am realistic. I can't anticipate or take care of things I'm totally unaware of. Luckily it doesn't keep me awake at night. Nothing does. It's waking and getting up I have problems with.'

17. THE SIMON COWELL I KNOW

Following one of Max's television appearances in 2001 he received a phone call from a young woman with a deep, throaty voice and strong Russian accent. She told him her name was Angela Ermakova and that she was a banking student. She called because German tennis legend Boris Becker was refusing to acknowledge that he was the father of her small daughter and she wanted to bring his denial to the attention of the public.

The child was the result of a brief now infamous encounter between Angela and Boris at the exclusive London restaurant Nobu in the summer of 1999. It had supposedly taken place in the broom cupboard, although the location was later changed to the stairs, and caused enormous public merriment.

It had lasted all of five minutes and it didn't cross Becker's mind that he would ever see Angela again. But in February 2000 she sent him a fax telling him in cryptic terms that she was due to give birth in a month's time. She wrote: 'Dear Mr Becker, You will recall a promotional project we discussed in Nobu, London, on June 30, 1999. The project is quite advanced and is scheduled for launch at the end of next month. It would be really good to hear your comments and thoughts for possible participation. Perhaps you could call.'

When Angela had contacted Max, he had initially asked what evidence she had. 'When you see me you won't need any evidence,' she laughed. She came to his office a day or two later bringing her little daughter in a pushchair. Angela was of mixed race, but her daughter Anna was the absolute spitting image of Boris. She had his red hair, pale skin colour, navy-blue eyes and even his almost invisible blonde eyelashes. Max burst out laughing. 'I wondered how on earth he thought he could get away with it? It was absolutely game, set and match to Angela.'

Max sold an exclusive interview with Angela who saw herself as an almost blameless victim, to the *Daily Mail*. The bombshell news made Becker's blood run cold and although he initially refused to believe the child was his, after the story appeared in the papers he agreed to DNA tests and subsequently admitted paternity.

As a result of the revelations, Becker's furious wife Barbara, who was seven months pregnant with their second child at the time, filed for divorce. Becker, a three-times Wimbledon champion, meanwhile tried to make excuses for his smutty behaviour. 'It was a very, very extreme moment in my life,' he said. 'I lost control. It hasn't happened before and it hasn't happened since. I had no idea what I was doing. It wasn't an affair. It was just "poom-bah-boom!"'

It became one of the most expensive 'poom-bah-booms' in history. Becker reportedly agreed to pay around £3million to support Anna and in a statement issued through a spokesperson said, 'I will do whatever I can to see that Anna is a happy little girl in the future.' He set up a trust fund for his daughter, pays for her to live in a £1million house with her mother, to attend private school and have a tutor for German and ballet lessons. He also tries to see her every couple of months.

'Angela could have made a career move out of selling the story of her cupboard love,' explains Max. 'But she made it clear she didn't want to do that. She just wanted to say how dare Becker accuse her of lying.'

'My dealings with Max were very short,' Angela agrees. 'I did one interview in England and one in Germany when my daughter was very small. All I wanted was justice for her and that Boris faced up to his responsibilities. Max achieved both of these things.'

For the first few years after her interviews Angela declined any more requests to talk about her situation, choosing instead to live a private life out of the headlines. But in April 2005 she arranged for five-year-old Anna to talk about her father to a German television station – something potentially more damaging than if she talked herself. 'I chose to let her speak in Germany because we don't live there, and I still prefer to remain quiet in London,' she explains.

Dressed in pink and wearing ballet shoes, frilly socks and ribbons in her hair, the little girl held up a picture of her father and said, 'This is my papa. He looks sweet. He has blue eyes. I look a lot like him.'

Although Anna is still the spitting image of Becker, Angela believes she and Anna also share similar features. 'I think Boris and I look alike, except he is white and I am black,' she says. She also believes he has some feeling for his daughter. 'Boris doesn't show them much on the outside, but when he sees her, yes, I believe he loves her. When she is old enough I will tell her that I loved her father and what happened was fate.

'I have taught Anna good manners and made sure she is always polite. It is important because as she grows older people are bound to criticise her. So I have to work hard to try to overcome the image that has been thrust on her. Boris has also given her a tennis racket and she has begun to play. She loves it, but she is still very young and it's too early to know how she will develop.'

Although 36-year-old Angela has no financial worries, she has not managed to move on. 'All I do is care for my daughter. It is very difficult to get into a relationship after what happened to me. I was so traumatised that I've not been able to trust another man.'

Later in 2001, however, it was left to another little girl to move the British public's hearts. And the story of her family is one that most highlights Max's ability to help ordinary people in extraordinary situations.

Max was contacted in June by a friend of Rina and Michael Attard. The couple, from the Maltese island of Gozo, had barely been out of the news since Rina, 29, gave birth to conjoined twins at St Mary's Hospital, Manchester, on 8 August 2000. Their tiny twins, Gracie and Rosie, were born with fused spines, were joined at the hip and shared a heart and pair of lungs.

The devout Catholic couple didn't want to separate the girls as they knew Rosie, the much weaker twin, couldn't survive, but the

Court of Appeal ruled that the operation could go ahead after they heard that if they were not separated, both children would die. The complex operation took place in November and Rosie died during the procedure.

'Gozo is a quiet island with what is to us an old-fashioned lifestyle, and when Rina and Michael came to see me it was obvious that they were from a different world and a different time. They had been under huge pressure to tell their story and had decided to go ahead. Although I usually warn my clients to expect to be attacked by the papers who don't get their story, in this instance I knew they would get nothing but sympathy from the press and the public.

'It was a fascinating human-interest story, with moral, ethical and religious implications, and not surprisingly I had the whole world knocking on my door wanting access to them. It was such a huge story that for the first time I arranged a double exclusive, doing a deal with both the *Mail on Sunday* and the *News of the World* to publish at the same time, because they had very different markets. I also tied the publication date with an interview on *Tonight with Trevor MacDonald*.

'The Attards were very grateful and I hope I helped them through their difficult time. I felt for them enormously and like everyone else I was totally caught up with what they were going through. I tried to make it as positive an experience as possible and to get them enough money that their future would be assured. I believe they earned over £400,000.'

Some of the money went into a trust for Gracie in case she needed further surgery. The family then went back to Gozo, where Gracie fully recovered from the operation. The following year Rina gave birth to another daughter they called Rosie in memory of her sister.

Looking back at that traumatic time, Michael Attard says he was very happy with Max's efforts on their behalf. 'It was very difficult for us. We were surrounded by so many people and we couldn't deal with all the attention. But as soon as my wife and I saw Max Clifford we thought he seemed a fair man and we trusted him. We were worried that the newspapers wouldn't treat us well, and were grateful for his reassurance.

'We agreed with how he wanted to handle our story, we were happy to leave it in his hands and were pleased with the results. Max made us very famous, but we don't want to be famous any more. We are happy to be an ordinary family. Journalists sometimes contact us wanting us to talk, but otherwise we live a normal life. The important thing is Gracie is fine, just like a little child should be.'

As well as dealing with the constant stream of stories and PR clients that flowed through his office at the start of the new century, Max also began to build up a close working relationship with Simon Cowell, the co-creator of *Pop Idol*, a reality TV talent contest for the pop stars of the future.

Cowell, 42, was already a successful producer on BMG Records with sales of 25 million albums, when he and former Spice Girls manager Simon Fuller developed *Pop Idol* for British television. Cowell very reluctantly agreed to be one of the judges.

'I had no desire to be in front of the cameras,' he says. 'I'd seen what can happen to people when they are on TV or get a record in the charts, particularly if like me you've lived a rather raunchy life in your twenties and thirties that could spark off a lot of kiss-and-tell stories. I was eventually persuaded but decided I needed someone to deal with all the press attention. So before the programme was aired I went to Max to get him on board. Most people go to a PR to get them more publicity; I specifically went to Max to get me less. I'd seen him on TV and heard him on the radio. He seemed a bright guy and I knew he'd worked with the Beatles, Sinatra and Muhammad Ali. Although most people saw him as someone who just sold stories to newspapers, I instinctively thought there was much more to him than that.

'I gave him a call in April 2001 and turned up a couple of days later to see him. I explained who I was and that I was going to do a show called *Pop Idol* and that I had a feeling that one or two girls from my past would want to sell their story and I needed someone to help me deal with all that plus give me general advice. I explained I wasn't looking for any publicity or someone to send out lots of press releases about me.'

'Although Simon was totally confident as a record executive, he'd had no experience of being on television,' says Max. 'He felt rather nervous and asked me if I thought he'd get murdered. I told him he had nothing to lose. If it didn't work, he could continue making fortunes from records and would quickly be forgotten.'

Simon appeared so calm in front of the cameras that it's now hard to believe that he – or Mr Nasty, as he was soon nicknamed for his withering put-downs of would-be pop stars on the show – ever felt a twinge of nerves about appearing in front of them, and was regularly calling Max for help.

'We discussed how critical he should be of the contestants,' adds Max. 'I told him to be himself and respond as he would if the person concerned had come to see him in his office. I advised him not to overdo it just for effect, but if he felt something, he should say it.

'I said be instinctive and natural and if he disagreed with the other judges, who were record producer Pete Waterman, Nicki Chapman, who had also worked alongside Simon Fuller, and radio DJ Dr Fox, he should say so too. He'd produced so many hit records that he had the credibility to back his judgment, so wasn't trying to be controversial just for the sake of it.

'I watched each programme. Afterwards we'd talk it through and I told him if I thought what he said sounded a bit fabricated. Although ninety-five per cent of the comments were Simon's I did at first give him the odd line. One was, "If only your ability matched your confidence." Another, "If you have a voice coach, sue him." But as the weeks went by, he didn't even need the odd line.

'One marvellous aspect of the show was that I could take lots of sick children and friends who were down on their luck to the studios, which they all loved. Simon was always delighted to have them around.'

Simon is very appreciative of Max's efforts. 'Max was and still is the first person I speak to after a TV appearance,' he says. 'A lot of PR people suck up to you and tell you what you want to hear, because you're paying them, but the relationship I have with Max is the opposite of that. He never flatters for the sake of flattering and will criticise when he thinks it's in my best interests. So I always listen carefully even if I don't always agree.

'Sometimes Max even says, "You weren't being too harsh, but you weren't the Simon I know and I'm sure you were thinking something else." We've spoken so often he knows more about the way I think than anybody else and is the first to spot when I have copped out for whatever reason. As well as watching the show on his own, he also sees it with friends and then gives me a consensus of what everyone thinks, which means I get a response from punters as well as a professional. It's good and helps me live in the real world. I don't want to exist in a bubble and pretend everything is great.

'We have a very balanced friendship and he has also taught me the relations side of public relations. That it's a two-way game and if you are relying on the media to promote your show, you have to accept that they will also be interested in you and not always in a complimentary way. And if you don't like it, don't go on TV. Max keeps telling me that the good outweighs the bad and I shouldn't moan. And that some people will like me and some won't and that I'm never going to please everyone.'

In practice it wasn't so easy. 'Although I was ready for all the kiss-and-tell stories to come out, after about six months, by which time the show was a huge hit, they seemed to be coming from every direction and I didn't like it. I phoned Max from Dublin one day to tell him it was too much. Instead of sympathising with me, he told me to think about what I had achieved over that time and not to take myself too seriously. He was right, it wasn't too bad, and I decided to handle it by stopping reading about myself. I didn't mind at all being called Mr Nasty. I know I am not. I don't drown kittens, I was just telling a few people they couldn't sing.

'In fact, he has managed to keep several stories by vindictive ex-girlfriends out of the papers and also tipped me off about other girls trying to set me up.'

Simon needed further hand-holding when he was asked to go on his first chat show in the spring of 2002. 'People might be surprised to learn that I am more shy off camera than I am on, particularly if I am meeting people for the first time and it is purely social.

'I was OK going on *GMTV* and BBC's *This Morning* because their items only last two or three minutes, but being asked to appear on the popular, funny Frank Skinner show and talk one-to-one for fifteen minutes was quite different. I was unsure whether or not to do it, especially as at the time the media coverage about me concentrated on the Mr Nasty aspect and how unpleasant I was supposed to be. But Max felt it was important for me to go on one show to justify what I did, so I agreed. A day or two before the set date he rang me to say he was going to bring Louise and a couple of friends along to the studio. With hindsight I now know he anticipated that chatting to them beforehand would take my mind off the interview.

'When he came into my dressing room I was obviously very nervous. It seemed such a weird situation for me to be in. I was confident talking about people's ability to sing, but not about myself, and didn't know how entertaining I was expected to be. Max told me I had nothing to worry about and put the whole thing into perspective. If you have a sense of perspective in life you can be in control. Luckily within thirty seconds of the interview starting I realised that the pressure was on Frank to make the interview entertaining, not on me and I was fine after that.

'Max was also good at calming me down when I got angry. He's seen so much and understands that the things that upset you at one moment in time are not those you should be upset about in the grand scheme of things. It's very easy when you're on television to become precious and paranoid and think that everything is a conspiracy and that people are out to get you. But he never once fanned that flame.

'When I phoned to say, "Guess what so-and-so said about me . . ." he'd just laugh. I remember during the first year of the show getting a phone call from the *Daily Mirror* at 9 p.m. one night when I was in the kitchen of my house in Holland Park. The journalist asked for a quote as the paper was going to be using a picture of me on the front page wearing ladies' underwear.

'He explained that my mother had given him the picture. In fact it was one of my brother and I at a "tarts and vicars" fancy-dress party in St Lucia. I'd gone as a tart and put my arms round my brother for the picture. I immediately saw the insinuation, particularly as there had been several untrue stories about me being gay. I immediately phoned Max. I was raging, but when he burst out laughing I did too, which was good. I'm sure if he had said, "This is terrible. We must stop it," I'd have got even more anxious.

'I was still cross with my mother for being stupid enough to give the picture to a tabloid journalist, even though she was in her 70s, but Max gently reprimanded me, saying, "She didn't mean to cause trouble. Don't phone her and give her a hard time. She didn't realise what she was doing." I listened and when I calmed down realised he was right about that too.'

Max adds: 'I explained to Simon that if he was seen to be precious about any kind of criticism people would quickly say he could give it but not take it. As it was how he had made his name, I told him to laugh at it, because if he didn't he would be making a rod for his own back.'

Renamed *American Idol* and with only the one judge Cowell made the leap across the Atlantic. The show appeared on US TV in the summer of 2002 and became an instant hit. An astonishing 31 million viewers watched the final in May 2004 and Simon was reported to have made £85million.

In the autumn of 2004 Simon launched *X Factor*, a talent show he created which differed from *Pop Idol* in that older performers, groups and individuals were allowed to compete. The winner would get a deal on his label. He invited band manager Louis Walsh and Sharon Osbourne, wife of Black Sabbath's Ozzy, to sit in judgment with him.

This time Max advised him to keep the launch low profile. '*Pop Idol* needed a huge amount of publicity to get it going, but I said he should take it steady this time round,' Max remembers. 'I compared it to a top football team like Arsenal going into the new season. You don't scream, you just do your best. You already have your platform and you don't need to shout out claims. He listened and it worked very well.'

Part of the show's appeal was the love–hate relationship that developed between Simon and Sharon. Although Simon appeared to cope on screen, he was regularly on the phone to Max about it. 'Max always said she was very good for the show but there were times I needed his help in dealing with her, particularly when she launched a prolonged attack on me on the show that lasted about four weeks. In turn she said I was after young girls, that I needed to come out of the closet, that I was a secret transvestite, a pervert, that I fancied her, and that Ozzy wanted to rip my head off. After the third week I told Max we had to put a stop to it and do something publicly in my defence, but he said, "Ignore it. Drop it." He was right.

'Instead I asked myself: "Are her accusations life threatening?" They weren't. Was the whole thing designed to piss me off? One hundred per cent. So why was she doing it? I think she was using me to get herself publicity. It was a shame because I thought we had a good relationship.

'Her worst accusation was that I was fixing the show, which was impossible and grossly unfair as there is an independent voting system. But the one thing I won't forgive her for is her outburst on the last night of the series when she viciously attacked winner Steve Brookstein, calling him a fake and saying he was too confident. I can look after myself but I had a big problem with her going after my artist for no good reason.

'It was clear to me that she needed a Max in her life. She would never have said it if she had been his client. It was obvious her comments were premeditated and, if she had discussed them with Max beforehand, he would have told her that on the night of the final, whether or not you are a fan of the finalists, it is their big moment and wrong to spoil it.

'It was so spiteful. Some have said she helped him win because the Brits like the underdog, but no one wants to win out of sympathy. Secondly, most people feel there is no smoke without fire, and I've seen people look at Steve and wonder if he is like she said he was.'

Max believes Sharon's comments were damaging to herself. 'It put a lot of fans off her. Her image on the show had been big-hearted and motherly, but she revealed a very nasty side and in the new series in September 2005 she will have to work hard to make people forget it.'

Simon is now more famous than the pop stars he helped to create, and generally much more relaxed on screen. 'Everyone who is on television finds that it affects their ego. You either end up a monster, or accept it as a period in your life and try not to become too much of an arsehole in the process. I have tried to do the latter and not take myself too seriously. To my amazement, through Max's help I've learned to enjoy the spotlight, especially as I don't think it's likely to last too much longer.

'The public will inevitably tire of my shows and then of me. So I might as well enjoy it while I've got it. It's very well paid and a good laugh, I get a decent table in a restaurant and ninety-nine per cent of the people who come up to me in the street shake my hand. Max also advised me to pace myself and explained it was a good idea to be out of the country for six months or so every year, that too much publicity was a bad thing and that if I disappeared for a bit and then returned people would be happy to see me and read about me. It's his secret for TV longevity.'

Simon and Max have also become friends. 'Nowadays we go out to dinner together not as client and PR person but because we enjoy each other's company. Max is a rogue, which I like, and not at all judgmental, so I am quite relaxed with him. Nor do I feel he's jealous of what I earn. Quite the opposite. He seems very happy for me.'

Max agrees. 'I am not at all resentful. I love it for him. I am doing extremely well and have never been jealous of other people's success. Jealousy and envy are such destructive qualities. They eat you up inside and put such a dark cloud around you, you can't see the sunshine. Fortunately they never affect me.'

Simon is so pleased to acknowledge Max's help that when he was interviewed by Piers Morgan on the television programme *Tabloid Tales* in May 2004 and asked what was the best career decision he's made he said, 'Hiring Max Clifford.'

Max was delighted. 'It was very nice of him. I help all kinds of people but they usually take all the credit for what I do. Simon is a breath of fresh air. It's rare that someone who is so successful remains both unaffected and appreciative.'

It was fortunate that Simon and Max worked so naturally and easily together as on the home front Max was desperately fighting what was to be the biggest battle of his life.

18. HEARTBREAK, HEARTACHE

February 2002 began much like any other month, but subsequent events gave Max intense heartache and sorrow and changed his life forever.

One evening when Max came home from work Liz mentioned that she'd hurt her back, she thought from either playing badminton or lifting up the garage door. Max wasn't initially too worried. Instead he expressed sympathy and suggested he bought an electrically operated door, which wouldn't be so heavy.

'We thought she'd probably damaged a vertebrae or pulled a muscle and didn't take too much notice,' he says. 'Liz had always been extremely fit. As well as playing badminton she took our dog for long walks every day and went to water aerobics twice a week. Although she'd been a smoker when she was younger, she'd stopped years previously and was always careful what she ate and drank.

'But over the following months instead of her back improving, it became increasingly painful. As we still assumed it was a sports injury I took her to see a sports physiotherapist. He examined her and told us he'd like her to see a specialist. We booked an appointment with a sports physician in July and he organised a series of x-rays.

'It became a dreadful month. Liz's sister Christine, who worked as an air hostess on Concorde, had been suffering from cancer, became seriously ill and died. The two sisters weren't close but Liz naturally wanted to go to the funeral. Christine lived in a very remote part of France and, as I didn't want Liz to have a difficult and tiring journey, I hired a private jet and we landed in a small aerodrome as close as possible to the cemetery.

'When we returned late that afternoon we drove straight to Ashtead hospital. We had an appointment at 7 p.m. to get the results of her x-rays. We still weren't unduly worried and fully expected to be told she had a slipped disc or something similar. We had no idea; we hadn't dreamed what the specialist would tell us.

'"I have bad news for you," he began. "We have discovered a secondary cancer. I'm afraid it's bone cancer and Liz will have to have more tests." We were shell-shocked. Apart from the aching back she didn't have any other symptoms. We then had to go home and I had the distressing task of telling Louise.

'The weekend that followed was the start of the hardest period of my life. Liz was so traumatised she could barely speak, while I kept trying to reassure her and tell her I was certain we could sort it out.

'We were referred to the Royal Marsden Hospital in Sutton where they discovered a tiny tumour in her lung. It was close to the bones and had started the whole thing off. It seemed cruel and ironic that Liz was now a patient at the same hospital I'd been involved with for so many years. That she would become a cancer sufferer was something that had never once crossed my mind.

'Unluckily, the type of cancer Liz had was a particularly nasty strain and was both very active and difficult to treat. The doctors told me from the start that the prognosis was bad and she probably wouldn't survive for more than six months. My life changed totally. Instead of looking forward to spending the rest of my life with the woman I loved, I now had to cope with the fact that we probably only had a few months left together. I can't possibly describe what I felt like.

'Somehow I pulled myself together and became determined to cushion and protect my Liz as much as humanly possible from anything negative, including the fact that she was dying. I only told her good things and pointed out how some patients who have a bad prognosis are still around years later.

But for me it was the most devastating thing that had ever happened. I've always been used to winning battles, but now it seemed I couldn't win the fight for the most important person in my life. I'd have done anything to change the prognosis, and accepting that I couldn't was incredibly hard for me to face up to. I kept saying to the doctors, "Surely there must be something somewhere in the world you can get to help her?" But there wasn't.

'I also felt incredibly angry but I forced myself not to complain or say, "Why me?" I faced up to it and tried to make Liz's life as good as I possibly could.'

Professor Powles felt deeply for his despairing friend. 'I often saw Max with Liz at the hospital during this terrible time. Her suffering was so great and the impotence Max felt at not being able to help her was terrible to witness.'

Max hopes and believes that Liz never knew she was dying. 'We talked about the cancer a lot, and I kept telling her that the doctors were making good progress. Right up to a couple of days before she died she was talking about our next trip to Spain and other plans she had for the summer.'

Liz was given chemotherapy and radiotherapy treatment for the first few months, but it failed to halt her decline. 'She began to deteriorate badly in the last two months of her life,' he says. 'She had no energy and far too soon the cancer specialist told me the end was near. I warned Louise and we tried to give each other strength. Although part of me hoped for a miracle right up to her death, once I knew there could be no happy ending I also wanted her suffering to be over as soon as possible.

'I couldn't bear to see what effect the cancer was having on her. She was a dignified woman who always wanted everything to be just so. I'm the sort of person who'll take the rubbish out in the morning in my dressing gown, with my hair all over the place and if someone walks by the house, I'll stand and chat without worrying about what I look like. But Liz would never do that. Before she left home for any reason, she made sure she was immaculate. My Liz was beautiful inside and out.

'She spent the last two weeks of her life at the Marsden and I was with her most of that time. I tried to take her out each day, either for a drive or a walk in her wheelchair, just as I had done with Louise when she was in hospital. By this time Liz had lost a lot of weight and looked very gaunt. It was horrible watching someone you love deteriorate like that, and although on the surface I tried to keep everything as normal as possible, I felt completely torn apart inside.

'It took a huge amount of energy for me to stay positive and to wrap myself around her and love and protect her. But I had to do it for her, just as I had always done it for Louise. For the first time in my life I hardly worked. I lost all enthusiasm for it. The girls in the office ran everything and only phoned me when they absolutely needed to. Instead I concentrated entirely on Liz.'

Before Liz became ill, she and Max had planned to have a big party to celebrate his sixtieth birthday on 6 April 2003. They had booked a large room at St George's tennis club in Weybridge. But when it became obvious how sick she was, Max cancelled it. He assumed Liz would be relieved, and in any event he didn't feel like celebrating.

Instead she was upset and tried to persuade him to have his party. At first he didn't listen, but one of her nurses told him that Liz kept saying how unhappy she was he'd cancelled it because of her and how much she wanted it to go ahead. So almost at the last minute, he decided to have his party at home instead.

He managed to find some caterers in Cobham and contacted everyone who had been on the original guest list. Almost no one had made alternative arrangements and nearly one hundred people turned up. They came partly to celebrate his birthday and partly, although no one said so publicly, to say goodbye to Liz. Perhaps, too, the party was Liz's own way of saying goodbye.

She was by now so desperately ill that a nurse from the hospital came to look after her. She had insisted on coming home for the whole of Sunday and when she arrived in the morning, she struggled to get involved with the arrangements. She even asked the caterers to wash and polish all her already clean plates before they were put out, as she wanted everything to meet her high standards.

Max enjoyed seeing his friends and family, although his heart was bleeding for Liz. By 6.30 p.m. Liz was so exhausted and in such pain that the nurse suggested she went back to the hospital rather than stay the night at home as had originally been planned. Liz, who so rarely showed her emotions, was so upset she cried.

Max and Louise spent most of the following day with Liz at the hospital. 'She was sleeping virtually all the time and the nurses gently told me she wouldn't last more than a few days,' Max recalls. 'By the time we left her at about midnight she had sunk into a coma.

I phoned the hospital at 6 a.m. the next morning to see how she was and told them that if anything suddenly changed I could be there in half an hour. Shortly after they called to say she had passed away. It was 6.15 a.m. on 8 April 2003.'

Louise heard the phone ring, and immediately got out of bed. Her bedroom was on the ground floor and, as Max came down from his bedroom upstairs, father and daughter met in the entrance hall. They didn't need to exchange a word. Instead they hugged each other tight and wept heart-wrenching tears. Then Max helped Louise get dressed and drove over to the hospital.

Max was initially very upset that he hadn't been with Liz during her last moments. 'I hadn't expected her to go quite so quickly, but I consoled myself that I was with her for nearly four decades and that as she was in a deep coma, she wouldn't have been aware of me anyway.

'So many people have since said she obviously just hung on for my birthday, but I don't know if that's true. But if she did, it shows what a wonderful person she was. She was cremated at Leatherhead crematorium on a beautiful sunny day. Making my speech to family and friends was one of the hardest things I've ever done, but I tried to make it as positive as I could, because the forty years we spent together was full of love and laughter, and a lot of people don't get a fraction of that. Although I'd barely worked from February to mid-May, towards the end of May, I began to get involved in one or two things again and found that the busier I got, the better I felt.

'I have, as usual managed to turn something so negative into a positive and now think how lucky I am to have such good memories of Liz – memories that no one can take away from me. I still miss everything about her, particularly her serenity, naturalness and understanding. Luckily I still feel she is with me in spirit, and I speak to her first thing in the morning and last thing at night.

'I keep her ashes in a container on a high shelf in my sitting room. Next to it is the birthday card she managed to organise for me. It reads: "You mean the world to me, you always have and you always will. Happy birthday. I love to snuggle you, hug and cuddle you. I love to love you lots. Liz." '

But Max didn't have much time to get over Liz's death, before Louise's health gave rise for concern.

Before Liz became ill, Max knew Louise's kidneys were failing as a result of the strong anti-inflammatory drugs she'd taken for so many years. Her doctors had said she needed a transplant. Max offered one of his kidneys and was devastated to discover that his blood group, A, was incompatible with Louise's, so he couldn't be a donor. 'I couldn't believe it,' he says. 'Louise and I were so close I thought we were bound to be compatible in every respect.

'Liz then volunteered and we were delighted to discover she and Louise shared the same blood group, O, but her cancer was diagnosed soon afterwards and, as a result, the operation couldn't go ahead.'

By the time Liz died, Louise only had about 20 per cent kidney function and, as a result, her blood pressure had shot up to a dangerous 220 over 160 (the average blood pressure in someone in their early 30s is around 120 over 80). Fortunately she didn't have to wait too long before a suitable kidney did become available and she had the transplant on 31 January 2004. It has been a remarkable success and has given her a much better quality of life and a lot more energy.

Nonetheless her health and welfare is always on Max's mind. 'Because of what she's been through, she needs me more than most thirty-something daughters need their fathers. I've arranged trust funds for her so she will always be fine financially, but I worry about who will take care of her if anything happens to me.

'Although she is an articulate and successful woman, and in the last few years has employed her own PAs in order to live life as independently as possible, she still needs looking after. There are many small things like lifting her up from chairs and taking her shoes off at night before she goes to sleep. I also worry if she's in the house on her own in case she falls over, and if I go away for a few days we have to arrange for a carer to stay with her. Not the sorts of thing most parents of a 34-year-old daughter think about.'

'Dad is very protective towards me,' Louise agrees. 'We are still tuned in to each other, but since my mother died I've realised I have to be the author of my own destiny rather than rely on Dad. I'm trying to do my own thing more, but it's quite difficult because Dad is such a strong, independent and entertaining person it's hard to find that in someone else. I have my own flat close to the family home, but moved back when Mum was ill and I have decided to stay on.'

Liz had always run everything at home, but after her death Max took on the responsibility for the domestic side of his life. It's been difficult. 'I haven't enjoyed getting involved with all the nitty-gritty. Liz dealt with all the cheques, bills and standing orders. The only thing I did regularly was the food shopping. I still do, but now it's on top of everything else.

'After Liz died I knew I had to get a housekeeper. It wasn't easy as I'm fussy and I don't like people being in my house. Nor did I want to advertise for someone, because I knew I'd get loads of replies and wouldn't know who I could trust.' So, as usual, he went with personal recommendations.

Inevitably once Liz had died Max also became the target of women of all ages and types. 'I changed into a successful single man. There have been several women who have wanted to comfort me and a few who wanted to comfort me for their own ends and assumed they were next in line.

'I was inundated with phone calls from women wanting to cook me dinner and take me out. Even,' he jokes, 'rub me down with *Sporting Life*. Two or three got close but the problem is they were close before and I haven't wanted to develop the relationship.

'People may think I am arrogant and overconfident, but I'm not stupid. I don't kid myself that I am God's gift to women. I have a wonderful lifestyle, which is hugely appealing to a lot of women, and quite a few would be prepared to put up with me to get the lifestyle. Luckily I can usually spot them one hundred miles away.

'The one person who has made a big difference is Jo Westwood, who became my PA a few months after Liz died. She has been tremendous. Jo, Louise and my office angels have played a huge part in helping me recover from my dreadful loss.

'I would love to get married again one day. I'm not the sort of person who just wants to live with someone, but she would have to be very special and very understanding to put up with someone like me.'

19. IMAGE IS EVERYTHING

The personality of a successful media guru is an extraordinary thing. Everyone from TV producers and journalists to the man in the street expects him to have a view about everything. Max is happy to oblige and over the years has mastered the art of the short sharp comment that is helpful, funny, perceptive or sarcastic as well as being full of common sense. He gives his views by the dozen to all branches of the media every day. But he made a small, but significant slip of the tongue when he was talking about Neil and Christine Hamilton and it resulted in him being sued for the first time in forty years.

The story began like so many others. Max had a phone call on 2 May 2001 from Nadine Milroy-Sloan, who said she had a story to sell. 'She came to see me and explained it was about a sex-based party she'd been invited to through a mutual friend of the Hamiltons. I told her to bring me some evidence. I thought no more about it, but a week later she called again to say she'd been the subject of a serious sexual assault and rape by the Hamiltons. She said she'd already been to the police and that they were looking into it. I told her if it was a police matter I couldn't get involved.

'That was basically it until August 2001 when the Hamiltons were arrested. They issued a statement giving details of what she claimed they had done and then mentioned my name in conjunction with my work for Mohamed Al Fayed and Freddie Starr. The fact that they did so, even if they did not accuse me, made me part of the rape allegations, which were nothing to do with me. As a result I was asked by the media to comment on the allegations.'

Max did scores of interviews. 'I kept saying it was a police matter and that if the police have arrested them there must be something to answer. That if they are innocent I hope they are proven innocent and if guilty, I hope that's proved too. I made virtually the same comment on GMTV. I was then asked if I believed the Hamiltons. I replied, "Of course not. You've only got to remember the cash-for-questions scandal when even their own parliamentary colleagues didn't believe them."' In 1994 Neil Hamilton, then a junior minister in the department of trade, was accused of taking cash from Mohamed Al Fayed to ask questions in parliament on his behalf. As a result he was forced to resign.

Max continues: 'Had I been asked whether I trusted Nadine Milroy-Sloan I would have said I didn't know her and didn't have a clue whether to trust her or not.'

The police found no evidence against the Hamiltons. They also discovered that Milroy-Sloan had a history of making false allegations and dropped the case on 28 August. Milroy-Sloan was later jailed for three years for perverting the course of justice.

The Hamiltons then proceeded with a claim for slander and libel against Max. 'My instinct was to sort it out quickly,' he says. 'They originally wanted ten thousand pounds and an apology. I'd have said, "All I ever meant was that you were liars," and that would have been it. Later on my lawyer said it was clear that on GMTV I meant lying about the cash for questions and they had no case against me. I rationalised that you don't employ a lawyer and disregard what he says.'

Max would have done well to stick to his original instincts. At a pre-trial hearing at the High Court, Mr Justice Eady ruled out parts of the defence and Max decided to cut his losses. He didn't apologise for his comments but had a statement read out in court admitting his remarks could have been taken to mean that Milroy-Sloan's sexual assault allegations were true. 'It was never my intention to suggest this as I had no direct knowledge whatsoever of the alleged events,' the statement read.

He didn't attend in person. 'What was the point? The matter had been decided. It was better for someone to read the statement out for me while I worked off my aggression on the tennis court.'

If Max had let the case go to court he might have won, but it was a risk and it could have set him back £1million including costs. Instead it cost in the region of £250,000, fortunately the same amount Max earned that very month. 'The point is,' he says, 'I made a mistake and put my hands up.

'After the court case Christine's autobiography *For Better for Worse* was published. In it she seems to imply that Mohamed Al Fayed and I were involved in the rape allegations and that Mohamed was prepared to offer Milroy-Sloan £100,000 if the allegations were true and could be proved. It's totally untrue. I had nothing to do with the allegations, nor did I even mention them to Al Fayed.'

He is no longer angry. 'I am aware that large sections of the British public are repulsed by the Hamiltons, but I've only ever found them figures of fun. Since Neil was thrown out of parliament, they have scratched a living ridiculing themselves. I think of them as pantomime figures like Widow Twankey and Buttons or the Ugly Sisters.'

Ironically Neil, Christine and Max have a common experience. They have been interviewed by Louis Theroux for his BBC 2 series *When Louis Met . . .*

By chance the Hamiltons were being filmed by Theroux when they were arrested, which resulted in a more dramatic encounter than had been anticipated. The programme with Max, however, was more like a game of chess. It took three and a half months to film and was broadcast in March 2002.

'Louis appeared to be working on his own agenda,' Max says. 'I found him to be a smarmy, patronising and extremely ambitious man. He'd chosen easy victims, comedians and politicians who were past their sell-by date or wanted to get back into the limelight and he then made fools of them. Although I wasn't an easy victim on the surface, he had all the cards because in the end he could decide what appeared on the screen and what was left out. I agreed to take part because I like a challenge. It keeps me sharp and on my toes. So it was a case of saying, "I know what you're trying to achieve. Let's see if I can achieve more than you."' It was Max's competitive instinct again.

He continues: 'For example, at one point when the cameras were rolling, he said, "I know Simon Cowell is homosexual, that's why he's brought you in to be his PR."

'I replied, "No, he isn't. But is it true you prefer men to women? Is that why your wife has left you? You can tell me." He yelled, "CUT!"

'That was the sort of battle we had. I think the programme took so long to film because he couldn't get enough on me. His game was to try to film things that would damage or humiliate me. He also tried hard to make me lose my temper, which I didn't, and show me up in any way he could to get people to laugh at me, in order to make good television. He'd already humiliated Paul Daniels, the Hamiltons and Ann Widdecombe and if he'd done the same to me, it would have been a triumph for him.

'I think it revealed more about him than me. He tried to hide behind a gawky, gangling schoolboy exterior but I thought he was a canny operator driven only by the desire to succeed and achieve good TV ratings. Afterwards I did several interviews about what had gone on. How he had assured me that the cameras were switched off when they weren't and pretended to be my best friend. Something that was about as effective as Colonel Sanders of KFC telling a chicken, "Trust me."

'From my point of view, when I wanted him to be somewhere he was, which meant I got plugs into the programme for lots of people, including Westlife, Simon Cowell and nine-year-old singer Declan Galbraith. I also took him along when I visited the Marsden Children's Clinic with Brian McFadden. That surprised him because he didn't know I was involved with the hospital. I was paid a fee of £5,000 for appearing on the programme, which I sent straight to the Marsden. The interesting point is that he hasn't made another series. Afterwards Theroux's estranged wife Susanna Kleeman came to see me. She said how much she'd enjoyed the programme and how he'd hated it. That he was pulling his hair out and screaming because he couldn't get me to do what he wanted, which, since she was no longer with him, she was pleased about. In fact the only long-term effect on me was that more people asked me to do PR for them.'

Max is far less concerned about his own image than he is about those who consult him. He prides himself on being able to change the fortunes of almost anything and anyone from a political party, to someone who has fallen out of public favour, or who needs a new look. He will, when necessary, become the image-maker's equivalent of a GP; sorting out specialists to help his clients with any addiction problems and even offering marriage guidance.

In December 2003 Charles Wardle, an ex-Tory and former minister who Max originally met through their mutual connection with Mohamed Al Fayed, asked Max on behalf of Nigel Farage, the front man for the anti-EU United Kingdom Independence Party (UKIP) if he would handle the party's public relations in the six-month run-up to the Euro elections.

Max agreed to meet Nigel over dinner in a Weybridge restaurant. 'He explained that UKIP had become increasingly frustrated that they couldn't get their message across and that they were constantly being linked with the racist British National Party. I said that although I was a Labour supporter, I didn't agree with their view on Europe, so I was happy to help get their anti-European message to the public via the media and would charge them £100,000 for the six months.

'Shortly afterwards I arranged to introduce Nigel to various editors, including Piers Morgan of the *Mirror*, Andy Coulson of the *News of the World*, Tina Weaver of the *Sunday Mirror*, Rebekah Wade of the *Sun* and Mark Thomas of the *Sunday People* so that they could talk to him directly and be more open to the views of the party. I also reduced UKIP's message to something simple that people could relate to. This was that we should be controlled by Westminster not by Brussels.

'It worked very well. UKIP started getting stuff in the papers that they hadn't been able to before, particularly the fact that they weren't associated with the BNP, which was a huge step. I knew the editors would try to work with me, because I provide them with so many stories. But I didn't kid myself. No editor would give space to people they thought were talking rubbish or were members of the BNP. What I managed to do was give UKIP a fighting chance to deliver their message, whereas before they didn't have that chance. It was then up to them to make the best of it.

'I also got involved with an old lady called Elizabeth Winkfield, also a member of UKIP, who contacted me about refusing to pay her council tax as a protest. I managed to get her full media coverage, and with some help from me she slipped in references to the party.' The stocky, redoubtable 83-year-old, who was dubbed the council tax martyr for her insistence that she would rather go to prison than pay the heavily increased rate, appeared in every paper and on innumerable news programmes.

Max, as usual, would only work on his terms. When he heard that actress Joan Collins had contacted UKIP and was interested in helping their cause, he made his own position clear. 'I gave them advice on how to deal with her, but then left it to them. I explained that she was an egomaniac, that they had to keep telling her she was the most beautiful woman in the world and that what she had achieved for them was beyond their wildest dreams. All that kind of nonsense. I also told them I wouldn't do it. I don't have two minutes to spend with people like that or cope with their constant demands and huge ego.'

Robert Kilroy-Silk also contacted UKIP. His BBC talk show was dropped following his column in the *Sunday Express*, in which he referred to Arabs as 'suicide bombers, limb-amputators [and] women repressors', and he offered the party his help. The irony was not lost on Max.

'I'd had enormous success in promoting the party and enabled them to reach a huge public and now there was someone I couldn't stand getting involved. I've wanted nothing to do with him since the fracas when I was on his morning programme. I told Nigel that there was only one person Kilroy-Silk was interested in, that he would get them a lot of publicity, but they should remember that all publicity isn't good publicity, and so it proved.

'I also said being their front man would be the perfect job for him; a lot of money and not much to do. Kilroy-Silk was annoyed, but that's the problem with employing me. I'm a free spirit and I can and frequently do upset people.'

Charles Wardle was amazed, delighted and far from upset by Max's efforts. 'I noticed that whenever Max appeared on television talking about other things he'd manage to mention UKIP. He'd say the Euro elections didn't count for a great deal, that the turnout would be low and that it was not an important vote, so why didn't people use it to make the point that they wanted to be in control of their own destiny.

'He kept plugging away and by the time we got to the June election, a groundswell had built up and the party came from nowhere with just two seats to winning twelve and almost several others. In political terms it was an astonishing feat. Almost miraculous.

'After the election the party decided they wanted to go their own way. Some felt they wouldn't get on with Max. But inevitably once Max was no longer involved the whole thing fell apart. Max knows what the media wants, he knows the editors. He understands audiences and readership. He can reduce a message to its simplest form so that there is a gut reaction. He has a sense of humour and lots of contacts, and contacts means influence.'

Kilroy-Silk split from the party in January 2005 and set up his own party, Veritas, which bombed in the May general election.

Max felt the UKIP results spoke for themselves. 'When people talk about my work they usually mention my success in putting Rebecca Loos in the spotlight, but what I did for UKIP was personally far more difficult and satisfying.'

Max also brought back the sparkle into the life of Gerald Ratner. Ratner had a fantastic High-Street jewellery business, but in 1991 made one of the biggest PR gaffes in retail history. At a speech to the Institute of Directors, he joked that one of his firm's products was 'total crap', and boasted that some of its earrings were 'cheaper than a prawn sandwich'.

The speech was instantly seized upon by the media and wiped an estimated £500million from the value of the company, which eventually went bust. Ratner took time out to heal his wounds. 'I never blamed the press for what happened, but it knocked me for six and took me a long time to get over,' he says.

He tried his hand at various businesses then, in 2003, decided to go back to his first love and start up an Internet jewellery business. 'I announced to the city in the summer of 2003 that I was going to launch the website geraldonline.com,' he says. 'There was a lot of publicity because I was selling jewellery again. But none of it was any good to me because the website wasn't up and running at the time. I'd only publicly mentioned what I was doing because I needed to raise money.

'As a result, when the website was ready in November, I couldn't get any publicity because the story had already been told. The success of a website totally depends on people knowing about it so I was desperate. A friend suggested I use Max, particularly as I was aiming at the mass market. I rang him and spoke to him straight away; there was none of this, "He's busy, call again in a week's time," and I was sitting in his office a couple of days later. I really needed him, because I had put myself in the lion's den.

'He immediately got me interviews in the *Sun* and the *Mirror*, the same papers that had been my worst enemies in 1991. I also had a profile in the *Observer* and I gave interviews on radio. I was amazed he had such a pull over the media, that the pieces about me were positive and that the journalists didn't hold my original comments against me.'

'I did a rags to riches, to rags, back to riches campaign,' Max explains. 'It worked incredibly well. The exposure was worth about three million pounds in publicity and it brought him back from the dead.'

Ratner is delighted. 'Max charged fifteen thousand pounds a month for four months. It was expensive but he did what I wanted him to do. The previous PR firm I'd used charged less than half, but they didn't achieve a fraction of what he did. After being in the wilderness for so long, I have to thank Max for kick-starting my business, which is now worth £25-30million and has become Britain's largest on-line jewellers. No one else could have done it.

'I now realise that when I got into my trouble in 1991 I should have gone straight to Max. I did call in a PR to try to put out the fire, but it didn't work. I think Max would have been the one person who could have dealt with it and saved me.'

Max is also possibly the only person who could handle the PR for both warring sides of a marriage while managing at the same time to keep both parties happy, a task that would try the most conciliatory of lawyers.

Max first met Brian McFadden in 2001 when he was still a member of Westlife, then the biggest boy band in the world. He approached the group to ask if they could sing for the children in the cancer unit at the Marsden as a Christmas treat. They readily agreed and were terrific with the children. 'Max opened my eyes and changed my attitude to life,' says Brian. 'It's very easy to get totally caught up in your own world when you are a successful singer, but seeing very sick children struggling to survive and showing such courage puts everything into perspective.'

Max got on particularly well with Brian and when he got into trouble on his stag night a few weeks later, prior to his marriage to ex-Atomic Kitten singer Kerry Katona, he immediately rang Max.

'He was supposed to have had oral sex with a stripper called Amy Barker and asked me to help,' remembers Max. 'Amy came to see me after the wedding and said she didn't want the story to come out, but that she desperately needed the money. I said I could arrange it so that she got the same money to keep it out of the papers as she would have from selling it and gave her a cheque for about £20,000. She then signed a confidentiality contract.

'But her lawyer, who knew she had signed the contract, went to the *Sunday People* and sold them the story. The then editor Neil Wallace, who knew of my involvement, instead of contacting me put the story straight in the paper. He explained afterwards he did it that way because he felt if he mentioned it to me first it might have put me in an awkward position. I stopped working with him so it meant he got one front-page story and missed out on loads of others. Where is the sense in that?

'Instead all hell broke lose and the new marriage nearly broke down under the strain. Kerry, who was already very insecure because of her disturbed childhood, became even more so. She began phoning Brian all the time for reassurance and to check up on him, which gradually got him down. It was a shame because they are both good-hearted, genuine and natural people.'

After Kerry's crowning as queen of *I'm a Celebrity, Get Me Out of Here* in 2004, Max negotiated a weekly column for her in *OK* magazine and arranged for her to do several interviews. 'He knew I didn't want to do too much and get overexposed, so he didn't push me,' remembers Kerry. 'He handled it all perfectly.'

Max also did PR for Brian when he left Westlife in the autumn of 2004 to go solo. Kerry and Brian's marriage broke up around the same time and they both contacted Max to ask him to look after them. 'I knew it would be difficult,' he says, 'but I anticipated that some of their so-called close friends would try to exploit their break-up. By representing the interests of both of them, I could stop the most damaging stories coming out or at worst soften them, either by buying the person off, or persuading editors not to run them with the promise of a more positive story to come. It got quite nasty at times, but I felt they needed to maintain good contact as they have two small kids, Molly and Lilly, to think about.'

'Max is one of the few people I totally trust,' says Brian. 'No one else could have handled the break-up of my marriage. He also helped us to stay good mates. I always know he has my interests at heart but sometimes I tease him and call him Emperor Maximus.'

'When Max first found out we were splitting up, he didn't want to accept the fact because there were children involved,' agrees Kerry. 'But once he realised it was inevitable, he was wonderful and he's been a great support to me.'

Kerry initially suffered a severe bout of depression after she and Brian broke up and spent some time in the psychiatric clinic The Priory. 'Max visited me,' she says. 'He brought me flowers and cards, took me out for meals and was very caring. He is one of those guys who, if you don't know him, you can think of him in quite a negative way and I know some people are scared of him. But he is one of the biggest softies I've ever met. He has never taken sides and always been fair. If it wasn't for Max I don't think Brian and I would be where we are today, which is huge friends.

'He always takes a close personal interest in me and when I find a new boyfriend he wants to vet him first and make sure he thinks he is OK. I can tell him anything, even very personal stuff. He looks after my career brilliantly too, but I never think of him as a businessman. To me he is a member of my family, like an uncle, or even a dad. If I ever get married again I want him to give me away.'

'I like them both very much,' Max adds, 'but the way I handle them is very different. Kerry is more emotional. Brian is more businesslike. So I am more like a dad to Kerry and more like an uncle to Brian.

'Kerry, who is twenty-five, is emotionally vulnerable and will always need a lot of support. Brian, who is only twenty-four, is more positive and self-contained. He wants to be single and a pop star. I was delighted to see that his first solo "Real To Me", which he wrote himself, went to the top of the charts in Europe and Scandinavia.'

Although Max was sorry their marriage had failed, he couldn't resist indulging in a little mischief. 'I'd had so many phone calls about their split that when I had a call from the Press Association at the end of a long day asking if they were getting back together, on the spur of the moment I said they were seeing a counsellor called Auntie Graham.

'I went on to say she was a transsexual and a recluse but that stars used her because she was so good. All of which was completely made up. The following day the *Sun* and *Mirror* did a piece about her as did *Hello!* As a result I had innumerable interview requests. One Irish TV station even offered £20,000 for an exclusive interview, but I said she couldn't go on TV because she was incontinent. I told Brian and Kerry what I was doing and it was one of the things that kept them laughing during such a miserable time.

'They have been getting on better with each other and I hope it stays like that. I know so much about their relationship that I'm like a marriage guidance counsellor. But I haven't tried to get them back together.'

Max's hand-holding skills were soon to be urgently required in a mesmerising love triangle that gripped the nation.

20. A NATIONAL SCANDAL

It was just the sort of sexy, over-the-top caper that could have been an episode of the TV soap drama *Footballers' Wives*. A sultry secretary falls for a football executive, then ditches him for the charismatic football manager. One finds out about the other and there is deceit, lies, treachery, betrayal, incriminating emails, underhand dealings, a Christmas office party and finally the arrival of Max Clifford to unravel the conspiracy and realign the characters.

In fact the reality was so extraordinary you couldn't have made it up, and the shenanigans between Faria Alam, 38, Mark Palios and Sven Goran Eriksson became one of the tabloid highlights of 2004.

Sultry Bangladeshi-born Faria started work as a secretary for David Davies, now the executive director of the Football Association, towards the end of 2003 when he was Director of Football Affairs. Within weeks she began an affair with chief executive Mark Palios, a divorced father of five. Faria sent telltale emails to her friends from the office, describing her new lover in glowing terms, without revealing his identity.

Soon afterwards she found herself at the FA Christmas dinner sitting between not one, but two of the most powerful men in football. Her lover Mark Palios was on one side and fabled England coach Sven Goran Eriksson on the other. Whatever small talk passed between them, both men were trying to score underneath the table. Legend has it that Palios was stroking Faria's thighs while at the same time Eriksson was rubbing his leg against hers.

After six months, in April 2004, Palios decided he no longer wanted to play and finished the relationship. Waiting on the subs bench was Eriksson, and their alleged relationship began shortly before Euro 2004. It's hard to keep a secret in the rumour-filled world of football and on 18 July the *News of the World* splashed with the news that Sven was having an affair, but didn't reveal the name of his lover. But the tabloid hacks followed the scent that led them to Faria and then Palios.

Max, who was in Spain when the story broke, was, as usual, inundated by calls from the media asking for his comments. He hadn't at the time met or spoken to Faria, but instead mischievously took the opportunity to promote Majestic. 'I said it was my understanding that Sven had been seen in Marbella looking at various villas owned by Majestic, the big property company in the area,' he says of the ruse. 'I was careful not to say I'd seen him, just that I'd heard others had.'

The phone call that propelled him straight into the eye of the scandal followed shortly afterwards. 'One of Faria's friends rang to ask if I'd give her some guidance. Faria then called me herself, told me all the papers were after her, that she hadn't been responsible for the story coming out and asked what she should do. I suggested she wait, keep her options open, and not be pressurised into doing a deal too quickly. But if she timed it right there would be a lot of money on offer.'

For the rest of the week, so-called friends of Faria's talked for four-figure sums to different tabloid papers about her relationship with a variety of men, most of whom she'd never even met.

'The result was,' says Max, 'that there was little choice but to sell her story. Her reputation had been destroyed.'

Faria stopped work on 20 July, following publication of the first report of the affair. 'I felt crushed and embarrassed when my name was subsequently revealed. It's not something anyone would want his or her family to read about and especially not a conservative family like mine,' she says.

'But Max told me that if they loved me enough they would understand and give me support. Fortunately my mother lives in Seattle, USA, so she didn't read everything. Max and I also talked in general terms about how I could turn round what had happened to me, learn from it and be stronger.'

Max returned to London on Sunday 1 August and saw Faria the following day. 'She was far more attractive in the flesh than in the pictures. She also brought along two lawyer friends who were advising her, Imran Khan and Steve Barker. The two men obviously had no time for each other and I made it clear that if I handled the story I'd do the whole thing myself or not at all. When other people get involved it becomes too messy. I explained I took twenty per cent.'

Faria was nervous. 'I'd seen Max on television and knew he'd dealt with so many major stories and represented so many big stars that I was shaking at the thought of meeting such a larger than life character. But he was very kind. He explained all the aspects of selling a story, including the inevitable repercussions in my life. He told me that if I was a wallflower-type it wouldn't be the right thing to do.

'Otherwise he was very quiet. I could feel him watching me and absorbing what I was like. I felt scared and wondered whether I was strong enough to go ahead, but as we talked I felt he was taking me under his wing and that gave me strength. The previous two weeks had been such a nightmare. Hoards of journalists had hung round my apartment and I was frightened to go out or even be seen at the window. My private life was being exposed in the European press as well as in the UK. I felt depressed, lonely and totally gutted.'

Max explained the pros of telling her story. 'I said it would counteract the damaging things that had been written about her and particularly the image that she was a nymphomaniac. I explained the money she'd earn would help compensate for the distress. She also asked what would happen to her relationship with Sven, who was still phoning her a lot. I said it would probably end it, because he is a very private man who wouldn't be happy with her talking about his personal life.'

Faria thought about what Max had said overnight and the next day asked him to handle the story for her. 'I was delighted,' he says. 'There I was, just a few months after the Beckham/Loos allegations, in the middle of another major story. I told her what the journalists would want to ask and that she should emphasise she wouldn't be talking but for the fact that the story was already out there.

'I reminded her that she'd told me that Sven was a much better lover than Palios, whereas everybody was reading that the opposite was true, but that it was up to her if she wanted to correct that.'

Clinching the deal didn't take long. Max again arranged a double exclusive by selling her story to both the *News of the World* and the *Mail on Sunday* for publication the coming Sunday.

'I spent just an hour on Wednesday sorting it out. The *News of the World* and the *Mail on Sunday* had each independently already offered £150,000. I pushed each offer up to £200,000. I then sewed up the television deal. The Trevor MacDonald programme offered £30,000, Sky £50,000. I went back and forth between them and by the end of the day Trevor MacDonald had increased their offer to well over £100,000 so they got it.'

Max sat with Faria for the first half-hour of the interview with the journalists from both papers. 'I wanted to make sure she felt relaxed, both for her sake and the journalists. The more comfortable she felt the better the interview would be.'

Faria was then whisked away to a hotel in Bath, where each journalist interviewed her individually and some pictures were taken. The plan was to keep her hidden for two weeks. Max spoke to her every day. 'She often felt very down and wanted to come back to London, but she couldn't. I told her to think about what she was going to do with the money and reassured her that her real friends would stick by her.'

Faria found the whole experience very difficult. 'I felt I was being pulled this way and that, particularly as we kept moving hotels to throw other journalists off the scent. Luckily Max was very supportive and I could always get through to him no matter how many times a day I called.'

Her titillating story filled the papers. She alleged that Eriksson took her to his Swedish mansion following England's defeat in Euro 2004. She described him as 'amazingly physical . . . very sensual . . . I was in ecstasy. It was the best sex of my life.' And no, he didn't use a condom.

Palios, by contrast, was damned. 'The game was over before it had begun . . . He was a rubbish lover.' She dubbed Nancy Dell'Olio, Sven's partner, 'a drag queen' and said Eriksson no longer had any feelings for her. When told about the story Nancy, who was holidaying on a yacht around the Greek islands, apparently fell to the deck in a faint.

The Football Association went into meltdown. FA Communications Director Colin Gibson and Mark Palios quit their jobs. Eriksson stayed put.

'When we were together Sven swore undying love to me,' Faria says, 'and until February 2005 was phoning me three or four times a day. He was trying to keep our relationship going, although he pretended to the outside world he wasn't. Between February and April he's phoned about once a week.'

Max, in his agony-uncle role, tried to tell her not to exaggerate the importance of his phone calls. 'I said if he really loved her he would have been more attentive and stood by her, and that I felt he was totally dominated by Nancy. When it comes to relationships men in powerful positions take a lot and give very little. But I can't imagine Sven minded about the revelation. He's come out as a superstud.'

Faria took the Football Association to an industrial tribunal claiming she was a victim of sexual discrimination, constructive dismissal, breach of contract and unequal pay. The case was heard in June 2005.

Determined to fight her corner she caused sensation in court by claiming that, in addition to having relationships with Palios and Eriksson, she'd also been sexually harassed by her immediate boss David Davies. The FA's lawyers hit back by revealing the contents of the e-mails Faria sent to her friends, detailing her sexual exploits, and calling her a sexual predator intent on manipulating powerful men.

But looking back, in spite of everything, Faria doesn't regret going to court. 'It was tough, particularly as I had so many people trying to bring me down in every possible way,' she says. 'It's no joke being up against a massive corporation like the Football Association. Not many women would have taken them on. I certainly wouldn't have if I didn't believe that I was in the right.

'I don't regret selling my story. Max served me well and I stand by what I said. The case made me see people in a different light. The only person I believe behaved decently was Mark Palios.'

The story has a curious epilogue. 'Early in 2005,' Max recalls, 'I was called by Karl Fowler, a friend of mine, who is a financial advisor to many big names including Sven. He asked if he could arrange a meeting between Sven, himself and me, as Sven wanted some PR advice. It took place shortly afterwards in Karl's Piccadilly offices. Sven was friendly and charming and we talked through his problems. I got the impression, though, that he wasn't the master of his own destiny and was under the control of Nancy and I decided it would make a tough job impossible for me. I learned many years ago that it wasn't worth representing any major figure who was under the control of a third party.'

Individuals wanting to sell stories about David and Victoria Beckham have been a regular part of Max's life for some years. Sometimes the person doesn't have sufficient proof of what they are saying or gets cold feet. But when Max was approached by the Beckhams' former nanny Abbie Gibson in April 2005 he agreed to take her on as a client. Abbie had looked after Victoria and David's two sons Brooklyn and Romeo for two years and came to see Max a couple of weeks after resigning her position.

'She wanted to show up the marriage for what it really was, not the stage-managed perfect relationship they've tried to portray. She was very straightforward, easy to deal with and I liked her.'

He sold the story to the *News of the World* for £125,000, but the day before it was due to appear the Beckhams tried to get an injunction, claiming Abbie was in breach of the confidentiality agreement she had signed when she took the job. The sitting judge, Mr Justice Langley, rejected their request. He said the story was in the public interest and in a landmark ruling agreed that the *News of the World* could publish her claims (although Abbie subsequently gave undertakings to the court not to disclose any more 'confidential' information pending trial or further order).

Abbie's sensational allegations centred on the devastating rows between the celebrity pair and she claimed that the marriage was on the rocks. She alleged David had had affairs not just with Rebecca Loos, but also beautician Dannielle Heath and at least one other woman. She also revealed that she was made to walk behind the couple when they were out with the children, so that the public wouldn't know Victoria didn't look after the children herself.

'I was surprised but pleased by the judge's decision,' says Max. 'It means that celebrities who use the media can't now complain when the media use them. The Beckhams have done so to reveal all kinds of information about their private lives, including that David wears Victoria's knickers. But as a result of the allegations people now know the truth.'

A few days after publication the Beckhams admitted they had threatened to split during a furious row. They also appealed against the judge's decision. Abbie has agreed to have her money frozen until the result of the hearing at the end of 2005.

As a result of Max's continued success and his expert handling of huge and difficult stories, he has become a much sought-after media guru and pundit whose comments extend well beyond the stories he is involved with. Not surprisingly, many other PRs are now trying to follow in his trailblazing footsteps. More want to be brokers rather than restrict their activities to the more gentle art of writing press releases and hosting press parties for their clients. Max couldn't be less concerned.

'Lots of them try to copy me. At a Christmas gathering a few years ago a PR called Ian Monk came up to me and said, "I am the next Max Clifford." I replied, "Why do you want to be the next Max Clifford? Don't you want to be the first Ian Monk? I wouldn't want to be the second anybody." A key difference between us is that the others tout for stories to sell, whereas my aim from the start has been to produce the goods rather than advertise. If you don't advertise people know you are busy enough not to need to.

'The number of subjects I've covered and the people I've dealt with is astonishing. I now get calls from all over the world including the United States and Australia asking for my help. I still enjoy what I do so much I feel it's cheating if I say it's hard work. It's a game, my hobby and my way of life. It's also a continual challenge. Like Johnny Haynes, I try to have as much influence and control as possible in everything I'm involved with and never want to stop working.'

He doesn't get the chance.

EPILOGUE

The mobile phone rang loud and clear in the flower-filled room of his modern detached house just outside Weybridge in Surrey. Max Clifford was eating one of his favourite oatmeal crunch biscuits and drinking a cup of strong tea. He brushed imaginary crumbs from his fingers and put the phone to his ear. 'Hello,' said the female voice at the other end. 'Is that Max Clifford? My name is Patricia and I may have a story to sell.'

So started the next potential newspaper exposé.

'Yes, this is Max,' he replied. 'Nicola in my office told me your mum contacted us and that you might call. First of all, did you sign a confidentiality contract? . . . How recently? . . . What does it prohibit you from doing? . . . Right. A lawyer will have to look at it to see what you can and can't say and do.

'But basically it comes down to this: if you do a story you'll obviously make a lot of money, but it could also mean the end of your career. You have to understand that. How much you'll make also depends on what you are going to say. There are other ways of doing the story. A "close friend" can reveal what has happened and they can't keep you from discussing everything with everybody.

'But these, as I said, are matters for lawyers . . . No, you shouldn't be sitting down with any journalist at this stage. He or she will be very nice and charming but you can say one thing and read ten quite different things. Once you talk to a journalist they can write anything they want whether you said it or not. A lot of people come to me because they've got fed up with reading what they are meant to have said about what they've done and who they've slept with when they haven't spoken to a soul . . .

'It is very simple; when any journalist tries to talk to you, tell them you have absolutely nothing to say. You can also say I am representing you and they should contact me . . . The point I am making is that it just gets them off your back.

'As for what is going to happen, well, you need to come to my office and see me and we will have a chat and go right through it . . . Where are you? . . . OK, so what *do* you want to do? . . . Well, I could possibly get someone to go down and talk it all through with you on the total understanding that nothing is going to appear. Then I could tell you the best way to do it . . .

'Look, you don't have to say anything you don't want to. What I am saying, Patricia, is that I am more than happy to give you guidance and professional advice, without it costing you anything at all and if nothing ever comes out, it's not a problem. It makes no difference to me. What it means is that at the end of the day you will be in a position to say you would or you wouldn't like to do it. You are totally in control. You can also insist on seeing the piece before it is printed and say, "I didn't mean that. I didn't say that." . . .

'That is why you have to control it from the start . . . Yes, I know how difficult it is and you feel you are walking into a minefield. But do you remember the recent big scandal with the FA about a girl who worked there who had an affair with Sven? For two weeks she read what other people were saying about her when she hadn't spoken to a soul. She then decided she had to put the record straight . . . Yes, she has made a lot of money . . . Yes, Rebecca Loos has made a lot of money too . . . Yes, she is presenting and acting in TV programmes . . . No, she is not ostracised . . .

'Yes, everyone is very friendly with Rebecca. When she went to a Save The Children charity ball at the Natural History Museum, Princess Anne came up and had a chat, Chris and Ingrid Tarrant were sitting at her table, and people from the BBC and Channel Four talked to her about other TV programmes she could present.

'Of course, her circumstances and yours are very different. That's why you need to control it and not let it control you . . . It's my job, love. If I had your job I wouldn't be able to do it. It's horses for courses . . . After forty years, the biggest part of my job is protection, keeping things out of the papers. I look after major stars and organisations. I do general PR and go on TV and talk about image and all kinds of things . . .

'OK, I'll arrange for someone to come down and have a chat with you about what you want to talk about and what your contract will let you talk about. We also need to see the confidentiality agreement. Should you go ahead, I can arrange that the newspaper that gets your story will also assume legal responsibility if you are sued by the people you are talking about. But it's not likely to happen because you know too much about their lives . . .

'You have my mobile number. If we do something in the future, press or TV, I would take twenty per cent of whatever I negotiate for you, which will be a lot more than you would get because I know the marketplace. But if you decide you can't or don't want to do anything it won't cost you a penny. If you want nothing to come out, nothing comes out. You decide. It's not a problem. Call me again if you want to . . .'

INDEX